Empirical Methods for Exploiting Parallel Texts

Empirical Methods for Exploiting Parallel Texts

I. Dan Melamed

The MIT Press
Cambridge, Massachusetts
London, England

This book was set in Times Roman by Windfall Software using ZzT$_E$X and was printed and bound in the United States of America.

Library of Congress Cataloging-in-Publication Data

Melamed, I. Dan.
  Empirical methods for exploiting parallel texts / I. Dan Melamed
      p.   cm.
  A thorough revision of the author's thesis (Ph.D.—1998).
  Includes bibliographical references and index.
  ISBN 0-262-13380-6 (hc.: alk. paper)
  1. Machine translation. 2. Linguistic models. I. Title.
P309.M45 2001
418′.02—dc21   00–038028

for Flora and Assir Melamed—my rock and my foundation

Contents

Acknowledgments

This book is a thorough revision of my 1998 Ph.D. dissertation. As with all dissertations, this one owed much to people who went out of their way to help me learn. I am particularly grateful to:

- Mitch Marcus, for creating the best imaginable research environment and for teaching me how to use it.

- My dissertation committee, for preventing me from making a fool of myself in print.

- The LINC lab empiricist gang. If I count carefully, I might find that half of the ideas in this book were germinated by Jason Eisner, and that the rest were proposed by Mike Collins, Adwait Ratnaparkhi, Lyle Ungar and David Yarowsky.

- Innumerable past and present students, staff, post-docs, visitors and faculty at the Institute for Research in Cognitive Science at the University of Pennsylvania and its member departments, who came to my CLiFF talks, read drafts of my papers, and helped me refine my crazy ideas into ideas that were not merely crazy but also useful.

- My collaborators and advisors outside of Penn. I have been very lucky to work with Pierre Isabelle and his team (now at University of Montreal), with Philip Resnik at Sun Labs and at UMIACS, and with Young-Suk Lee of MIT Lincoln Labs. Some of the ideas in this book can be directly traced to correspondence with Ken Church at AT&T Research, Ido Dagan at Bar-Ilan University, George Foster at University of Toronto, and Djoerd Hiemstra at University of Twente.

- My undergraduate mentor Graeme Hirst, for encouraging my nascent interest in computational linguistics, thereby propelling me towards an exciting research career.

- Peter Jackson and my colleagues in the Computer Science Research Department of West Group, for their support and encouragement during the rewriting and editing stages.

- The anonymous reviewers who read the manuscript so carefully and who gave me many new insights.

Empirical Methods for Exploiting Parallel Texts

1 Introduction

One of the most exciting promises of research in artificial intelligence is computers that can understand natural human language. The main obstacle to fulfilling this promise has been the difficulty of modeling linguistic phenomena in sufficient detail. Natural language follows few hard and fast rules. Therefore, a good model must account for tendencies and likelihoods. Although people use language all the time, they cannot accurately assign probability distributions over linguistic data by introspection.

Fortunately, the amount of computing power available for research has been steadily doubling since the 1980s and there has been a dramatic increase in the amount of linguistic data available online. These resources have made possible a new approach to the language modeling problem—the empirical approach. If people cannot specify statistical language models by introspection, perhaps computers can induce the models from data.

One kind of raw material that has become much more plentiful since the birth of the Web is parallel texts in multiple languages (Resnik, 1999). A text and its translation constitute a *bitext*. Bitexts are one of the richest sources of linguistic knowledge because the translation of a text into another language can be viewed as a detailed annotation of what that text means. One might think that if that other language is also a natural language, then a computer is no further ahead, because it cannot understand the annotation any more than it can understand the original text. However, just the knowledge that the two data streams are semantically equivalent leads to a kind of understanding that enables computers to perform an important class of "intelligent" functions.

In particular, many functions that involve two or more languages can now be automated to some degree. Easier tasks, such as finding corresponding regions of parallel texts, can now be fully automated. On the other extreme of the difficulty continuum, the Web has spawned a number of online services that perform fully automatic translation from one language to another, with varying degrees of success. The Web has also created a demand for new kinds of multilingual functions, such as cross-language information retrieval, that computers are far better suited to perform than people. All these functions require knowledge of semantic equivalence across languages.

Formally, semantic equivalence between different languages or parts thereof is a mathematical relation called *translational equivalence*. The relation holds between expressions with the same meaning. The expressions can be as small as individual morphemes or as large as entire texts and speeches. To achieve the kind of limited understanding described above, it is first necessary to break down translational equivalence between texts into equivalence between smaller text units. The present work is about automatic discovery and exploitation of translational equivalence between words.

Translational equivalence can range over token pairs or type pairs. *Tokens* are instances of linguistic units in particular positions in particular texts. *Types* are abstract sets of tokens with identical appearance. For example, the first word in this sentence is a For token. That token and all other For tokens in this book and in other English texts constitute the word type **For**. With any kind of data, a computer must know something about the properties of types to infer properties of tokens, and vice versa. Using knowledge about types to find their tokens is usually called pattern recognition. Using information about tokens to induce models of their types is called learning. This book is organized around the type-token symbiosis.

Part I of the book deals with pattern recognition—using knowledge about types to infer knowledge about tokens. Even a very rough approximation of translational equivalence among word types is sufficient to recognize translationally equivalent tokens. Chapter 2 shows how to find corresponding word tokens in bitext automatically using, e.g., only the cognate heuristic and/or a few hundred entries automatically extracted from an on-line bilingual dictionary. Chapter 3 shows how correspondence among word tokens can be quickly and accurately extended to correspondence among longer bitext segments such as sentences. Chapter 4 shows how the techniques developed in chapter 2 can be applied to build a translators' tool for automatically detecting omissions in translations. Omission detection is typical of the kind of problem whose solution was previously thought to require full understanding of two languages, but that now can be approached with bitext-driven empirical methods.

Part II of the book deals with issues at the type-token interface. Chapter 5 describes how a *model of co-occurrence* can abstract a translational equivalence relation at the token level to a translational equivalence relation at the type level. Almost all published methods of learning translational equivalence among word types, including the methods in this book, start by considering what pairs of word tokens co-occur in corresponding regions of the training bitext. Counting co-occurrences correctly is crucial, but the most commonly used counting method turns out to be suboptimal for most applications. Chapter 5 exposes the problem and offers some solutions. It also shows how to count cooccurrences in *arbitrary* bitexts, not just in the restricted class of bitexts most often addressed in the literature to date.

The other chapter in part II describes a project undertaken to manually annotate translational equivalence at the token level in a significant subset of a large bitext. I use these annotations in subsequent chapters as a gold standard for evaluating various models of translational equivalence among word types. The annotation style guide appears as appendix A. The annotations themselves are freely downloadable for research purposes.

Part III of the book is about *models of translational equivalence* among word types (or *translation models*,[1] for short). Chapter 7 describes how to exploit two properties of bitext to improve translation model accuracy. The chapter also shows how a statistical model can incorporate various kinds of pre-existing knowledge that might be available about particular language pairs. Even the simplest kinds of language-specific knowledge, such as the distinction between content words and function words, are shown to reliably boost translation model accuracy. Chapter 8 tackles another long-standing problem: how to estimate translational equivalence, given that many word sequences are translated non-compositionally. The solution lies in an information-theoretic method for automatically discovering these non-compositional compounds and then treating them as atomic words within the methods of chapter 7. Chapter 9 develops a new method for unsupervised word-sense discrimination, in order to enable word-to-word translation models to account for polysemy.

The main innovations in this book have been rigorously evaluated and shown to advance the state of the art on the relevant criteria. Significant quantitative improvements in engineering methods often translate into qualitative improvements. Occasionally, a quantitative improvement will make a new application feasible by tipping the cost-efficiency balance, whether financial cost or computational cost. I hope that each reader will envision at least one new application of the ideas in this book, in addition to the ones I have proposed here.

Throughout the book, $\mathcal{CALLIGRAPHIC}$ letters denote text corpora and other sets of sets; CAPITAL letters denote collections, including sequences and bags; *italics* denote scalar variables; and the Helvetica font denotes literals. I also distinguish between types and tokens by using bold face for the former and plain font for the latter.

I TRANSLATIONAL EQUIVALENCE AMONG WORD TOKENS

2 A Geometric Approach to Mapping Bitext Correspondence

The first step in most empirical work in multilingual natural language processing (NLP) is to find sets of corresponding word tokens in the two halves of a bitext (*bitext maps*). Bitext mapping can be viewed as a form of pattern recognition. As in other kinds of pattern recognition, success hinges on three tasks: signal generation, noise filtering, and search. Given effective signal generators and noise filters, it is possible to map bitext correspondence with high accuracy using a greedy algorithm that runs in linear space and time. This chapter presents the Smooth Injective Map Recognizer (SIMR), a generic pattern recognition algorithm that is particularly well-suited to mapping bitext correspondence.

2.1 Introduction

Existing translations contain more solutions to more translation problems than any other existing resource (Isabelle, 1992).

Although the above statement concerned translation problems faced by human translators, recent research (Brown et al., 1993b; Melamed, 1996a; Al-Onaizan et al., 1999) suggests that it also applies to problems in machine translation. Texts that are available in two languages (*bitexts*) (Harris, 1988) also play a pivotal role in various less automated applications. For example, bilingual lexicographers can use bitexts to discover new cross-language lexicalization patterns (Catizone et al., 1989; Gale & Church, 1991b); students of foreign languages can use one half of a bitext to practice their reading skills, referring to the other half for translation when they get stuck (Nerbonne et al., 1997). Bitexts are of little use, however, without an automatic method for matching corresponding text units in their two halves.

The bitext-mapping problem can be formulated in terms of pattern recognition. From this point of view, the success of a bitext-mapping algorithm hinges on three tasks: signal generation, noise filtering, and search. This chapter presents the Smooth Injective Map Recognizer (SIMR), a generic pattern-recognition algorithm that is particularly well-suited to mapping bitext correspondence. SIMR demonstrates that, given effective signal generators and noise filters, it is possible to map bitext correspondence with high accuracy in linear space and time. If necessary, SIMR can be used with the Geometric Segment Alignment (GSA) algorithm described in chapter 3, which uses segment boundary information to reduce general bitext maps to segment alignments. Evaluation on pre-existing gold standards has shown that SIMR's bitext maps and GSA's alignments are more accurate than those of comparable algorithms in the literature.

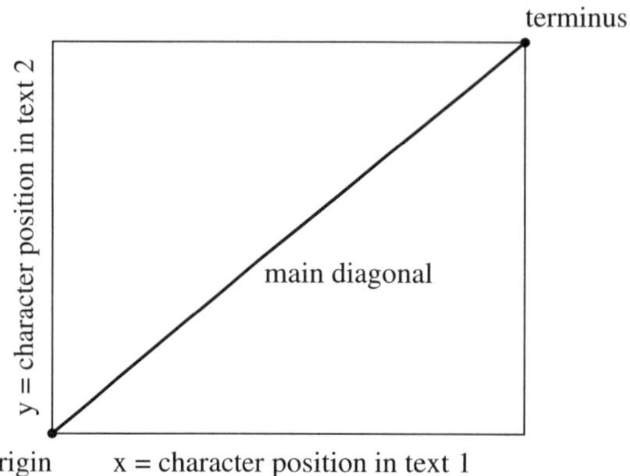

Figure 2.1
A bitext space.

The chapter begins with a geometric interpretation of the bitext-mapping problem and a discussion of previous work. SIMR is detailed in section 2.4 and evaluated in section 2.6.

2.2 Bitext Geometry

Each bitext defines a rectangular *bitext space*, as illustrated in figure 2.1. The lower left corner of the rectangle is the *origin* of the bitext space and represents the two texts' beginnings. The upper right corner is the *terminus* and represents the texts' ends. The line between the origin and the terminus is the *main diagonal*. The slope of the main diagonal is the *bitext slope*.

Each bitext space is spanned by a pair of *axes*. The lengths of the axes are the lengths of the two component texts. The axes of a bitext space are measured in characters, because text lengths measured in characters correlate better than text lengths measured in tokens (Gale & Church, 1991a). This correlation is important for geometric bitext-mapping heuristics, such as those described in section 2.4.4. Although the axes are measured in characters, I will argue that word tokens are the optimum level of analysis for bitext mapping. By convention, each token is assigned the position of its median character.

Each bitext space contains a number of *true points of correspondence (TPCs)*, other than the origin and the terminus. TPCs exist both at the coordinates of matching text units and at the coordinates of matching text unit boundaries. If a token at position p on the x-axis and a token at position q on the y-axis are translations of each other, then the coordinate (p, q) in the bitext space is a TPC.[1] If a sentence on the x-axis ends at character r and the corresponding sentence on the y-axis ends at character s, then the coordinate $(r + .5, s + .5)$ is a TPC. The .5 is added because it is the inter-sentence boundaries that correspond, rather than the final characters of the sentences. Similarly, TPCs arise from corresponding boundaries between paragraphs, chapters, list items, etc. Groups of TPCs with a roughly linear arrangement in the bitext space are called *chains*.

Bitext maps are injective (1-to-1) partial functions in bitext spaces. A complete set of TPCs for a particular bitext is the *true bitext map (TBM)*. The purpose of a *bitext mapping algorithm* is to produce bitext maps that are the best possible approximations of each bitext's TBM.

2.3 Previous Work

Early bitext mapping algorithms focused on finding corresponding sentences (Debili & Sammouda, 1992; Kay & Röscheisen, 1993). Although sentence maps are too coarse for some bitext applications (e.g., the one in chapter 4 and the one described by Macklovitch [1995]), sentences were a relatively easy starting point, because their order rarely changes during translation. Therefore, most sentence-mapping algorithms ignore the possibility of crossing correspondences and aim to produce only an alignment. Given parallel texts U and V, an *alignment* is a segmentation of U and V into n segments each, so that for each i, $1 \leq i \leq n$, u_i and v_i are mutual translations. An *aligned segment pair* a_i is an ordered pair (u_i, v_i). Thus, an alignment A can also be defined as a sequence of aligned segments: $A \equiv \langle a_1, \ldots, a_n \rangle$. In 1991, two teams of researchers independently discovered that sentences from bitexts involving clean translations can be aligned with high accuracy just by matching sentence sequences with similar lengths (Brown et al., 1991a; Gale & Church, 1991a). Both teams approached the alignment problem via maximum likelihood estimation, but used different models.

Brown et al. (1991a) formulated the problem as a hidden Markov model (HMM), based on a two-stage generative process. Stage one generated some number of aligned segment pairs; stage two decided how many segments from each half of the bitext to put in each aligned segment pair. Brown et al. (1991a) took advantage of various lexical "anchors" in the bitext that they were experimenting with. These anchors were also generated by the HMM, according to their respective probability functions. All the hidden variables were estimated using the EM algorithm (Dempster et al., 1977).

Gale & Church (1991a) began with a less structured model and proceeded to estimate its parameters through a series of approximations. Given the set $\mathcal{A}$ of all possible alignments, the maximum likelihood alignment is

$$A_{\max} = \arg \max_{A \in \mathcal{A}} \Pr(A|U, V). \tag{2.1}$$

Gale & Church first assumed that the probability of any aligned segment pair is independent of any other segment pair:

$$A_{\max} = \arg \max_{A \in \mathcal{A}} \prod_{i=1}^{|A|} \Pr(a_i|u_i, v_i). \tag{2.2}$$

Next, they assumed that the only feature of u_i and v_i that influences the probability of their alignment is a function $d(u_i, v_i)$ of the difference in their lengths, in characters:

$$A_{\max} = \arg \max_{A \in \mathcal{A}} \prod_{i=1}^{|A|} \Pr(a_i|d(u_i, v_i)). \tag{2.3}$$

By Bayes' rule, we find that

$$A_{\max} = \arg \max_{A \in \mathcal{A}} \prod_{i=1}^{|A|} \frac{\Pr(d(u_i, v_i)|a_i) \Pr(a_i)}{\Pr(d(u_i, v_i))}. \tag{2.4}$$

Ignoring the normalizing constant $\Pr(d(u_i, v_i))$ and taking the logarithm, Gale & Church arrived at

$$A_{\max} = \arg \max_{A \in \mathcal{A}} \sum_{i=1}^{|A|} \log \Pr(d(u_i, v_i)|a_i) \Pr(a_i). \tag{2.5}$$

Gale & Church empirically estimated the distributions $\Pr(d(u_i, v_i)|a_i)$ and $\Pr(a_i)$ from a hand-aligned training bitext and then used dynamic programming to solve equation (2.5).

The length-based alignment algorithms work remarkably well on language pairs like French/English and German/English, considering how little information they use. However, length correlations are not as high when either of the

Table 2.1
Alignment algorithms that don't look at the words can fumble in bitext regions like this vote record.
Source: Chen (1993)

English	French
⋮	⋮
Mr. McInnis?	M. McInnis?
Yes.	Oui.
Mr. Saunders?	M. Saunders?
No.	Non.
Mr. Cossitt?	M. Cossitt?
Yes.	Oui.
⋮	⋮

languages involved does not use a phonetically based alphabet (e.g., Chinese). Even in language pairs where the length correlation is high, length-based algorithms can fumble in bitext regions that contain many segments of similar length, like the vote record in table 2.1. The only way to ensure a correct alignment in such cases is to look at the words. For this reason, Chen (1993) added a statistical translation model to the Brown et al. alignment algorithm, and Wu (1994) added a translation lexicon to the Gale & Church alignment algorithm.

A translation lexicon T can be represented as a sequence of t entries, where each entry is a pair of words: $T \equiv \langle (x_1, y_1), \ldots, (x_t, y_t) \rangle$. Roughly speaking, Wu (1994) extended the method of Gale & Church (1991a) by a matching function $m(u, v, j)$ that was equal to one whenever $x_j \in u$ and $y_j \in v$ for lexicon entry (x_j, y_j), and zero otherwise. The information in the matching function was then used along with the information in $d(u_i, v_i)$ to condition the probability of alignments in equation (2.3):

$$A_{\max} = \arg \max_{A \in \mathcal{A}} \prod_{i=1}^{|A|} \Pr(a_i | d(u_i, v_i); m(u_i, v_i, 1), \ldots, m(u_i, v_i, t)). \qquad (2.6)$$

From this point, (Wu) proceeded along the lines of equations (2.4) and (2.5) and the dynamic programming solution.

Another interesting approach is possible when part-of-speech taggers are available for both languages. The insight that parts of speech are usually preserved in translation enabled Papageorgiou et al. (1994) to design an alignment algorithm that maximizes the number of matching parts of speech in aligned segments. It is difficult to compare this algorithm's performance to that of other algorithms in the literature, because results were reported only for a relatively easy bitext. On this bitext, the algorithm's performance was nearly perfect. A translation model between parts of speech would not help on bitext regions like the one in table 2.1.

The alignment algorithms described above work nearly perfectly given clean bitexts that have easily detectable sentence boundaries. However, bitext mapping at the sentence level is not an option for many bitexts (Church, 1993). Sentences are often difficult to detect, especially when punctuation is missing due to OCR errors. More importantly, bitexts often contain lists, tables, titles, endnotes, citations and/or mark-up codes that foil sentence alignment methods. Church's solution was to map bitext correspondence at the level of the smallest text units—characters. Characters match across languages to the extent that they participate in orthographic cognates—words with similar meanings and spellings in different languages. Since there are far more characters than sentences in any bitext, the quadratic computational complexity of this approach presented an efficiency problem. Church showed how to use a high-band filter to find a rough bitext map quickly.

Church's rough bitext maps were intended for input into Dagan et al. (1993b)'s slower algorithm for refinement. Dagan et al. used the rough bitext map to define a distance-based model of co-occurrence (see chapter 5). Then they adapted Brown et al. (1993b)'s statistical translation Model 2 to work with this model of co-occurrence. The information in the translation model was more reliable than character-level cognate information, so it produced a higher signal-to-noise ratio in the bitext space. Therefore, Dagan et al. (1993b) were able to filter out many of the imperfections of the initial bitext map.

A limitation of Church's method, and therefore also of (Dagan et al.)'s method, is that orthographic cognates exist only among languages with similar alphabets (Church et al., 1993). Fung has investigated ways to make these methods useful when cognates cannot be found. First, she introduced the K-vec algorithm (Fung & Church, 1994), which used a rough model of co-occurrence to bootstrap a small translation lexicon. The translation lexicon indicated points of correspondence in the bitext map, much the same way as matching character n-grams. These points of correspondence could then be further refined using the methods previously developed by Church (1993) and Dagan et al. (1993b). Later, Fung & McKeown (1994) improved K-vec by employing relative position offsets, instead of a fixed model of co-occurrence. This strategy made the algorithm more robust for more noisy bitexts.

2.4 The Smooth Injective Map Recognizer (SIMR)

2.4.1 Overview

SIMR borrows several insights from previous work. Like the algorithms of Gale & Church (1991a) and Brown et al. (1991a), SIMR exploits the correlation between the lengths of mutual translations. Like `char_align` (Church, 1993), SIMR infers bitext maps from likely points of correspondence between the two texts, points that are plotted in a two-dimensional space of possibilities. Unlike previous methods, however, SIMR greedily searches for only a small chain of correspondence points at a time.

The search begins in a small search rectangle in the bitext space whose diagonal is parallel to the main diagonal. The search for each chain alternates between a generation phase and a recognition phase. In the generation phase, SIMR generates candidate points of correspondence within the search rectangle that satisfy the supplied matching predicate, as explained in section 2.4.2 below. In the recognition phase, SIMR invokes the chain-recognition heuristic to select the most likely chain of *true* points of correspondence (TPCs) among the generated points. The most likely chain of TPCs is the set of points whose geometric arrangement most resembles the typical arrangement of TPCs. The parameters of the chain recognition heuristic are optimized on a small training bitext. If no suitable chains are found, the search rectangle is proportionally expanded by the minimum possible amount and the generation-recognition cycle is repeated. The rectangle keeps expanding until at least one acceptable chain is found. If more than one acceptable chain is found in the same cycle, SIMR accepts the chain whose points are least dispersed around its least-squares line. Each time SIMR accepts a chain, it moves the search rectangle to another region of the bitext space to search for the next chain.

SIMR employs a simple heuristic to select regions of the bitext space to search. To a first approximation, TBMs are monotonically increasing functions. This means that if SIMR accepts one chain, it should look for others either above and to the right or below and to the left of the one it has just found. All SIMR needs is a place to start the trace, and a good place to start is at the beginning. Since the origin of the bitext space is always a TPC, the first search rectangle is anchored at the origin. Subsequent search rectangles are anchored at the top right corner of the previously found chain, as shown in figure 2.2.

The expanding-rectangle search strategy makes SIMR robust in the face of TBM discontinuities. Figure 2.2 shows a segment of the TBM that contains

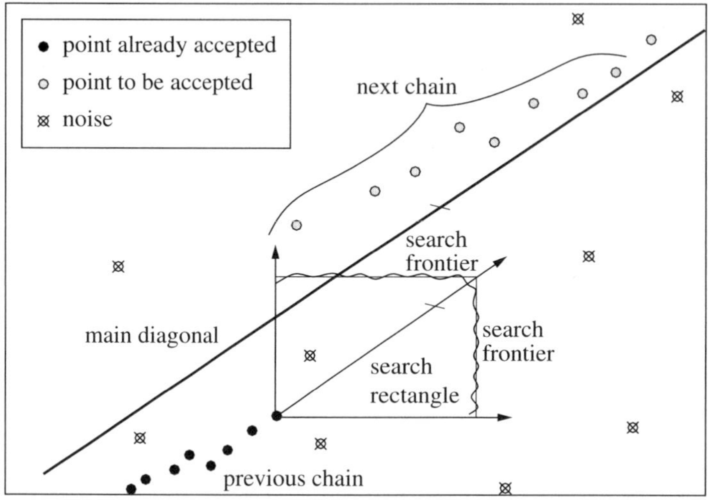

Figure 2.2
SIMR's "expanding rectangle" search strategy. The search rectangle is anchored at the top right
corner of the previously accepted chain. Its diagonal remains parallel to the main diagonal.

a vertical gap (an omission in the text on the x-axis). As the search rectangle
grows, it will eventually intersect with the TBM, even if the discontinuity is
quite large.[2] The noise filter described in section 2.4.3 reduces the chances that
SIMR will be led astray by false points of correspondence.

2.4.2   Point Generation

Before SIMR can decide where to generate candidate points of correspondence, it must be told which pairs of words have coordinates within the boundaries of the current search rectangle. The mapping from tokens to axis positions
is performed by a language-specific *axis generator* (see section 2.7.2). SIMR
calls one of its matching predicates on each pair of tokens whose coordinate
falls within the search rectangle. A *matching predicate* is a heuristic for deciding whether two given tokens might be mutual translations. Two kinds of
information that a matching predicate can rely on most often are cognates and
translation lexicons.

Two word tokens are *orthographic cognates* if they have the same meaning and similar spellings. Similarity of spelling can be measured in more or
less complicated ways. The first published attempt to exploit cognates for
bitext-mapping purposes (Simard et al., 1992) deemed two alphabetic tokens

cognates if their first four characters were identical. This criterion proved surprisingly effective, given its simplicity. However, like all heuristics, it produced some false positives and some false negatives. An example of a false negative is the word pair government and gouvernement. The false positives were often words differing greatly in length, like conseil and conservative. These examples suggest that a more accurate cognate matching criterion can be driven by approximate string matching. For example, McEnery & Oakes (1995) threshold the Dice coefficient of matching character bigrams in each pair of candidate cognates. The matching predicates in SIMR's current implementation threshold the Longest Common Subsequence Ratio (LCSR).

The LCSR of two tokens is the ratio of the length of their longest (not necessarily contiguous) common subsequence (LCS) and the length of the longer token. In symbols,

$$LCSR(A, B) = \frac{\text{length}[LCS(A, B)]}{\max[\text{length}(A), \text{length}(B)]}. \tag{2.7}$$

For example, gouvernement, which is 12 characters long, has 10 characters that appear in the same order in government, so the LCSR for these two words is 10/12. On the other hand, the LCSR for conseil and conservative is only 6/12. A simple dynamic programming algorithm can compute the LCS in $O(n^2)$ (Bellman, 1957). A rather more complicated algorithm can compute it in $O(n \log \log n)$ time on average (Hunt & Szymanski, 1977).

When dealing with language pairs that have different alphabets, the matching predicate can employ *phonetic cognates*. When language L1 borrows a word from language L2, the word is usually written in L1 similarly to the way it sounds in L2. Thus, French and Russian /pɔrtmɔne/ are cognates, as are English /sɪstəm/ and Japanese /šisutemu/. For many languages, it is not difficult to construct an approximate mapping from the orthography to its underlying phonological form. Given such a mapping for L1 and L2, it is possible to identify cognates despite incomparable orthographies.

Knight & Graehl (1997) have shown that it is possible to find phonetic cognates even between languages whose writing systems are as different as those of English and Japanese. They have built a weighted finite-state automaton (WFSA), based on empirically estimated probability distributions, for back-transliterating English loan words written in katakana into their original English form. The WFSA efficiently represents a large number of transliteration probabilities between words written in the katakana and Roman alphabets. Standard finite-state techniques can efficiently find the most likely path through the WFSA from a given Japanese word written in katakana to a given English word. The weight of the most likely path is an estimate of the probability that the former is a transliteration of the latter. Thresholding this probability would lead to a phonetic cognate-matching predicate for English/Japanese bitexts. The threshold would need to be optimized together with SIMR's other parameters, in the same way that the LCSR threshold is currently optimized (see section 2.5).

Cognates are more common in bitexts from more similar language pairs, and from text genres where more word borrowing occurs, such as technical texts. In the non-technical Canadian Hansards (parliamentary debate transcripts published in English and in French), an LCSR cutoff of .58 finds cognates for roughly one quarter of all text tokens. Even distantly related languages like English and Czech share a large number of orthographic cognates in the form of proper nouns, numerals and punctuation. When one or both of the languages involved is written in pictographs, cognates can still be found among punctuation and numerals. However, these kinds of cognates are usually too sparse to build an accurate bitext map from.

When the matching predicate cannot generate enough candidate correspondence points based on cognates, its signal can be strengthened by a *seed translation lexicon*—a simple list of word pairs that are believed to be mutual translations. Seed translation lexicons can be extracted from machine-readable bilingual dictionaries (MRBDs) in the rare cases where MRBDs are available. In other cases, they can be constructed automatically or semi-automatically using any of several published methods (Fung & Church, 1994; Fung, 1995b; Melamed, 1996a; Resnik & Melamed, 1997).[3] A matching predicate based on a seed translation lexicon deems two candidate tokens to be mutual translations if the token pair appears in the lexicon. Since the matching predicate need not be perfectly accurate, the seed translation lexicons need not be perfectly accurate either.

All the matching predicates described above can be fine-tuned with stoplists for one or both languages. For example, closed-class words are unlikely to have cognates. Indeed, French/English words like a, an, on, and par often produce spurious points of correspondence. The same problem is caused by *faux amis* ("false friends") (Macklovitch, 1995), words with similar spellings but *different* meanings in different languages. For example, the French word librarie means bookstore, not library, and actuel means current, not actual. A matching predicate can use a list of closed-class words and/or a list of pairs of *faux amis* to filter out spurious matches.

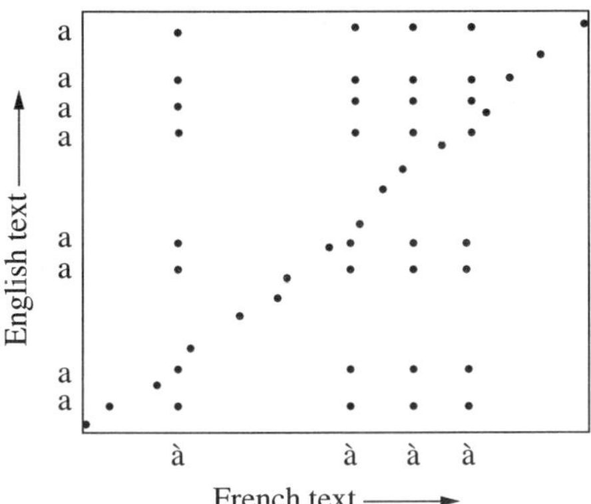

Figure 2.3
Frequent word types cause false points of correspondence that line up in rows and columns.

2.4.3 Noise Filter

Inspection of several bitext spaces has revealed a common noise pattern, illustrated in figure 2.3. It consists of correspondence points that line up in rows or columns associated with frequent word types. Word types like the English article *a* can produce one or more correspondence points for almost every sentence in the opposite text. Only one point of correspondence in each row and column can be correct; the rest are noise. It is difficult to measure exactly how much noise is generated by frequent tokens, and the proportion is different for every bitext. Informal inspection of some bitext spaces indicated that frequent tokens are often responsible for the lion's share of the noise. Reducing this source of noise makes it much easier for SIMR to stay on track.

Other bitext-mapping algorithms mitigate this source of noise either by assigning lower weights to correspondence points associated with frequent word types (Church, 1993) or by deleting frequent word types from the bitext altogether (Dagan et al., 1993b). However, a word type that is relatively frequent overall can be rare in some parts of the text. In those parts, the word type can provide valuable clues to correspondence. On the other hand, many tokens of a relatively rare type can be concentrated in a short segment of the text, resulting in many false correspondence points. The varying concentration of identical tokens suggests that more localized noise filters would be more effective. SIMR's localized search strategy provides a vehicle for a localized noise filter.

The filter is based on the *maximum point ambiguity level* parameter. For each point $p = (x, y)$, let X be the number of points in column x within the

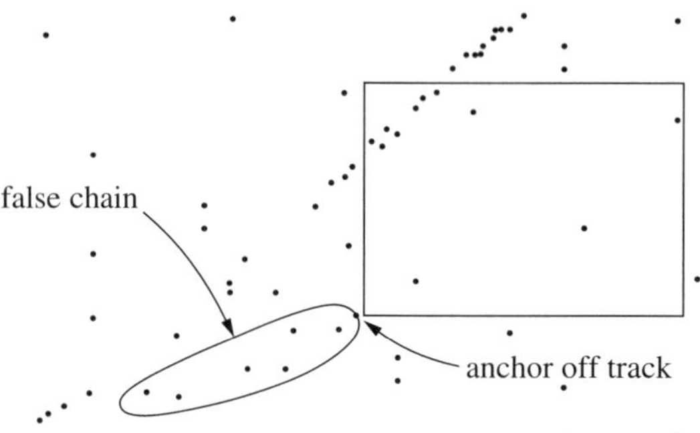

Figure 2.4
SIMR's noise filter makes an important contribution to the signal-to-noise ratio in the bitext space. Even if one chain of false points of correspondence slips by the chain recognition heuristic, the expanding rectangle is likely to find its way back to the TBM trace before the chain recognition heuristic accepts another chain.

search rectangle, and let Y be the number of points in row y within the search rectangle. The ambiguity level of p is defined as $X + Y - 2$. In particular, if p is the only point in its row and in its column, then its ambiguity level is zero. The chain recognition heuristic ignores points whose ambiguity level is too high. What makes this a localized filter is that only points within the search rectangle count toward one another's ambiguity level. The ambiguity level of a given point can change when the search rectangle expands or moves.

The noise filter ensures that false points of correspondence are relatively sparse, as illustrated in figure 2.4. Even if one chain of false points of correspondence slips by the chain-recognition heuristic, the expanding rectangle is likely to find its way back to the TBM trace before the chain-recognition heuristic accepts another chain. If the matching predicate generates a reasonably strong signal, then the signal-to-noise ratio will be high and SIMR is not likely to get lost, even though it is a greedy algorithm with no ability to look ahead.

2.4.4   Point Selection

After noise filtering, most TPC chains conform to the pattern illustrated in figure 2.5. The pattern can be characterized by three properties:

• **Injectivity:** No two points in a chain of TPCs can have the same x- or y-co-ordinates.

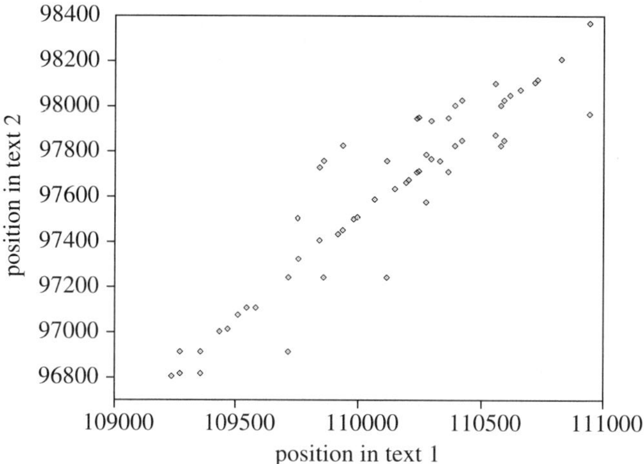

Figure 2.5
Typical pattern of candidate points of correspondence in a bitext space, after noise filtering. The true points of correspondence trace the true bitext map parallel to the main diagonal.

• **Linearity**: TPCs tend to line up straight. Recall that sets of points with a roughly linear arrangement are called **chains**.

• **Low Variance of Slope**: The slope of a TPC chain is rarely very different from the bitext slope.

SIMR exploits these properties to decide which chains might be TPC chains. First, chains that lack the injectivity property are rejected outright. The remaining chains are filtered using two threshold parameters: *maximum point dispersal* and *maximum angle deviation*. The linearity of each chain is measured as the root mean squared distance of the chain's points from the chain's least-squares line. If this distance exceeds the maximum point dispersal threshold, the chain is rejected. The angle of each chain's least-squares line is compared to the arctangent of the bitext slope. If the difference exceeds the maximum angle deviation threshold, the chain is rejected.

2.4.5 Reduction of the Search Space

In a search rectangle containing n points, there are 2^n possible chains—too many to search by brute force. The properties of TPCs listed above provide two ways to constrain the search.

The Linearity property leads to a constraint on the chain size. Chains of only a few points are unreliable, because they often line up straight by co-incidence. Chains that are too long span too much of the TBM to be well approximated by a line. SIMR uses a fixed chain size k, $6 \leq k \leq 11$. The exact value of k is optimized together with the other parameters, as described in section 2.5. Fixing the chain size at k reduces the number of candidate chains to $\binom{n}{k} = \frac{n!}{(n-k)!k!}$.

For typical values of n and k, $\binom{n}{k}$ can still reach into the millions. The Low Variance of Slope property suggests another constraint: SIMR should consider only chains that are roughly parallel to the main diagonal. Two lines are parallel if the perpendicular displacement between them is constant. So chains that are roughly parallel to the main diagonal will consist of points that all have roughly the same displacement[4] from the main diagonal. Points with similar displacement can be grouped together by sorting, as illustrated in figure 2.6. Then, chains that are most parallel to the main diagonal will be contiguous subsequences of the sorted point sequence. In a region of the bitext space containing n points, there will be only $n - k + 1$ such subsequences of length

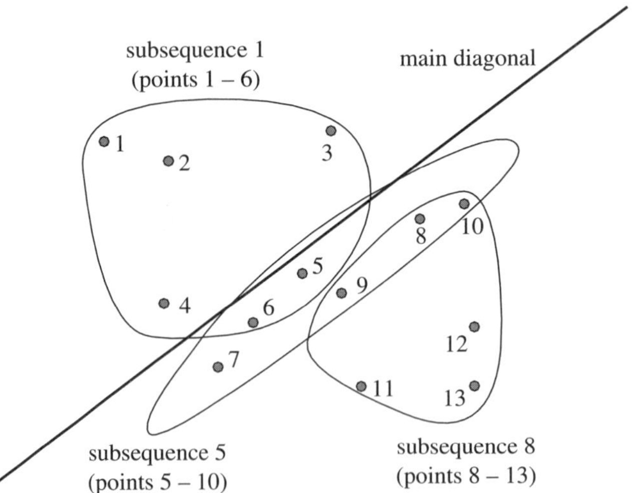

Figure 2.6
The chain recognition heuristic exploits the Low Variance of Slope property of TPC chains. The candidate points of correspondence are numbered according to their displacement from the main diagonal. The chain most nearly parallel to the main diagonal is always one of the contiguous subsequences of this ordering. For a fixed chain size of 6, there are $13 - 6 + 1 = 8$ contiguous subsequences in this region of 13 points. Of these 8, the fifth subsequence is the best chain.

k. The most computationally expensive step in the chain recognition process is the insertion of candidate points into the sorted point sequence.

2.4.6 Enhancements

The following sections describe two of the more interesting enhancements in the current SIMR implementation.

Overlapping Chains SIMR's fixed chain size imposes a rather arbitrary fragmentation on the TBM trace. Each chain starts at the top-right corner of the previously found chain, but these chain boundaries are independent of discontinuities or angle variations in the TBM trace. Therefore, SIMR is likely to miss TPCs wherever the TBM is not linear. One way to make SIMR more robust is to start the search rectangle just above the *lowest* point of the previously found chain, instead of just above the highest point. If the chain size is fixed at k, then each linear stretch of s TPCs results in $s - k + 1$ overlapping chains.

Unfortunately, this solution introduces another problem: Two overlapping chains can be inconsistent. The injective property of TBMs implies that whenever two (interpolated) chains overlap in the x or y dimension but are not identical in the region of overlap, then one of the chains must be wrong. To resolve such conflicts, SIMR employs a post-processing algorithm to eliminate conflicting chains one at a time, until all remaining chains are pairwise consistent. The conflict-resolution algorithm is based on the heuristic that chains that conflict with a larger number of other chains are more likely to be wrong. The algorithm sorts all chains on how many other chains they conflict with and eliminates them in this sort order, one at a time, until no conflicts remain. Whenever two or more chains are tied in the sort order, the conflict resolution algorithm eliminates all but the chain with the least point dispersal.

Additional Search Passes To ensure that SIMR rejects spurious chains, the maximum angle deviation threshold must be set low. However, like any heuristic filter, this one will reject some perfectly valid candidates. If a more precise bitext map is desired, some of these valid chains can be recovered during an extra sweep through the bitext space. Since bitext maps are mostly injective, valid chains that are rejected by the angle deviation filter usually occur between two accepted chains, as shown in figure 2.7. If chains C and D are accepted as valid, then the slope of the TBM between the end of chain C and the start of chain D must be much closer to the slope of chain X than to the slope of the main diagonal. Chain X should be accepted. During a second pass through the

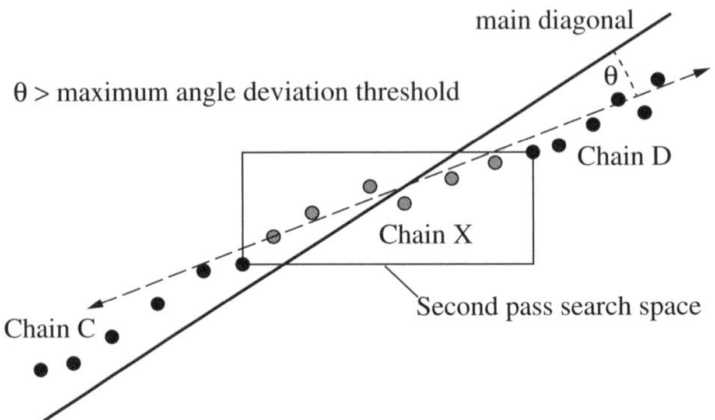

Figure 2.7
Chain X is perfectly valid, even though it has a highly deviant slope. Such chains can be recovered
by re-searching regions between accepted chains. The slope of the *local* main diagonal can be quite
different from the slope of the *global* main diagonal.

bitext space, SIMR searches for sandwiched chains in any space between two
accepted chains that is large enough to accommodate another chain. This sub-
space of the bitext space will have its own main diagonal. The slope of this
local main diagonal can be quite different from the slope of the *global* main
diagonal.

An additional search through the bitext space also enables SIMR to recover chains that were missed because of an inversion in the translation. Non-
monotonic TBM segments result in a characteristic map pattern, as a conse-
quence of the injectivity of bitext maps. SIMR has no problem with small non-
monotonic segments inside chains. However, the expanding rectangle search
strategy can miss larger non-monotonic segments that do not fit inside one
chain. In figure 2.8, the vertical range of segment j corresponds to a vertical
gap in SIMR's first-pass map. The horizontal range of segment j corresponds
to a horizontal gap in SIMR's first-pass map. Similarly, any non-monotonic
segment of the TBM will occupy the intersection of a vertical gap and a horizontal gap in the monotonic first-pass map. Furthermore, switched segments
are usually adjacent and relatively short. Therefore, to recover non-monotonic
segments of the TBM, SIMR need only search gap intersections that are close
to the first-pass map. There are usually very few such intersections that are
large enough to accommodate new chains, so the second-pass search requires
only a small fraction of the computational effort of the first pass.

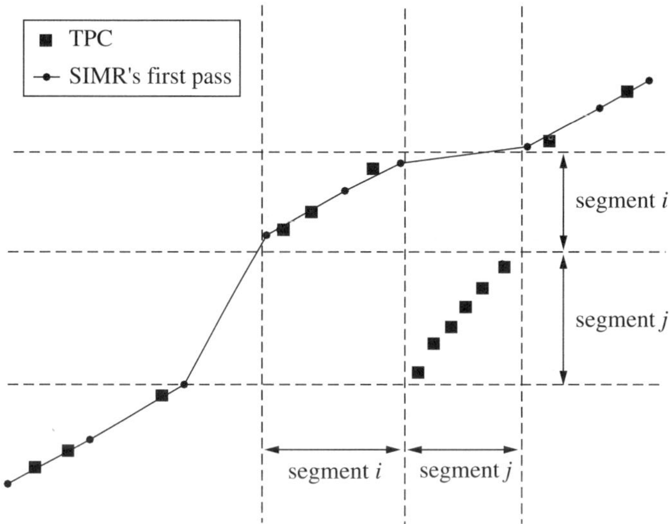

Figure 2.8
Segments i and j switched places during translation. Any non monotonic segment of the TBM will occupy the intersection of a vertical gap and a horizontal gap in the monotonic first-pass map. These larger non-monotonic segments can be recovered during a second sweep through the bitext space.

2.5 Parameter Optimization

SIMR's parameters—the fixed chain size, the LCSR threshold used in the matching predicate, and the thresholds for maximum point dispersal, maximum angle deviation, and maximum point ambiguity—interact in complicated ways. Ideally, SIMR should be reparameterized so that its parameters are pairwise independent. Then it may be possible to optimize the parameters analytically, or at least in a probabilistic framework. For now, the easiest way to optimize these parameters is via simulated annealing (Vidal, 1993), a simple general framework for optimizing highly interdependent parameter sets.

Simulated annealing requires an objective function to optimize. The objective function for bitext mapping should measure the difference between the TBM and the interpolated bitext maps produced with the current parameter set. In geometric terms, the difference is a distance. The distance between a bitext map and each TPC can be defined in a number of ways. The simplest metrics are the horizontal distance and the vertical distance, but these metrics measure

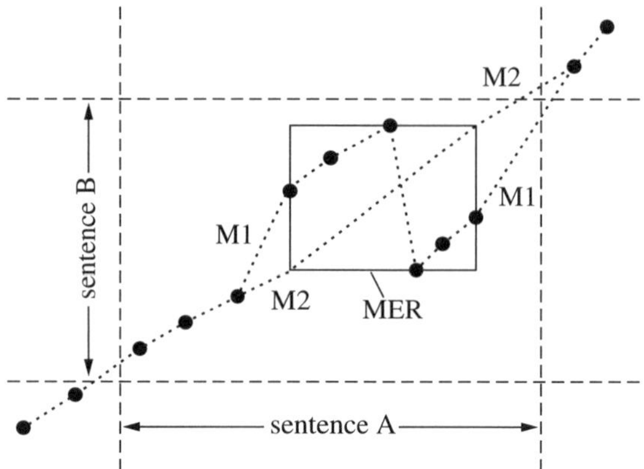

Figure 2.9
Two text segments at the end of Sentence A were switched during translation, resulting in a non-monotonic segment. To interpolate injective bitext maps, non-monotonic segments must be encapsulated in Minimum Enclosing Rectangles (MERs). A unique bitext map can then be interpolated by using the lower left and upper right corners of the MER (map M2), instead of the non-monotonic correspondence points (function M1).

the error with respect to only one language or the other. A more robust average is the distance perpendicular to the main diagonal. In order to penalize large errors more heavily, root-mean-squared (RMS) distance should be minimized instead of mean distance.

There is a slight complication in the computation of distances between two partial functions: Linear interpolation is not well-defined for non-monotonic sets of points. It would be incorrect to simply connect the dots left to right, because the resulting function may not be injective. To interpolate injective bitext maps, non-monotonic segments must be encapsulated in Minimum Enclosing Rectangles (MERs), as shown in figure 2.9. A unique bitext map results from interpolating between the lower left and upper right corners of the MER, instead of using the non-monotonic correspondence points.

2.6 Evaluation

SIMR's parameters were optimized by simulated annealing, as described in the previous section. A separate optimization was performed on separate training bitexts for each of four language pairs. SIMR was then evaluated on previously unseen test bitexts in the four language pairs. The evaluation metric and the objective function for optimization were the root-mean-squared distance,

Table 2.2
SIMR accuracy on training bitexts for four language pairs.

Language pair	Number of training TPCs	Training genre	RMS error in characters
French / English	598	marketing report	6.6
Spanish / English	562	software manuals	5.5
Korean / English	615	military manuals	3.9
Chinese / English	678, 915, 695	the Bible	7.9, 6.5, 7.8

Table 2.3
SIMR error estimates on different text genres in four language pairs.

Language pair	Bitext or genre	Number of test TPCs	RMS Error in characters
French / English	parliamentary debates	7123	5.7
	CITI technical reports	365, 305, 176	4.4, 2.6, 9.9
	other technical reports	561, 1393	21, 14
	court transcripts	1377	3.9
	U.N. annual report	2049	12
	I.L.O. report	7129	6.4
Spanish / English	software manuals	376, 151, 100, 349	4.6, 0.67, 5.2, 4.7
Korean / English	military manuals	40, 88, 186, 299	2.6, 7.1, 25, 7.8
	military messages	192	0.53
Chinese / English	I Corinthians	437	17
	II Corinthians	257	11
	Daniel	357	12
	Ecclesiastes	222	9.1
	Ezra	280	59
	Hebrews	303	14
	Nehemiah	406	50
	Revelations	404	6.8
	Romans	433	14
	Zechariah	211	15

in characters, between each TPC and the interpolated bitext map produced by SIMR, where the distance was measured perpendicular to the main diagonal. Tables 2.2 and 2.3 report SIMR's errors on the training and test bitexts, respectively.

The TBM samples used for training and testing were derived from segment alignments. The Chinese/English alignments were based on Biblical verse boundaries, which are constant across languages. The bitexts in the other three language pairs had been manually aligned by bilingual annotators (Melamed, 1997b). The alignments were converted into sets of coordinates in the bitext space by pairing the character positions at the ends of aligned segment pairs.

This TBM sampling method artificially reduced the error estimates. Most of the aligned segments were sentences, which ended with a period. Whenever SIMR matched the periods correctly, the interpolated bitext map was pulled close to the TPC, even though it may have been much farther off in the middle of the sentence. Thus, the results in table 2.3 should be considered only relative to each other and to other results obtained under the same experimental conditions. It would be impressive indeed if any bitext mapping algorithm's actual RMS error were less than one character on bitexts involving languages with different word order, such as English/Korean.

The matching predicates for French/English and Spanish/English relied on an LCSR threshold to find cognates. Seed translation lexicons were used for Korean/English and Chinese/English, with 5228 entries in the former and 7997 in the latter. The Korean text contained some roman character strings, so the matching predicate for Korean/English also generated candidate points of correspondence whenever one of these strings coordinated in the search rectangle with an identical string in the English half of the bitext. In addition, English, French, Spanish and Korean stop-lists were used to prevent matches of closed-class words. The translation lexicons and stop-lists had been developed independently of the training and test bitexts.

The French/English part of the evaluation was performed on bitexts from the publicly available *corpus de bi-texte anglais-français (BAF)* (Simard & Plamondon, 1996). SIMR's error distribution on the "parliamentary debates" bitext in this collection is given in table 2.4. This distribution can be compared to the error distributions reported for the same test set by Dagan et al. (1993b). Dagan et al. (1993b) report parts of their error distribution in words, rather than in characters: "In 55% of the cases, there is no error in word_align's output (distance of 0), in 73% the distance from the correct alignment is at most 1, and in 84% the distance is at most 3." These distances were measured horizontally from the bitext map rather than perpendicularly to the main diagonal. Given the bitext slope for that bitext and a conservative estimate of six characters per word (including the space between words), each horizontal word of error corresponds to just over four characters of error perpendicular to the main diagonal. Thus, Dagan et al. (1993b)'s "no error" is the same as two characters of error or less, i.e., less than half a word. One word of error is the same as an error of up to six characters, and three words of error are equivalent to

Table 2.4
SIMR's error distribution on the French/English "parliamentary debates" bitext. Errors were measured perpendicular to the main diagonal.

Number of test points	Error range in characters	Fraction of test points
1	-101	.0001
2	-80 to -70	.0003
1	-70 to -60	.0001
5	-60 to -50	.0007
4	-50 to -40	.0006
6	-40 to -30	.0008
9	-30 to -20	.0013
29	-20 to -10	.0041
3057	-10 to 0	.4292
3902	0 to 10	.5478
43	10 to 20	.0060
28	20 to 30	.0039
17	30 to 40	.0024
5	40 to 50	.0007
8	50 to 60	.0011
1	60 to 70	.0001
1	70 to 80	.0001
1	80 to 90	.0001
1	90 to 100	.0001
1	110 to 120	.0001
1	185	.0001
7123	*-101 to 185*	*1.000*

$4 \cdot 3\frac{1}{2} = 14$ characters. On this basis, table 2.5 compares the accuracy of SIMR and `word_align`.[5]

Another interesting comparison is in terms of maximum error. Certain applications of bitext maps, like the one described in chapter 4, can tolerate many small errors but no large ones. As shown in table 2.4, SIMR's bitext map was never off by more than 185 characters from any of the 7123 segment boundaries. 185 characters is about 1.5 times the length of an average sentence (see chapter 4). `word_align`'s input is the output of `char_align` and Dagan et al. (1993b) have reported that `word_align` cannot escape from `char_align`'s worst errors. An independent implementation of `char_align` (Simard, 1995) erred by more than one thousand characters on the same bitext.

The Spanish/English and Korean/English bitexts were hand-aligned when SIMR was being ported to these language pairs. The Spanish/English bitexts were drawn from the Sun Solaris AnswerBooks and hand-aligned by Philip

Table 2.5
Comparison of error distributions for *SIMR* and word_align on the parliamentary debates bitext.

Algorithm	Error of at most 2 characters	Error of at most 6 characters	Error of at most 14 characters
word_align	55%	73%	84%
SIMR	93%	97%	98%

Resnik. The Korean/English bitexts were provided by MIT's Lincoln Laboratories and hand-aligned by Young-Suk Lee. Table 2.3 shows that SIMR's performance on Spanish/English and Korean/English bitexts is no worse than its performance on French/English bitexts.

The Chinese/English bitexts were acquired with the help of Resnik et al. (1997), who compiled the most common 66 books of the Bible online in a variety of languages. Biblical text exhibits a variety of genres and styles, so I decided to use three different texts for training and cross-validation. On the basis of previous experience (Melamed, 1996b), I decided to train on books that had between 500 and 1000 aligned segments (verses). The books of Proverbs, Mark, and II Samuel were selected at random from this subset. I wanted to test SIMR on a variety of bitexts as quickly as possible. Therefore, for testing, I decided to use all the books of the Bible that had less than 500 verses, of which there were ten.

With the exception of Ezra and Nehemiah, SIMR's accuracy on all the books was comparable to its accuracy on bitexts in other language pairs and other genres (Melamed, 1997b). The two exceptions were surprising and disappointing. Bitext mapping is typically used in a pipeline with other processes, rather than as an end in itself, so it is unacceptable for a bitext-mapping algorithm to fail two times out of ten. I undertook some error analysis in order to learn more.

The porting guidelines (Melamed, 1996b) describe a general error-hunting strategy that can be used to debug training data intended for optimizing SIMR's parameters. I used this strategy to analyze the test data. I found that SIMR got both the Ezra and Nehemiah bitext maps mostly right. However, both of the problematic bitexts contained short segments in which SIMR made several large errors in a row. The RMS error metric is very sensitive to large errors, even if they are few in number.

Next, I looked at the bitexts themselves in the region where SIMR was far off the mark. The problem, illustrated in figure 2.10, became readily apparent. The

10:38: From the descendants of Binnui: Shimei,
10:39: Shelemiah, Nathan, Adaiah,
10:40: Macnadebai, Shashai, Sharai,
10:41: Azarel, Shelemiah, Shemariah,
10:42: Shallum, Amariah and Joseph.
10:43: From the descendants of Nebo: Jeiel, Mattithiah, Zabad, Zebina, Jaddai,
    Joel and Benaiah.

Figure 2.10
Genealogy excerpt from the New International Version of the book of Ezra.

Bible contains a number of passages describing genealogies, which contain little besides names and punctuation. The names were not in the Chinese/English seed translation lexicon. Punctuation marks alone could not provide a sufficiently strong signal for SIMR to follow. SIMR essentially skipped over these regions of the bitext space, unable to find any suitable chains of correspondence points there. Interpolation of SIMR's bitext map across the gaps was a poor approximation to the TBM for these bitexts.

The error analysis above provides some justification for absolving SIMR of its performance on Ezra and Nehemiah, and for considering its performance on the other bitexts as more indicative. First, the problem arose from a quirk in the bitext (exceedingly long strings of proper nouns) that is unlikely to be encountered in other bitexts. Second, the problem is solvable. Proper nouns that are translated into Chinese from another language are usually written so as to retain much of their pronunciation. Therefore, proper nouns can be matched across Chinese/English bitexts as phonetic cognates (Knight & Graehl, 1997; Chen et al., 1998; Wan & Verspoor, 1998). A matching predicate that can supplement its translation lexicon with phonetic cognates could provide an even stronger signal. In addition to preventing large errors in the rare cases encountered here, the stronger signal can improve SIMR's performance on more typical bitexts.

The results in table 2.3 were obtained using a version of SIMR that included all the enhancements described in section 2.4.6. It is interesting to consider the degree to which each enhancement improves performance. I remapped the French/English bitexts listed in table 2.3 with two stripped-down versions of SIMR. One version was basic SIMR without any enhancements. The other version incorporated overlapping chains, but performed only one search pass. The deterioration in performance varied widely. For example, on the parliamentary debates bitext, the RMS error rose from 5.7 to 16 when only one search pass was allowed, but rose only another two points to 18 using non-overlapping chains. In contrast, on the U.N. Annual Report bitext, the extra search passes made no difference at all but non-overlapping chains increased the RMS error from 12 to 40. For most of the other bitexts, each enhancement reduced the RMS error by a few characters, compared to the basic version. However, the improvement was not universal: the RMS error of the basic SIMR was 19 for the "other technical report" on which the enhanced SIMR scored 21. The expected value of the enhancements is difficult to predict, because each enhancement is aimed at solving a particular pattern recognition problem, and each problem may or may not occur in a given bitext. The relationship between geometric patterns in TPC chains and syntactic properties of bitexts is a ripe research topic.

2.7   Implementation of SIMR for New Language Pairs

SIMR can be ported to a new language pair in three steps.

2.7.1   Step 1: Construct Matching Predicate

The original SIMR implementation for French/English included matching predicates that could use cognates and/or translation lexicons. For language pairs in which lexical cognates are frequent, a cognate-based matching predicate should suffice. In other cases, SIMR can use a seed translation lexicon to boost the number of candidate points of correspondence produced in the generation phase. The matching predicate for Spanish/English uses only cognates. For Korean/English and Chinese/English, SIMR takes advantage of punctuation and numeral cognates but supplements them with a translation lexicon.

Although the Korean/English translation lexicon contains 5228 entries, fewer than 150 entries were used to map the Korean/English bitexts in table 2.3. Most of these 150 entries were used only once. Similar usage ratios were observed for Chinese/English. It seems likely that a much smaller translation lexicon can be equally effective, if the entries in this lexicon are more relevant to the bitexts being mapped. If this conjecture is true, then a bilingual lexicographer should be able to build a matching predicate for any pair of languages in a matter of hours.

2.7.2   Step 2: Construct Axis Generators

In order for SIMR to generate candidate points of correspondence in the search rectangle, it needs to know which token pairs' coordinates fall within the search rectangle. Therefore, it needs to know the position of each token within each of the two texts. It is the axis generator's job to map the two halves of the bitext to positions on the x- and y-axes of the bitext space, before SIMR starts searching for TPC chains. Axis generators need to be built only once per language, rather than once per language pair. However, they should be designed with the matching predicate in mind.

If the matching predicate uses cognates, then every word that might have a cognate in the other half of the bitext should be assigned its own axis position. This rule applies to punctuation and numbers as well as to "lexical" cognates. In the case of lexical cognates, the axis generator typically needs to invoke a language-specific tokenization program to identify words in the text. If no such program is available in advance, then writing it may constitute a significant part of the porting effort. The effort may be lessened, however, by the realization that it is acceptable for the tokenization program to overgenerate, just as it is for the matching predicate.

For example, when tokenizing German text, it is not necessary for the tokenizer to know which compound words are translated as a unit. If a German lexicon indicates that a word has another word as a substring, then the tokenizer should simply generate an extra axis position for that substring. More specifically, suppose we want to tokenize the German word Kindergarten, a noun-noun compound that literally means children's garden. Kindergarten is translated into some languages as a unit; e.g., English has borrowed it verbatim. In other languages, the concept is expressed compositionally; e.g., the French translation is jardin d'enfants, three words that literally mean garden of children. Suppose we have a German lexicon in which the component nouns Kinder and Garten are also listed. To maximize the chances of Kindergarten in the German half of a bitext being matched to a cognate in the opposite half of the bitext, independently of the language of that other half, the tokenizer should generate one axis position for Kindergarten and extra axis positions for Kinder and for garten. If the axis generator sees Kindergarten stretching from the 50th character to the 62nd character in a German text, it should output (53.5, kinder) and (59.5, garten), as well as (56.5, kindergarten).

When lexical cognates are not being used, the axis generator need only identify punctuation, numerals, and those character strings in the text that also appear on the relevant side of the translation lexicon.[6] It would be pointless to plot other words on the axes because the matching predicate could never match them anyway. Therefore, for languages like Chinese and Japanese, which are written without spaces between words, tokenization boils down to string matching. In this manner, SIMR circumvents the difficult word-identification problems in these languages.

An important source of error for SIMR is "non-linguistic" text, such as white space or tables of numbers. During translation, such text is usually copied rather than translated, resulting in TBM segments whose slope is exactly 1. These segments can constitute a large enough portion of the TBM to severely skew the slope of the main diagonal. Thus, they can fool SIMR into searching the whole bitext space for TPC chains whose slope is close to 1, even though most of the bitext map between "linguistic" parts of the bitext has a very different slope. Sometimes the translation of non-linguistic text is completely erratic, especially where white space is concerned.

A simple solution to this problem is to delete the non-linguistic text. After SIMR produces a map for the resulting bitext, a post-processor scales the points in the map to account for the deleted text segments. The current implementation of SIMR treats only white space in the above manner, because strings of white space are easy to identify. A general method for classifying a given string as linguistic or non-linguistic can be adopted from language identification methods (e.g. Elworthy, 1998). Given a character-level language model, it is straightforward to compute the likelihood $\frac{\Pr(string|language)}{\Pr(string|\neg language)}$ that a string was generated by the language in question. This likelihood will be less than 1 in all or most of the substrings in a non-linguistic text region.

2.7.3   Step 3: Reoptimize Parameters

The last step in the porting process is to reoptimize SIMR's numerical parameters. The most tedious part of the porting process is the construction of TBMs against which SIMR's parameters can be optimized and tested. The easiest way to construct these gold standards is to extract them from pairs of hand-aligned text segments: The final character positions of each segment in an aligned pair are the coordinates of a TPC. Over the course of two porting efforts, I developed and refined tools and methods that allow a bilingual annotator to construct the required TBMs very efficiently from a raw bitext (Melamed, 1996b). The procedure was used to hand-align 1338 Spanish/English segments in about five hours and 1224 Korean/English segments in about twelve hours. These amounts of hand-aligned data sufficed for training, cross-validation, and testing. Using the established methodology, it should be possible to create enough hand-aligned data to port SIMR to any language pair in under two days.

2.8   Conclusion

The Smooth Injective Map Recognizer (SIMR) is based on innovative approaches to each of the three main components of a bitext-mapping algorithm: signal generation, noise filtering, and search. The advances in signal generation stemmed from the use of word-based matching predicates. When word-pair coordinates are plotted in a Cartesian bitext space, the geometric heuristics of existing sentence alignment algorithms can be exploited just as easily and to a greater extent at the word level. The cognate heuristic of character-based bitext-mapping algorithms also works better at the word level, because cognateness can be defined more precisely in terms of words, e.g., using the Longest Common Subsequence Ratio. Most importantly, matching heuristics based on existing translation lexicons can be defined only at the word level. When neither cognates nor sentence boundaries can be found, we can still map bitexts in any pair of languages using a small hand-constructed translation lexicon. To complement word-based matching predicates, I have proposed localized noise filtering. Localized noise filters are more accurate than global ones because they are sensitive to local variations in noise distributions. The combination of a strong signal and an accurate noise filter makes localized search heuristics possible. Localized search heuristics can directly exploit the geometric tendencies of TPC chains in order to search the bitext space in linear space and time, a level of efficiency that is particularly important for large bitexts.

SIMR also advances the state of the art of bitext mapping on several other criteria. Evaluation on pre-existing gold standards has shown that SIMR can map bitexts with high accuracy in a variety of language pairs and text genres without getting lost. SIMR is robust in the face of translation irregularities like omissions and allows crossing correspondences to account for word-order differences. SIMR encapsulates its language-specific heuristics, so that it can be ported to any language pair with minimal effort (Melamed, 1997b). These features make SIMR one of the mostly widely applicable bitext-mapping algorithms published to date.

There are numerous ways to improve the methods presented here. For example, the current highly interdependent parameter set makes it too complicated for SIMR to exploit graded information that is available in the signal, such as the actual LCSRs, the actual angle deviations, and the actual point dispersals. All SIMR can do now is compare these quantities to a threshold. If SIMR were reparameterized so that its parameters were pairwise independent, then it would be possible to optimize the coefficients of a linear combination of graded parameters. Efficient use of more of the information in the signal would probably lead to better performance. Thus, the details of the current implementation are less important than the general approach to bitext mapping advocated here.

3 Application: Alignment

Many existing translators' tools and machine translation strategies depend on aligned text segments. An alignment does not permit crossing correspondences, so it is a special case of the more general correspondence relation. This chapter presents the Geometric Segment Alignment (GSA) algorithm, which uses segment boundary information to reduce general bitext maps to accurate segment alignments. Evaluation on a pre-existing gold standard has shown that GSA produces more accurate alignments than previously published algorithms that were tested the same way. GSA's expected running time is linear in the size of the input, faster than dynamic programming methods, which take $O(n^2)$. Therefore, it is not necessary to partially pre-align large bitexts manually before input to GSA.

3.1 Introduction

SIMR has no idea that words are often used to make sentences. It just outputs a series of corresponding token positions, leaving users free to draw their own conclusions about how the texts' larger units correspond. However, many existing translators' tools and machine translation strategies depend on aligned sentences or other aligned text segments. What can SIMR do for them? Formally, an alignment is a correspondence relation that does not permit crossing correspondences. This chapter presents the Geometric Segment Alignment (GSA) algorithm, which uses segment boundary information to reduce the correspondence relation in SIMR's output to a segment alignment. The GSA algorithm can be applied equally well to sentences, paragraphs, lists of items, or any other text units for which boundary information is available.

3.2 Correspondence is Richer Than Alignment

A set of correspondence points, supplemented with segment boundary information, expresses *segment correspondence*, which is a richer representation than segment alignment. Figure 3.1 illustrates how segment boundaries form a grid over the bitext space. Each cell in the grid represents the intersection of two segments, one from each half of the bitext. A point of correspondence inside cell (X, y) indicates that some token in segment X corresponds with some token in segment y; i.e., segments X and y correspond. For example, figure 3.1 indicates that segment e corresponds with segments G and H.

In contrast to a correspondence relation, "an *alignment* is a segmentation of the two texts such that the nth segment of one text is the translation of the nth segment of the other" (Simard et al., 1992). For example, given the token

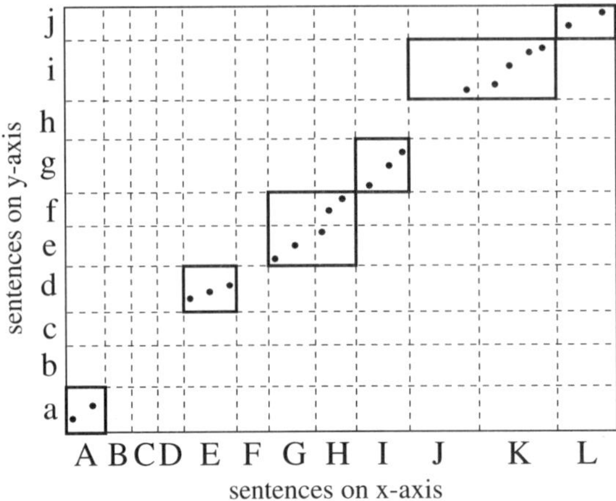

Figure 3.1
Segment boundaries form a grid over the bitext space. Each cell in the grid represents the product
of two segments, one from each half of the bitext. A point of correspondence inside cell (X, y)
indicates that some token in segment X corresponds to some token in segment y; i.e., the segments X and y correspond. So, for example, segment E corresponds with segment d. The aligned
blocks are outlined with solid lines.

correspondences in figure 3.1, the segment $\langle G, H \rangle$ should be aligned with the
segment $\langle e, f \rangle$. If segments $\langle X_1, \ldots, X_n \rangle$ align with segments $\langle y_1, \ldots, y_n \rangle$,
then $((\langle X_1, \ldots, X_n \rangle, \langle y_1, \ldots, y_n \rangle))$ is an *aligned block*. In geometric terms,
aligned blocks are rectangular regions of the bitext space such that the sides
of the rectangles coincide with segment boundaries, and such that no two rectangles overlap either vertically or horizontally. The aligned blocks in figure 3.1
are enclosed by solid lines.

SIMR's initial output has more expressive power than the alignment that
can be derived from it. One illustration of this difference is that segment correspondence can represent order inversions, but segment alignment cannot.
Inversions occur surprisingly often in real bitexts, even for sentence-size segments (Church, 1993). Figure 3.1 provides another illustration. If, instead of
the point in cell (H,e), there were a point in cell (G,f), the correct alignment
for that region would still be $((\langle G, H \rangle, \langle e, f \rangle))$. If there were points of correspondence in both (H,e) and (G,f), the correct alignment would remain the same.
Yet the three cases are clearly different. If a lexicographer wanted to see a word
in segment G in its bilingual context, it would be useful to know whether segment f is relevant.

3.3   The Geometric Segment Alignment (GSA) Algorithm

Given a sequence of segment boundaries for each half of a bitext, the *Geometric Segment Alignment (GSA)* algorithm reduces sets of correspondence points to segment alignments. The algorithm's first step is to perform a transitive closure over the input correspondence relation. For instance, if the input contains (G,e), (H,e), and (H,f), then GSA adds the pairing (G,f). Next, GSA forces all segments to be contiguous: If segment Y corresponds with segments x and z but not y, the pairing (Y, y) is added. In geometric terms, these two operations arrange all cells that contain points of correspondence into non-overlapping rectangles, while adding as few cells as possible. The result is an alignment relation.

A complete set of TPCs, together with appropriate boundary information, guarantees a perfect alignment. Alas, the points of correspondence postulated by SIMR arc ncither complete nor noise-fiee. SIMR makes errors of omission and errors of commission. Fortunately, the noise in SIMR's output causes alignment errors in predictable ways. GSA employs several backing-off heuristics to reduce the number of errors.

Typical errors of commission are stray points of correspondence like the one in cell (H, e) in figure 3.1. This point indicates that $\langle G, H \rangle$ and $\langle e, f \rangle$ should form a 2×2 aligned block, whereas the lengths of the component segments suggest that a pair of 1×1 blocks is more likely. In a separate development bitext, I have found that SIMR is usually wrong in these cases. To reduce such errors, GSA asks Gale & Church's length-based alignment algorithm (Gale & Church, 1991a; Simard, 1995) for a second opinion on any aligned block that is not 1×1. Whenever the length-based algorithm prefers a more fine-grained alignment, its judgment overrules SIMR's opinion.

Typical errors of omission are illustrated in figure 3.1 by the complete absence of correspondence points between segments $\langle B, C, D \rangle$ and $\langle b, c \rangle$. This empty block of segments is sandwiched between aligned blocks. It is highly likely that at least some of these segments are mutual translations, despite SIMR's failure to find any points of correspondence between them. Therefore, GSA treats all sandwiched empty blocks as aligned blocks. If an empty block is not 1×1, GSA re-aligns it using Gale & Church's a length-based algorithm, just as it would re-align any other many-to-many aligned block.

The most problematic cases involve an error of omission adjacent to an error of commission, as in blocks $(\langle \rangle, \langle h \rangle)$ and $(\langle J, K \rangle, \langle i \rangle)$. If the point in cell (J,i) should really be in cell (J,h), then re-alignment inside the erroneous blocks would not solve the problem. A naive solution is to merge these blocks and then to re-align them using a length-based method. Unfortunately, this kind of alignment pattern, i.e., 0×1 followed by 2×1, is surprisingly often correct. Length-based methods assign low probabilities to such pattern sequences and usually get them wrong. Therefore, GSA also considers the confidence level with which the length-based alignment algorithm reports its re-alignment. If this confidence level is sufficiently high, GSA accepts the length-based re-alignment; otherwise, the alignment indicated by SIMR's points of correspondence is retained. The minimum confidence at which GSA trusts the length-based re-alignment is a GSA parameter, which has been optimized on a separate development bitext.

3.4   Evaluation

GSA processed two bitext maps produced by SIMR using two different matching predicates. The first matching predicate relied only on cognates that pass a certain LCSR threshold, as described in section 2.4.2. The second matching predicate was like the first, except that it also generated a point of correspondence whenever the input token pair appeared as an entry in a translation lexicon. The translation lexicon was automatically extracted from an MRBD (Cousin et al., 1991).

Bitexts involving millions of segments are becoming more and more common. Before comparing bitext alignment algorithms in terms of accuracy, it is important to compare their asymptotic running times. In order to run a quadratic-time alignment algorithm in a reasonable amount of time on a large bitext, the bitext must be pre-segmented into a set of smaller bitexts. When a bitext contains no easily recognizable "anchors," such as paragraphs or sections, this first-pass alignment must be done manually.

Given a reasonably good bitext map, GSA's expected running time is linear in the number of input segment boundaries. In all the bitexts on which GSA was trained and tested, the points of correspondence in SIMR's output were sufficiently dense and precise that GSA backed off to a quadratic-time alignment algorithm only for very small aligned blocks. For example, when the seed translation lexicon was used in SIMR's matching predicate, the largest aligned block that needed to be re-aligned was 5×5 segments. Without the seed trans-

Bitext	Algorithm	Errors, given aligned paragraphs	%	Errors, not given aligned paragraphs	%
"easy"	Gale & Church (1991a)	not available		128	1.8
Hansard	Simard et al. (1992)	114	1.6	171	2.4
($n = 7123$)	SIMR/GSA	104	1.5	115	1.6
	SIMR/GSA with MRBD	80	1.1	90	1.3
"hard"	Gale & Church (1991a)	not available		80	3.0
Hansard	Simard et al. (1992)	50	1.9	102	3.8
($n = 2693$)	SIMR/GSA	50	1.9	61	2.3
	SIMR/GSA with MRBD	45	1.7	48	1.8

Table 3.1
Comparison of bitext alignment algorithms' accuracy. One error is counted for each aligned block in the reference alignment that is missing from the test alignment.

lation lexicon, the largest re-aligned block was 7×7 segments. Thus, GSA can obviate the need to pre-align large bitexts manually.

Table 3.1 compares GSA's accuracy on the "easy" and "hard" French/ English bitexts with the accuracy of two other alignment algorithms, as reported by Simard et al. (1992). The error metric counts one error for each aligned block in the reference alignment that is missing from the test alignment. To take into account the possibility of modularizing the overall alignment task into paragraph alignment followed by sentence alignment, Simard et al. (1992) reported the accuracy of their sentence alignment algorithm when a perfect alignment at the paragraph level is given. SIMR/GSA was also tested in this manner, yielding the second set of comparisons in table 3.1.

Due to the scarcity of hand-aligned training bitexts at my disposal, GSA's backing-off heuristics are somewhat ad hoc. Even so, GSA performs at least as well as, and usually better than, other alignment algorithms for which comparable results have been published. Chen (1993) has also published a quantitative evaluation of his alignment algorithm on these reference bitexts, but his evaluation was done post hoc. Since the results here are based on a gold standard, they are not comparable to Chen's results. Among other reasons, error rates based on a gold standard are sometimes inflated by errors in the gold standard, as was indeed the case for the gold standard used here (see chapter 4). It is also an open question whether GSA performs better than the algorithm proposed by Wu (1994). The two algorithms have not yet been evaluated on the same test data. For now, I can offer only a theoretical reason why SIMR+GSA should be more accurate than the algorithms of Chen and Wu: Bitext maps lead to alignment more directly than a translation model (Chen, 1993) or a translation lexicon (Wu, 1994), because both segment alignments and bitext maps are relations between token instances, rather than between token types.

3.5 Conclusion

Admittedly, GSA is useful only when a good bitext map is available. In such cases, there are three reasons to favor GSA over other options for alignment: One, it is simply more accurate. Two, its expected running time is linear in the size of the bitext. Therefore, three, it is not necessary to pre-align large bitexts manually before input to GSA.

More important than GSA's current performance is GSA's potential performance. With a bigger development bitext, more effective backing-off heuristics can be developed. More precise input could also make a difference: GSA's performance will improve in lockstep with SIMR's performance.

4   Application: Automatic Detection of Omissions in Translations

ADOMIT is an algorithm for Automatic Detection of OMIssions in Translations. The algorithm relies solely on geometric analysis of bitext maps and uses no linguistic information. This property allows it to deal equally well with omissions that do not correspond to linguistic units, such as might result from word-processing mishaps. ADOMIT has proven its worth by discovering errors in a hand-constructed gold standard for evaluating bitext mapping algorithms. Quantitative evaluation on simulated omissions has shown that ADOMIT can find a large enough proportion of typical omissions to be of great practical benefit. The technique is easy to implement and easy to integrate into a translator's work routine.

4.1 Introduction

Omissions in translations arise in several ways. A tired translator can accidentally skip a sentence or a paragraph in a large text. Pressing a wrong key can cause a word-processing system to delete several lines without warning. Such anomalies can usually be detected by careful proof-reading. However, price competition is forcing translation bureaus to cut down on this labor-intensive practice. An automatic method of detecting omissions can be a great help in maintaining translation quality.

ADOMIT is an algorithm for Automatic Detection of OMIssions in Translations. ADOMIT rests on principles of geometry, and uses no linguistic information. This property allows it to deal equally well with omissions that do not correspond to linguistic units, such as might result from word-processing mishaps. ADOMIT is limited only by the quality of the available bitext map.

The chapter begins by describing the geometric properties of bitext maps that make possible the Basic Method for detecting omissions. Section 4.3 shows that the Basic Method can reliably detect alignment errors in hand-aligned bitexts. Section 4.4 suggests how the omission detection technique can be embodied in a translators' tool. The main obstacle to perfect omission detection is noise in bitext maps, which is characterized in section 4.5. ADOMIT is a more robust variation of the Basic Method. Section 4.6 explains how ADOMIT filters out some of the noise in bitext maps, section 4.7 describes my method for simulating omissions, and section 4.8 demonstrates ADOMIT's performance and its value as a quality-control tool.

4.2 The Basic Method

Any algorithm for detecting omissions in a translation must use a process of elimination: It must first decide which segments of the original text *have*

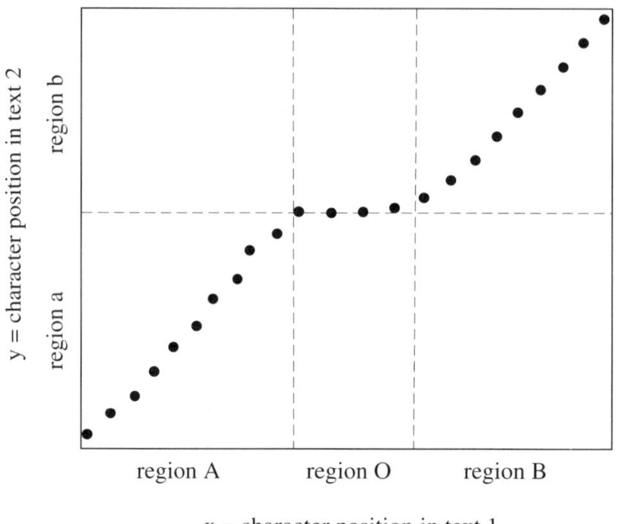

Figure 4.1
An omission in bitext space. Regions A and B correspond to regions a and b, respectively. Region O has no corresponding region on the vertical axis.

corresponding segments in the translation. This decision requires a detailed description of the correspondence between units of the original text and units of the translation, i.e., a bitext map. Omissions in translations give rise to distinctive patterns in bitext maps, as illustrated in figure 4.1. The nearly horizontal part of the bitext map in region O takes up almost no part of the vertical axis. This region represents a section of the text on the horizontal axis that has no corresponding section in the text on the vertical axis—the very definition of an omission. The slope between the end points of the region is unusually low. An omission in the text on the horizontal axis would manifest itself as a nearly vertical region of the bitext map. These unusual slope conditions are the key to detecting omissions.

Given a noise-free bitext map, omissions are easy to detect. First, a bitext space is constructed by placing the original text on the x-axis and the translation on the y-axis. Second, the known points of correspondence are plotted in the bitext space. Each adjacent pair of points delimits a segment of the bitext map. Any segment whose slope is unusually low is probably an omission. This notion can be made precise by specifying a slope angle threshold t. So, third, segments with slope angle $a < t$ are flagged as *omitted segments*.

4.3 Noise-Free Bitext Maps

The only way to ensure that a bitext map is noise-free is to construct one by hand. Simard et al. (1992) hand-aligned corresponding sentences in two excerpts of the Canadian Hansards (parliamentary debate transcripts available in English and French). For historical reasons, these bitexts are called "easy" and "hard" in the literature. The sentence-based alignments were converted to character-based alignments by noting the corresponding character positions at the end of each pair of aligned sentences. The result was two hand-constructed bitext maps. Several researchers besides me have used these particular bitext maps as a gold standard for evaluating bitext mapping and alignment algorithms (Simard et al., 1992; Church, 1993; Dagan et al., 1993b).

Surprisingly, ADOMIT found a number of errors in these hand-aligned bitexts, both in the alignment and in the original translation. ADOMIT processed both halves of both bitexts using slope angle thresholds of $5°$, $10°$, $15°$, $20°$, and $25°$. For each run, ADOMIT produced a list of the bitext map's segments whose slope angles were below the specified threshold t. The output for the French half of the "easy" bitext, with $t = 15°$, consisted of the following 10 items:

```
(26869, 29175) to (26917, 29176)
(42075, 45647) to (42179, 45648)
(44172, 47794) to (44236, 47795)
(211071, 230935) to (211379, 231007)
(211725, 231714) to (211795, 231715)
(319179, 348672) to (319207, 348673)
(436118, 479850) to (436163, 479857)
(453064, 499175) to (453116, 499176)
(504626, 556847) to (504663, 556848)
(658098, 726197) to (658225, 726198)
```

Each ordered pair is a coordinate in the bitext space; each pair of coordinates delimits one omitted segment. Examination of these 10 pairs of character ranges in the bitext revealed that

- four omitted segments pointed to omissions in the original translation;

- four omitted segments pointed to alignment errors;

- one omitted segment pointed to an omission that apparently caused an alignment error (i.e., one of each);

• one omitted segment pointed to a piece of text that was duplicated in the original but translated only once.

With $t = 10°$, nine of the 10 segments in the list still came up; eight out of 10 remained with $t = 5°$. Similar errors were discovered in the other half of the "easy" bitext and in the "hard" bitext, including one omission of more than 450 characters. Other segments appeared in the list for $t > 15°$. None of the other segments were outright omissions or misalignments. However, all of them corresponded to non-literal translations or paraphrases. For instance, with $t = 20°$, ADOMIT discovered a case in which "Why is the government doing this?" was translated as "Pourquoi?"

The hand-aligned bitexts were also used to measure ADOMIT's recall. The human aligners indicated omissions in the original translation by 1–0 alignments (Gale & Church, 1991a; Isabelle, 1995). ADOMIT did not use this information; the algorithm has no notion of a line of text. However, a simple cross-check showed that ADOMIT found all of the omissions. The README file distributed with the bitexts admitted that the "human aligners weren't infallible" and predicted "probably no more than five or so" alignment errors. ADOMIT corroborated this prediction by finding exactly five alignment errors. Thus, ADOMIT achieved perfect recall on both kinds of errors.

4.4 A Translator's Tool

As any translator knows, many omissions are intentional. Translations are seldom word for word. Metaphors and idioms usually cannot be translated literally, so paraphrasing is common. Sometimes a paraphrased translation is much shorter or much longer than the original. Segments of the bitext map that represent such translations have slope characteristics similar to omissions, even though the translations may be perfectly valid. These cases are termed *intended omissions* to distinguish them from omission errors. To be useful, the omission detection algorithm must be able to tell the difference between intended and unintended omissions.

Fortunately, the two kinds of omissions have different length distributions. Intended omissions are seldom longer than a few words, whereas accidental omissions are often on the order of a sentence or more. So, a simple heuristic for separating the accidental omissions from the intended omissions is to sort all the omitted segments from longest to shortest. The longer accidental omissions will float to the top of the sorted list.

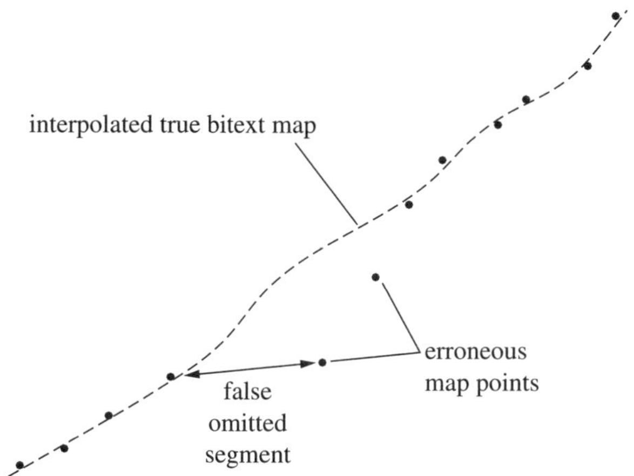

Figure 4.2
An undetectable error in the bitext map. A real omission could result in the same map pattern as
these erroneous points.

Translators can search for omissions when they finish a translation, just
as they might run a spelling checker. A translator can find omission errors
by scanning the sorted list of omitted segments from the top and examining
the relevant regions of the bitext. Each time the list points to an accidental
omission, the translator can make an appropriate correction in the translation.
If the translation is reasonably complete, the accidental omissions will quickly
stop appearing in the list and the correction process can stop. Only the smallest
errors of omission will remain.

4.5   Noisy Bitext Maps

The results of section 4.3 demonstrate ADOMIT's potential. However, such
stellar performance is only possible with a nearly perfect bitext map. Such
bitext maps rarely exist outside the laboratory; today's best automatic methods
for finding bitext maps are far from perfect. At least two kinds of map errors
can interfere with omission detection. One kind results in spurious omitted
segments, while the other hides real omissions.

Figure 4.2 shows how erroneous points in a bitext map can be indistinguish-
able from omitted segments. When such errors occur in the map, ADOMIT
cannot help but announce an omission where there isn't one. This kind of map
error is the main obstacle to the algorithm's precision.

The other kind of map error is the main obstacle to the algorithm's recall. A typical manifestation is illustrated in figure 4.1. The map segments in Region O contradict the injective property of bitext maps. Most of the points in Region O are probably noise, because they map many positions on the x-axis to just a few positions on the y-axis. Such spurious points break up large omitted segments into sequences of small ones. When the omitted segments are sorted by length for presentation to the translator, the fragmented omitted segments sink to the bottom of the list, along with segments that correspond to small intended omissions. The translator is likely to stop scanning the sorted list of omissions before reaching them.

4.6   ADOMIT

ADOMIT alleviates the fragmentation problem by finding and ignoring extraneous map points. A couple of definitions help to explain the technique. Recall that omitted segments are defined with respect to a chosen slope angle threshold t: Any segment of the bitext map with slope angle less than t is an omitted segment. An omitted segment that contains extraneous points can be characterized as a sequence of minimal omitted segments, interspersed with one or more interfering segments. The following terms are illustrated in figure 4.3. A *minimal omitted segment* is an omitted segment between two adjacent points in the bitext map. A *maximal omitted segment* is an omitted segment that is not a proper subsegment of another omitted segment. *Interfering segments* are subsegments of maximal omitted segments with a slope angle *above* the chosen threshold. Interfering segments are always delimited

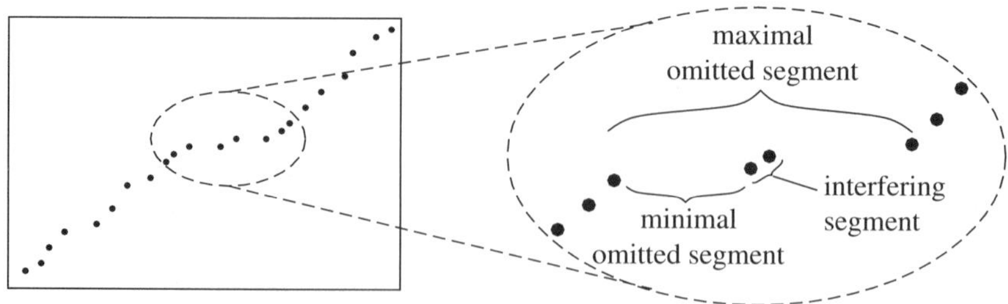

Figure 4.3
Fragmentation of omitted segments. Maximal omitted segments would be easy to find, were it not for interfering segments.

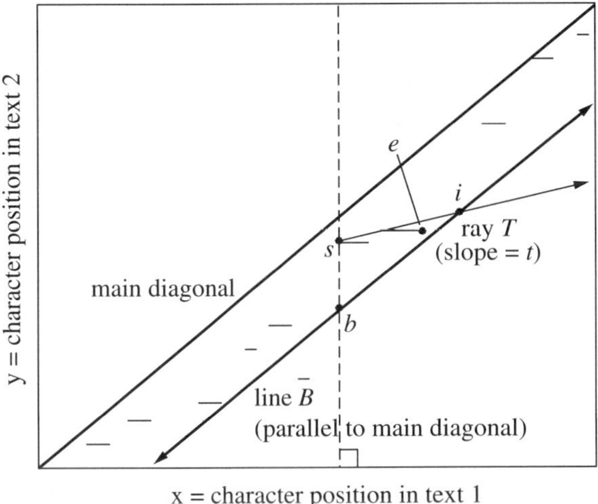

Figure 4.4
An efficient search for maximal omitted segments. The array of minimal omitted segments lies above line $\bar{B}$. Any sequence of segments starting at s, such that the slope angle of the whole sequence is less than t, must end at some point e in the triangle $\triangle sib$.

by extraneous map points. If it were not for interfering segments, the fragmentation problem could be solved by simply concatenating adjacent minimal omitted segments. Using these definitions, the problem of reconstructing maximal omitted segments can be stated as follows: Which sequences of minimal omitted segments resulted from fragmentation of a maximal omitted segment?

A maximal omitted segment must have a slope angle below the chosen threshold t. So the problem can be solved by considering each pair of minimal omitted segments to see if the slope angle between the starting point of the first and the end point of the second is less than t. This brute-force solution requires approximately $\frac{1}{2}n^2$ comparisons. Since a large bitext can have tens of thousands of minimal omitted segments, a faster method is desirable.

Theorem 1 suggests a fast algorithm to search for pairs of minimal omitted segments that are farthest apart and that may have resulted from fragmentation of a maximal omitted segment. The theorem is illustrated in figure 4.4. B and T are mnemonics for "bottom" and "top."

THEOREM 4.1 Let A be the array of all minimal omitted segments, sorted by the abscissa of the left end point. Let $\bar{B}$ be a line in the bitext space whose slope equals the bitext slope, such that all the segments in A lie above $\bar{B}$. Let s be the left endpoint of a segment in A. Let $\vec{T}$ be a ray starting at s with a slope angle equal to the chosen threshold t. Let i be the intersection of $\bar{B}$ and $\vec{T}$. Let b be the point on $\bar{B}$ with the same abscissa as s. Now, a maximal omitted segment starting at s must end at some point e in the triangle $\triangle sib$.

Proof   Suppose e is outside $\triangle sib$. Then e must be to the left of segment $\bar{bs}$, below segment $\bar{bi}$, or above segment $\bar{si}$. s is defined as the left end point, so e cannot be to the left of s. By definition of $\bar{B}$, e cannot be below segment $\bar{bi}$. If e were above segment $\bar{si}$, then the slope angle of segment $\bar{se}$ would be greater than the slope angle of $\vec{T} = t$, so $\bar{se}$ could not be an omitted segment.   ∎

ADOMIT exploits theorem 4.1 as follows. Each minimal omitted segment z in A is considered in turn. Starting at z, ADOMIT searches the array A for the last (i.e., rightmost) segment whose right end point e is in the triangle $\triangle sib$. Usually, this segment will be z itself, in which case the single minimal omitted segment is deemed a maximal omitted segment. When e is not on the same minimal omitted segment as s, ADOMIT concatenates all the segments between s and e to form a maximal omitted segment. The search starting from segment z can stop as soon as it encounters a segment with a right end point higher than i. For useful values of t, each search will span no more than a handful of candidate end points. Processing the entire array A in this manner produces the desired set of maximal omitted segments very quickly.

4.7   Simulation of Omissions

To accurately evaluate a system for detecting omissions in translations, it is necessary to use a bitext with many omissions whose locations are known in advance. For perfect validity, the omissions should be those of a real translator, working on a real translation, detected by a perfect proof-reader. Unfortunately, first drafts of translations that had been subjected to careful revision were not readily available. Therefore, the evaluation proceeded by simulation. The advantage of a simulation was complete control over the lengths and relative positions of omissions. This is important because the noise in a bitext map is more likely to obscure a short omission than a long one.

The simulated omissions' lengths were chosen to represent the lengths of typical sentences and paragraphs in real texts. A corpus of 61479 *Le Monde* paragraphs yielded a median French paragraph length of 553 characters. I had no corpus of French sentences, so I estimated the median French sentence length less directly. A corpus of 43747 *Wall Street Journal* sentences yielded a median English sentence length of 126 characters. This number was multiplied by 1.103, the ratio of text lengths in the "easy" Hansard bitext, to yield a median French sentence length of 139. Of course, the lengths of sentences and paragraphs in other text genres will vary.

The placement of simulated omissions in the text was governed by the assumption that translators' errors of omission occur independently of one another. This assumption implied that it was reasonable to scatter the simulated omissions in a single text. To simplify subsequent evaluation, the omissions were spaced at least 1000 characters apart. Such a distribution of simulated omissions simplified the experimental design, because performance on a fixed number of omissions in one text would be the same as performance on the same number of omissions scattered among multiple texts. As a result, the bitext-mapping algorithm had to be run only once per parameter set, instead of separately for each of the omissions in that parameter set.

Sentence-length omissions were simulated by deleting 100 segments from the French half of the "easy" Hansard bitext, 139 characters per segment. The position of each simulated omission was randomly generated from a uniform distribution, except that a minimum buffer zone of 1000 characters was enforced between consecutive omissions. The "easy" bitext was selected because it is the one for which the densest hand-constructed true bitext map (TBM) was available.[1] The TBM was used to find the segments in the English half of the bitext that corresponded to the deleted French segments. For the purposes of the simulation, these English segments served as the "true" omitted segments. The same procedure was used to simulate paragraph-length omissions, this time deleting segments of 533 characters each.

4.8 Evaluation

A useful evaluation of any omission detection algorithm must take the human factor into account. A translator is unlikely to slog through a long series of false alarms to make sure that there are no more true omissions in the translation. Several consecutive false omissions will deter the translator from searching any further. On average, the more consecutive false omissions it takes for a translator to give up, the more true omissions she will find. Thus, recall on this tasks correlates with the translator's patience. Translator patience was one of the independent variables in this experiment, quantified in terms of the number of consecutive false omissions that the translator will tolerate.

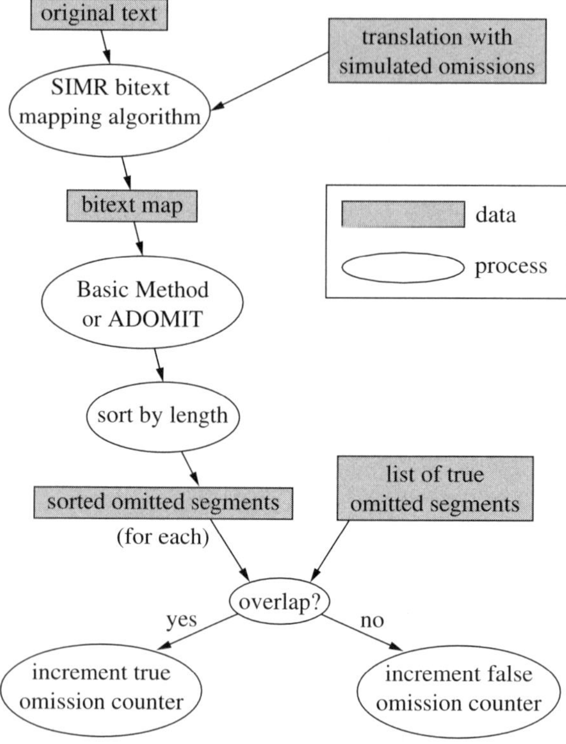

Figure 4.5
Evaluation method for simulated omissions.

Separate evaluations were carried out for the Basic Method and for ADOMIT. Each algorithm was evaluated on the two different omission lengths. The evaluation of each algorithm on each omission length was carried out according to the following method, as illustrated in figure 4.5:

1. The SIMR bitext mapping algorithm in section 2.4 was used to find a map between the original English text and the French text containing the simulated omissions.[2]

2. The bitext map resulting from step 1 was fed into the omission detection algorithm, which flagged what it thought were omitted segments. The flagged omitted segments, which varied in length because of noise in the bitext map, were sorted in order of decreasing length.

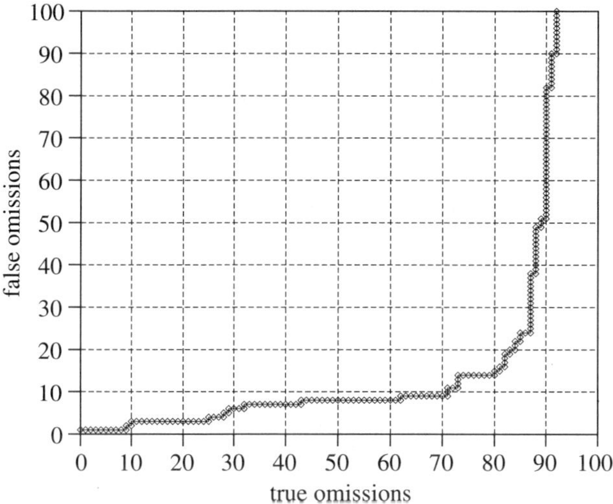

Figure 4.6
An example of the order of "true" and "false" omissions when sorted by length. Horizontal runs
correspond to consecutive "true" omissions in the output; vertical runs correspond to consecutive
"false" omissions. In this example, the first run of more than three "false" omissions occurs only
after 87 "true" omissions.

3. Each omitted segment in the list output by step 2 was compared, in order, to
the list of true omitted segments. If any of the true omitted segments overlapped
the flagged omitted segment, the "true omissions" counter was incremented.
Otherwise, the "false omissions" counter was incremented. An example of the
resulting pattern of increments is shown in figure 4.6.

4. The pattern of increments was further analyzed to find the first point at
which the "false omissions" counter was incremented three times in a row.
The value of the "true omissions" counter at that point represented the recall
achieved by translators who give up after three consecutive false omissions. To
measure the recall that would be achieved by more patient translators, the "true
omissions" counter was also recorded at the first run of four consecutive false
omissions and at the first run of five.

5. Steps 1 to 4 were repeated on 10 different sets of simulated omissions in
order to measure 95% confidence intervals.

The low slope angle thresholds used in section 4.3 are suboptimal in the presence of noise, because much of the noise results in segments of very low slope.

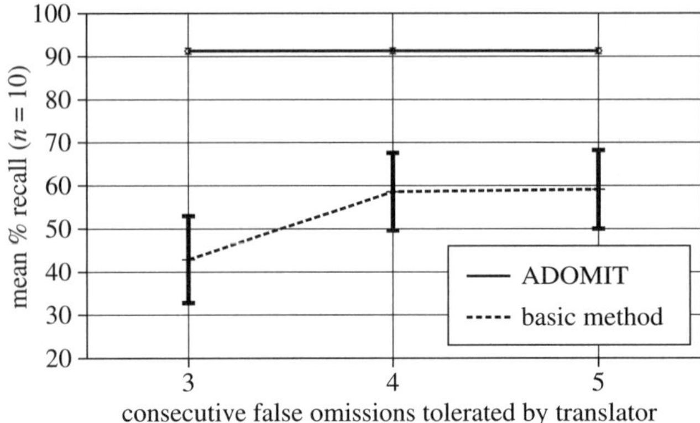

Figure 4.7
Mean recall scores for simulated paragraph-size (553-character) omissions for translators with varying degrees of patience. Error bars represent 95% confidence intervals.

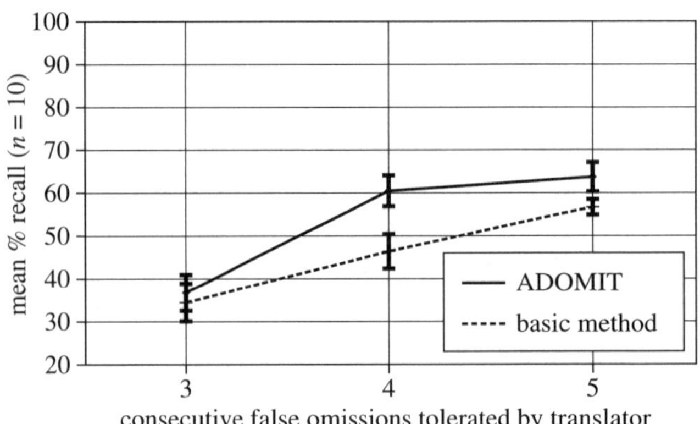

Figure 4.8
Mean recall scores for simulated sentence-size (139-character) omissions for translators with varying degrees of patience. Error bars represent 95% confidence intervals.

New thresholds were reoptimized for ADOMIT and for the Basic Method using a separate development bitext. The algorithms were never informed of the length or number of simulated omissions, nor that all the omissions were of the same length in a given text.

Figures 4.7 and 4.8 plot the mean recall scores for translators with different amounts of patience. ADOMIT outperformed the Basic Method by up to 48 percentage points. ADOMIT is also more robust, as indicated by its narrower confidence intervals. The results shows that ADOMIT can help translators catch more than 90% of all paragraph-size omissions and more than half of all sentence-size omissions.

4.9 Conclusion

ADOMIT demonstrates that bitext maps have applications other than inducing statistical translation models, and that accurate high-resolution bitext maps are more valuable than mere alignments. Given a perfect bitext map, ADOMIT can reliably detect even the smallest errors of omission. Given SIMR's bitext maps, ADOMIT finds enough typical omissions to be a valuable quality control tool for translators and translation bureaus.

II THE TYPE-TOKEN INTERFACE

5 Models of Co-occurrence

A *model of co-occurrence* in bitext is a boolean predicate that indicates whether a given pair of word *tokens* co-occur in corresponding regions of the bitext space. Co-occurrence is a precondition for the possibility that two tokens might be mutual translations. Models of co-occurrence are the glue that binds methods for mapping bitext correspondence and methods for estimating translation models into an integrated system for exploiting parallel texts. Different models of co-occurrence are possible, depending on the kind of bitext map available, the language-specific information available, and the assumptions made about the nature of translational equivalence. Although most statistical translation models are based on models of co-occurrence, modeling co-occurrence optimally is more difficult than may at first appear.

5.1 Introduction

Most methods for estimating translation models from bitext start with the following intuition: Words that are translations of each other are more likely to appear in corresponding bitext regions than other pairs of words. The intuition is simple, but its correct exploitation turns out to be rather subtle. Most of the literature on translation model estimation presumes that corresponding regions of the input bitexts are represented by neatly aligned segments. As discussed in chapter 2, however, most of the bitexts available today are not easy to align. Moreover, imposing an alignment relation on such bitexts is inefficient, because alignments cannot capture crossing correspondences among text segments.

Chapter 2 proposed methods for producing general bitext maps for arbitrary bitexts. The present chapter shows how to use bitext maps and other information to construct a model of co-occurrence. A *model of co-occurrence* is a boolean predicate that indicates whether a given pair of word *tokens* co-occur in corresponding regions of the bitext space. Co-occurrence is a precondition for the possibility that two tokens might be mutual translations. Models of co-occurrence are the glue that binds methods for mapping bitext correspondence and methods for estimating translation models into an integrated system for exploiting parallel texts. When the model of co-occurrence is modularized away from the translation model, it also becomes easier to study translation model estimation methods per se.

Different models of co-occurrence are possible, depending on the kind of bitext map available, the language-specific information available, and the assumptions made about the nature of translational equivalence. The following three sections explore these three variables.

5.2 Relevant Regions of the Bitext Space

By definition of "mutual translations," corresponding regions of a text and its translation contain word token pairs that are mutual translations. Therefore, a general representation of bitext correspondence is the natural concept on which to build a model of where mutual translations co-occur. The most general representation of bitext correspondence is a bitext map, as described in section 2.2. Token pairs whose coordinates are part of the true bitext map (TBM) are mutual translations, by definition of the TBM. The a priori likelihood that two tokens are mutual translations is inversely correlated with the distance between the tokens' coordinate in the bitext space and the interpolated TBM.

It may be possible to develop translation model estimation methods that are initialized with a graded model of co-occurrence. However, all models in this book and all models I've seen in the literature are initialized with a boolean co-occurrence model—they want to know either that two tokens co-occur or that they do not. A boolean co-occurrence predicate can be defined by setting a threshold δ on the distance from the interpolated bitext map. Any token pair whose coordinate is closer than δ to the bitext map would be considered to co-occur by this predicate. The optimal value of δ varies with the language pair,

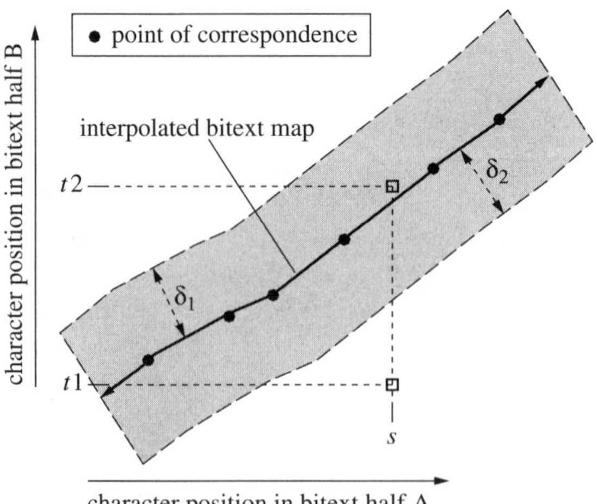

Figure 5.1
Distance-based model of co-occurrence. Word token pairs whose coordinates lie in the shaded region count as co-occurrences. Thus, $(s, t2)$ co-occur, but $(s, t1)$ do not.

the bitext genre and the application. More generally, different thresholds δ_1 and δ_2 can be applied on each side of the TBM. Figure 5.1 illustrates what I call the *distance-based model of co-occurrence*. Dagan et al. (1993b) were the first to use a distance-based model of co-occurrence, although they measured the distance in words rather than in characters.

General bitext mapping algorithms are a relatively recent invention. So far, most researchers interested in co-occurrence of mutual translations have relied on bitexts in which sentence boundaries (or other text unit boundaries) were easy to find (e.g. Gale & Church, 1991b; Kumano & Hirakawa, 1994; Fung, 1995b; Melamed, 1995). Aligned text segments suggest a *boundary-based model of co-occurrence*, as illustrated in figure 5.2.

For bitexts involving languages with similar word order, a more accurate *combined model of co-occurrence* can be built using both segment boundary information and the map-distance threshold. As shown in figure 5.3, each of these constraints eliminates the noise from a characteristic region of the bitext space.

5.3 Co-occurrence Counting Methods

Both the boundary-based and distance-based constraints restrict the region of the bitext space where tokens may be considered to co-occur. Yet these constraints do not answer the question of how to count co-occurrences within the restricted regions. It is somewhat surprising that this is a question at all, and

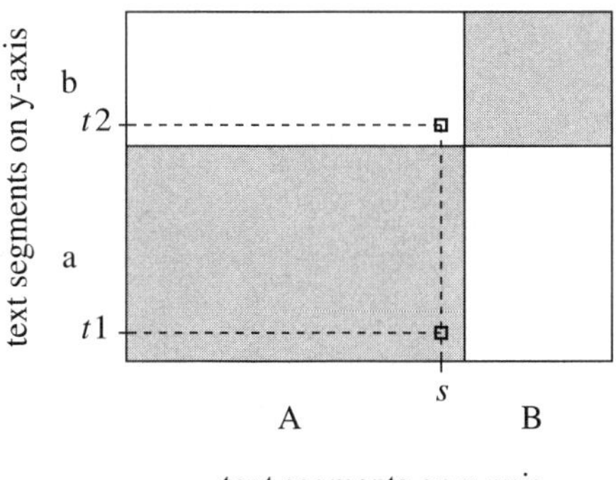

Figure 5.2
Boundary-based model of co-occurrence. Word token pairs whose coordinates lie in shaded regions count as co-occurrences. In contrast with figure 5.1, $(s, t1)$ co-occur but $(s, t2)$ do not.

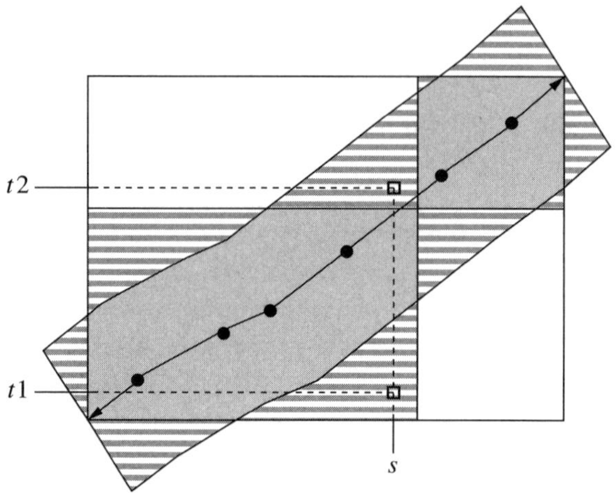

Figure 5.3
Combined model of co-occurrence. Word token pairs whose coordinates lie in shaded regions count as co-occurrences. In contrast with figures 5.1 and 5.2, neither $(s, t1)$ nor $(s, t2)$ co-occur. Striped regions indicate eliminated sources of noise.

most authors ignore it. However, when authors specify their translation model estimation algorithms in sufficient detail to answer this question, the most frequent answer (given, e.g., by Brown et al., 1993b; Dagan et al., 1993b; Kupiec, 1993; Melamed, 1995) turns out to be suboptimal for most applications.

The problem is easiest to illustrate under the boundary-based model of co-occurrence. Given two aligned text segments, the most common way to count co-occurrences is by multiplication:

$$cooc(\mathbf{u}, \mathbf{v}) = e(\mathbf{u}) \cdot f(\mathbf{v}), \tag{5.1}$$

where $e(\mathbf{u})$ and $f(\mathbf{v})$ are the frequencies of occurrence of $\mathbf{u}$ and $\mathbf{v}$ in their respective segments. This method works fine for most $\mathbf{u}$ and $\mathbf{v}$, where $e(\mathbf{u})$ and $f(\mathbf{v})$ are either 0 or 1, and equation (5.1) returns 1 just in case both words occur. The problem arises when $e(\mathbf{u}) > 1$ and $f(\mathbf{v}) > 1$. For example, if $e(\mathbf{u}) = f(\mathbf{v}) = 3$, then according to equation (5.1), $cooc(\mathbf{u}, \mathbf{v}) = 9$!

A nonlinear relationship between co-occurrence counts and marginal frequency counts is not a problem for Brown et al. (1993b)'s Model 1, because its search space is everywhere concave, so it has only one local optimum (Brown et al., 1993b, equation 74). It is straightforward to estimate Model 1's globally optimal parameter values, as long as all the relevant co-occurrence counts are initialized to more than zero. For all other translation models that I'm aware of, the search space has many local optima, so it is important to choose favorable initial conditions.

Loosely speaking, the best initial conditions for a statistical model are those that are closest to the globally optimal parameter values. If maximum likelihood estimation is used to search for the optimum parameters, then, all else equal, the best initialization is the relative frequency of whatever phenomena are being modeled. For translation models, this line of reasoning suggests co-occurrence counts that grow linearly with marginal frequencies. If the two aligned segments in the example above are really translations of each other, then it is most likely that each of the occurrences of $\mathbf{u}$ is a translation of just one of the occurrences of $\mathbf{v}$. Although it may not be known which of the three v's each u corresponds to, the number of times that $\mathbf{u}$ and $\mathbf{v}$ co-occur as possible translations of each other in that segment pair must be 3.

There are various ways to arrive at $cooc(\mathbf{u}, \mathbf{v}) = 3$. Two of the simplest ways are

$$cooc(\mathbf{u}, \mathbf{v}) = \min[e(\mathbf{u}), f(\mathbf{v})] \tag{5.2}$$

and

$$cooc(\mathbf{u}, \mathbf{v}) = \max[e(\mathbf{u}), f(\mathbf{v})]. \tag{5.3}$$

Equation (5.2) is based on the simplifying assumption that each word is translated to at most one other word.[1] Equation (5.3) is based on the simplifying assumption that each word is translated to at least one other word. Either simplifying assumption yields more generally useful co-occurrence counts than the multiplication method in equation (5.1).

Counting co-occurrences is more difficult under a distance-based co-occurrence model, because there are no aligned segments and consequently no useful definition for $e()$ and $f()$. Furthermore, under a distance-based co-occurrence model, the co-occurrence relation is not transitive. As illustrated in figure 5.4, it is possible that t_1 co-occurs with s_1, s_1 co-occurs with t_2, t_2 co-occurs with s_2, but t_1 does not co-occur with s_2. The correct counting method becomes clearer if the problem is recast in graph-theoretic terms. Let the words in each half of the bitext represent the vertices on one side of a bipartite graph. Let there be edges between each pair of words whose co-ordinates are closer than δ to the bitext map. Now, under the "at most one" assumption of equation (5.2), each co-occurrence is represented by an edge in the graph's

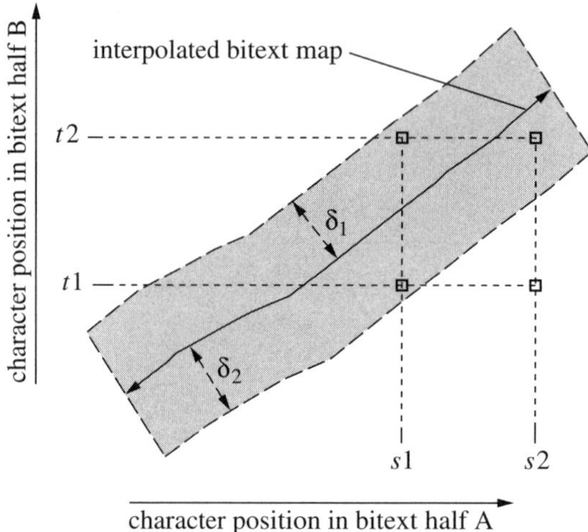

Figure 5.4
Under a distance-based model of co-occurrence, the co-occurrence relation is not transitive.

maximum matching.[2] Under the "at least one" assumption of equation (5.3), each co-occurrence is represented by an edge in the graph's smallest vertex cover. Maximum matching can be computed in polynomial time for any graph (Ahuja et al., 1993). Vertex cover can be solved in polynomial time for bipartite graphs.[3] It's likely that the solutions to both problems can be found very quickly by exploiting the ordering among the nodes. That is, the search space can be drastically reduced by noting that if s_2 falls between s_1 and s_3, and t_1 co-occurs with s_1 but not with s_2, then t_1 cannot co-occur with s_3. It is of no importance that maximum matchings and minimum vertex covers may be non-unique—by definition, all solutions have the same number of edges, and this number is the correct co-occurrence count.

5.4 Language-Specific Filters

Co-occurrence is a universal precondition for translational equivalence among word tokens in bitexts. Other preconditions may be imposed if certain language-specific resources are available (Melamed, 1995). For example, parts of speech tend to be preserved in translation (Papageorgiou et al., 1994). If part-of-speech taggers are available for both languages in a bitext, and if cases in which one part of speech is translated to another are not important for the intended application, then we can rule out the possibility of translational equivalence for all token pairs involving different parts of speech. A more obvious source of language-specific information is a machine-readable bilingual dictionary (MRBD). If token a in one half of the bitext is found to co-occur with token b in the other half, and (a, b) is an entry in the MRBD, then it is highly likely that the tokens a and b are indeed mutual translations. In this case, there is no point considering the co-occurrence of a or b with any other token. Similarly, exclusive candidacy can be granted to cognate token pairs (see section 2.4.2).

All the translation models in this book are based on co-occurrence counts. None of them rely on any language-specific resource. However, more accurate models may result if the co-occurrence counts are biased with language-specific knowledge. Without loss of generality, whenever I refer to co-occurrence counts in the rest of this book, I can refer to co-occurrence counts that have been filtered using whatever language-specific resources happen to be available. It does not matter if there are dependencies among the different knowledge sources, as long as each is used as a simple filter on the co-occurrence relation (Melamed, 1995).

5.5 Conclusion

In this short chapter, I have investigated methods for modeling word token co-occurrence. Models of co-occurrence are a necessary precursor to all the most accurate translation models in the literature and all the translation models in this book. So far, most researchers have relied on only a restricted form of co-occurrence, based on a restricted kind of bitext map, applicable to only a limited class of bitexts. I have shown how a more general co-occurrence model can be based on any bitext map, and thus on any bitext.

The correct method for counting the number of times that two words co-occur turns out to be rather subtle, especially for more general co-occurrence models. As noted in section 5.3, many published translation models have been based on suboptimal models of co-occurrence. This chapter has exposed their shortcomings and shown how to improve them.

6 Manual Annotation of Translational Equivalence

Bilingual annotators were paid to link roughly sixteen thousand corresponding words between on-line versions of the Bible in modern French and modern English. These annotations are freely available to the research community to serve as a standard data set for developing and testing translation lexicons and statistical translation models. This chapter describes the annotated bitext, the specially designed annotation tool, and the strategies employed to increase the consistency of the annotations. The annotation process was repeated five times by different annotators. Inter-annotator agreement rates indicate that the annotations are reasonably reliable and that the method is easy to replicate. The gold standard annotations can be freely downloaded from `http://www.cis.upenn.edu/~melamed`.

6.1 Introduction

Appropriately encoded expert opinions about which parts of a text and its translation are semantically equivalent can accelerate progress in several areas of computational linguistics. First, researchers in translation theory and lexical semantics can mine such data for insights about cross-linguistic lexicalization patterns. Second, Resnik & Yarowsky (1997) have suggested that cross-linguistic lexicalization patterns are an excellent criterion for deciding what sense distinctions should be made by monolingual word-sense disambiguation algorithms. My own motivation was in a third area. Until now, translation lexicons and statistical translation models have been evaluated either subjectively (e.g. White & O'Connell, 1993) or using only approximate metrics, such as perplexity with respect to other models (Brown et al., 1993b). One might think that machine-readable bilingual dictionaries could be used to evaluate representations of translational equivalence. Unfortunately, bilingual dictionaries can only approximate this relation, because the complete translational equivalence relation for any pair of languages is too large to describe in print and evolves too rapidly for lexicographers to keep pace. More significantly, dictionaries provide no indication of the relative importance of different translations for each head word.

To enable objective and more accurate comparisons of different translation models, I have designed a method for constructing a close approximation of token-level translational equivalence for a given bitext. The design allows abstraction of the word–token relation to the corresponding word–type relation, so that evaluation can be performed both at the type and token levels. The design has been implemented to link roughly 16000 corresponding words between online versions of the Bible in modern French and modern English. As explained in section 6.2, this text was selected to facilitate widespread use and standardization, which was neither a goal nor an outcome of a similar earlier project (Sadler & Vendelmans, 1990). A further distinguishing characteristic of the present work is its emphasis on measurable consistency. Inter-annotator agreement rates are reported in section 6.5.

Construction of a gold standard of this sort turned out to be very challenging for two reasons. First, translational equivalence is a rather subjective notion, so it would have been difficult for annotators to reach consensus about word-level correspondence without a detailed style guide, such as the one in appendix A. Development of an unbiased style guide for this task is itself very challenging, as evidenced by the intense debate on this topic during the second campaign of the ARCADE competition (Langlais et al., 1998). Second, there is no simple way for annotators to record word correspondences that isn't highly error-prone. To reduce data-entry errors, I designed the special annotation tool described in section 6.3.

6.2   The Gold-Standard Bitext

The first step in creating the gold standard was to choose a bitext. To make my results easy to replicate, I decided to work with the Bible. The Bible is the most widely translated text in the world, and it exists in electronic form in many languages. Replication of experiments with the Bible is facilitated by its canonical segmentation into verses, which is constant across all translations.[1] After some simple reformatting, e.g., using the tools described by Resnik et al. (1997), the verse segmentation can serve as a ready-made, indisputable and fairly detailed bitext map. Among the many languages in which the Bible is available online, I chose to work with two with which I have some familiarity: modern French and modern English. For modern English I used the New International Version (NIV) and for modern French the Edition Louis Segond, 1910 (LSG).[2]

Next, I had to decide which parts of the bitext to annotate. My decision on which books to include was guided by two practical considerations. First, most online versions include a particular set of 66 books (Resnik et al., 1997). From these 66, I excluded Ecclesiastes, Hosea and Job, because these books are not very well understood, and so their translations are often extremely inconsistent (Aster, 1997). The remaining 63 books comprise 29614 verses. My choice of verses among these 29614 was motivated by the desire to make the gold standard useful for evaluating non-probabilistic translation lexicons. I will argue in section 7.7.2 that the accuracy of an automatically induced translation lexicon can be evaluated only in terms of the bitext from which it was induced: Reliable evaluation of a word's entry in the lexicon requires knowledge of all of that word's translations in the bitext. Therefore, I decided to annotate a set of verses that includes all instances of a set of randomly selected word types. However, the set of word types was not completely random, because I also wanted to make the gold standard useful for investigating the effect of word frequency on the accuracy of translation lexicon construction methods.

To meet all these goals, I used the following procedure to select verses that contain a random sample of word types, stratified by word frequency.

1. I pre-processed both halves of the Bible bitext to separate punctuation symbols from the words to which they were adjacent and to split elided forms (hyphenated words, contractions, French du and aux, etc.) into multiple tokens. To keep the bitext easy for the annotators to read, I did not lemmatize inflected forms. The resulting bitext comprised 814451 tokens in the English half and 896717 tokens in the French half, of 14817 and 21372 types, respectively.

2. I computed a histogram of the words in the English Bible.

3. I randomly selected a *focus set* of 100 word types, consisting of 25 types that occurred only once, 25 types that occurred twice, 25 types that occurred three times and 25 types that occurred four times.

4. I extracted the English verses containing all the instances of all the words in the focus set, and the French translations of those verses.

5. Step 4 resulted in some verses being selected more than once, because they contained more than one of the words in the focus set. I eliminated the duplications by discarding the lower-frequency word in each conflict and resampling from the word types with that frequency.

The 100 types in the final focus set are listed in table 6.1. The tokens of these word types are contained in $(1 + 2 + 3 + 4) * 25 = 250$ verse pairs. By design, all the possible correct translations of the focus words in the bitext can be automatically extracted from the annotations of these 250 verse pairs. Including the focus words, the 250 verses in the gold standard comprise 7510 English word tokens and 8191 French word tokens, of 1714 and 1912 distinct types, respectively.

Table 6.1
Word types in the gold standard's focus set.

Frequency 1	Frequency 2	Frequency 3	Frequency 4
Akkad	Alexandrian	Beginning	Anointed
Arnan	Around	Cover	Derbe
Ashterathite	Carites	Formerly	Izharites
Bimhal	Dressed	Gatam	Jeriah
Cun	Exalt	Inquire	Mikloth
Ephai	Finish	agrees	assurance
Ethiopians	Halak	deceivers	burnished
Harnepher	Helam	defended	circle
Impress	Jahleel	defiling	defender
Jairite	Jokmeam	drain	dens
Jeberekiah	Kehelathah	engulfed	examined
Manaen	Plague	equity	failing
Nekeb	Zeus	evident	herald
apt	brandish	goldsmiths	leadership
eyesight	fulfilling	intense	loathe
handmill	hotly	partners	radiance
improperly	intelligible	profound	rallied
journeys	ledges	progress	refusing
origins	lit	rout	secretaries
parade	pardoned	stared	student
readily	petitioned	starting	stumbles
unending	reappears	swirling	thankful
unsatisfied	thwarts	thistles	topaz
unsuited	undoing	tingle	violently
visitors	unscathed	woodcutters	wisely

6.3   The Blinker Annotation Tool

To promote consistent annotation, I needed an effective way to link corresponding words in the bitext. I could have just asked bilingual annotators to
type in pairs of numbers corresponding to the word positions of mutual translations in their respective verses. However, such a data entry process would be so
error-prone as to render the annotations highly unreliable. Instead, I designed
the Blinker ("bilingual linker"), a mouse-driven graphical annotation tool. Implemented at the University of Maryland under the direction of Philip Resnik,
the Blinker allowed annotators to "link" any number of words to each other.
First, the words are selected with the left mouse button. When the right mouse
button is clicked, the Blinker links all the selected words by lines drawn between them on the screen. Words that were omitted from the translation were

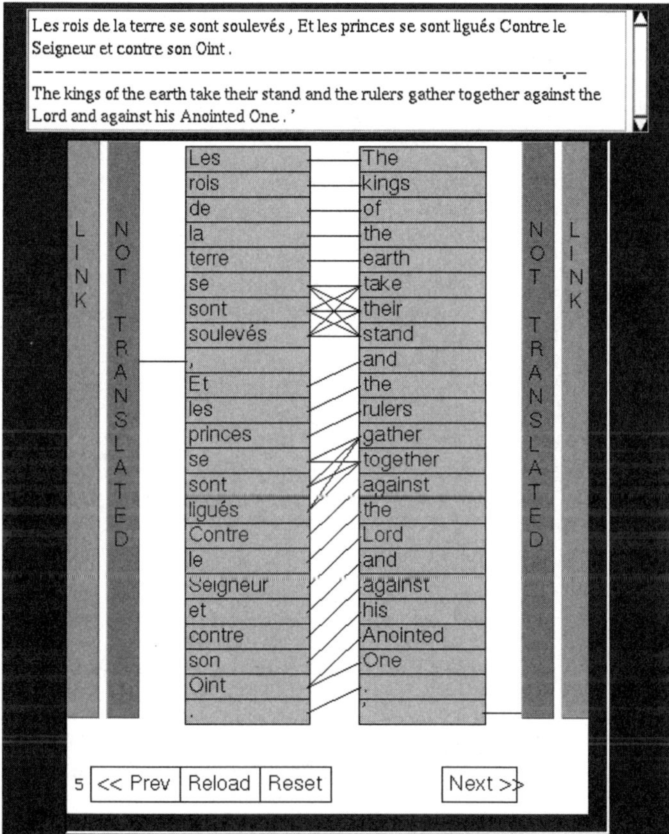

Figure 6.1
A Blinker session.

indicated by a link to one of the "Not Translated" bars. The Blinker makes
heavy use of color-coding, but a greyscale screen capture of a Blinker session
is shown in figure 6.1. Detailed instructions for using the Blinker are given in
figure 6.2.

6.4   Methods for Increasing Reliability

Translational equivalence is often difficult to determine at the word level.
Many words are translated only as part of larger text units, and even Biblical

How to Use the Blinker

The Blinker (for "bilingual linker") is a mouse-driven graphical user interface. Here's how to use it:

- To specify the correspondence between two or more words,

    1. Select the words you want by clicking on them with the LEFT mouse button. The boxes around the words will turn pink. (Note: Clicking on a word again will "unselect" it.)

    2. Either click on one of the Link bars, or click the MIDDLE or RIGHT mouse button. The Blinker will draw lines between the words that you've selected and color their boxes light blue.

- To specify that a word is not translated, click on the word (it will turn pink), and then click on the Not Translated bar beside it. The Blinker will draw a line from the word to the Not Translated bar.

- If you ever change your mind, you can simply re-link words that you've already linked. The Blinker will delete all the links previously associated with those words and draw the new links that you've specified.

- You will see four buttons at the bottom of each verse pair.

    1. When you've finished specifying all the correspondences for a pair of verses, click the Next >> button at the bottom. The Blinker will verify that all the words on both sides have been accounted for, and then present you with the next pair of verses in the set.

    2. The << Prev button allows you to return to previous verse pairs in the same set.

    3. The Reset button allows you to erase all the links in the verse pair currently on the screen.

    4. The Reload button allows you to reload the most recent links for the whole set of verse pairs, e.g. after you've pressed Reset or when you return to a set after taking a break.

    Your work is permanently saved whenever you press Next >>, << Prev or Reload.

Figure 6.2
Blinker instructions.

translations are sometimes inconsistent or incomplete. Therefore, I adopted several measures to increase the reliability of the gold-standard annotations.

First, instead of relying on only one or two annotators, I recruited as many as I could find—seven—with the intent of creating multiple annotations for the same data. Each set of annotations could be compared to the others, in order to identify deviations from the norm. The replication of effort also made it possible to evaluate the gold standard itself in terms of inter-annotator agreement rates.

Second, I designed the Blinker to prevent an annotator from proceeding to the next verse pair until all the words in the current verse pair were annotated. If an annotator felt that a given word did not have a translational equivalent in the opposite verse, he or she had to explicitly mark the word as "Not Translated." This forced-choice annotation method can be contrasted with the strategy adopted in the Penn Treebank project for part-of-speech (POS) annotation (Marcus et al., 1993). Most of the Penn Treebank was annotated for POS only once, and the annotation method was to manually correct the output of an automatic POS tagger. Marcus et al. (1993) reported that this method produced more reliable annotations than manual POS tagging from scratch. However, a reliable "corrective" annotation method is only possible given a reasonably good first approximation. Such an approximation might have been achieved by one of the translation models described in chapter 7, but only at the expense of biasing the gold standard towards a particular translation model, which would have defeated the purpose of the project. Another justification for the forced-choice approach is the overwhelming bias towards a "no-link" annotation—the vast majority of word pairs are not linked. When I attempted the task myself, I was amazed at how many words I forgot to link. A disadvantage of the forced-choice approach is that forced decisions are not reliable when they are difficult. The reliability of the gold standard is discussed in section 6.5.

My third strategy for increasing the reliability of the gold standard was borrowed from the Penn Treebank project (Marcus et al., 1993): I constructed an annotation style guide, which appears as appendix A. To reduce experimenter bias, the guide was based largely on the intuitions of the annotators:

1. I wrote a draft version of the General Guidelines, shown in section A.1.

2. Two groups of annotators each annotated a set of ten randomly selected verse pairs from the Bible bitext, using the draft General Guidelines. There were seven annotators, so one set of 10 verse pairs was annotated four times

and the other three times. These dry-run annotations also served to acclimate the annotators to the task.

3. The different annotations for each verse pair were automatically compared.

4. I manually analyzed the differences and identified the major sources of variation in the annotations.

5. I reconvened four of the seven annotators and presented them with examples of the different kinds of variation, one kind at a time. We briefly discussed each kind of variation, and then the annotators voted on the preferred annotation style.

6. I compiled the votes and the examples on which they were based into the Detailed Guidelines in section A.2. I also added some clarifying examples post hoc.

7. When the annotators began annotating the gold standard, they reported a few additional difficult cases. By email, I solicited votes on the preferred annotation style for these difficult cases from all the annotators. The majority opinions were incorporated into the style guide.

The annotators were encouraged to conform to the style guide by a financial incentive plan. They were offered a bonus for each "difficult" verse-pair on which their rate of agreement with other annotators was the highest. The definition of "difficult" was left intentionally vague, to prevent any attempts at collaborative cheating.

6.5   Inter-Annotator Agreement

Annotators A1, A2 and A3 annotated all 250 verse pairs. The other four annotators could not devote so much time to the project. To accommodate them, verse pairs 1 through 100 were annotated by annotators A4 and A6, while verse pairs 101 through 250 were annotated by annotators A5 and A7. I report separate inter-annotator agreement statistics for verse pairs up to #100 and for verse pairs starting with #101.

The simplest way to measure agreement would have been to compute a single rate for each pair of annotators over whichever parts of the gold standard they both annotated. However, standard deviations could not be computed this way. The next simplest way to measure agreement would have been to compute separate agreement rates for each of the 250 verse pairs, and then to find the means and standard deviations of these 250 rates. However, this approach would have inflated the agreement rates, because links in shorter verse pairs were easier to assign and therefore less likely to diverge. Since there were fewer links in shorter verse pairs, each of these "easier" links would have influenced the mean agreement rate more than the links in long verse pairs. A more accurate method for measuring agreement lay between these two extremes. I divided part 1 of the gold standard into 10 sets of 10 verse pairs each, and part 2 into 10 sets of 15 verse pairs each. I pooled the links in each set of verses and computed 10 agreement rates for each pair of annotators for each part of the gold standard. Then, I computed the means and standard deviations of the 10 rates for each pair of annotators for each part of the gold standard.

A straightforward metric for measuring agreement rates can be derived from the recall and precision measures widely used in the information retrieval literature. When comparing a set of "test" elements X to a set of "correct" elements Y,

$$\text{precision}(X|Y) = \frac{|X \cap Y|}{|X|}, \tag{6.1}$$

$$\text{recall}(X|Y) = \frac{|X \cap Y|}{|Y|}. \tag{6.2}$$

X and Y can be fuzzy sets, such as probability distributions, in which case $|X|$ is defined as the sum of the weights of the elements in X and $|X \cap Y|$ is the sum of the weights of the elements shared by X and Y. Equations (6.1) and (6.2) differ only in the set whose size is used as the denominator. If neither X nor Y is privileged, or if precision and recall are equally important, we can compute a symmetric measure of agreement D as the harmonic mean of precision and recall:

$$D(X, Y) = \frac{2}{\frac{1}{\text{Precision}(X|Y)} + \frac{1}{\text{Recall}(X|Y)}} = \frac{2 * |X \cap Y|}{|X| + |Y|}. \tag{6.3}$$

D is the set-theoretic equivalent of the Dice coefficient (Dice, 1945) and conveniently ranges from zero to one.

From an information-processing point of view, the input to the annotators was a set of aligned text segments and their output was a set of pairs of corresponding word positions. So, inter-annotator agreement should be measured in terms of the similarity between sets of pairs of corresponding word positions. There is a small problem with counting pairs of word positions at face value, however, which is related to the problem with the naive method of counting co-occurrences using equation (5.1). The annotators of the gold standard could link each word to as many other words as they wished (e.g., "take their stand" in figure 6.1). Therefore, an evaluation metric that treats all link tokens as equally important would place undue importance on words that were linked more than once.

One solution to this problem is to attach a weight $w(u, v)$ to each link token (u, v), where

$$w(u, v) = \frac{1}{\max[\mathit{fanout}(u), \mathit{fanout}(v)]}. \tag{6.4}$$

The *fanout* function returns the number of links attached to its argument. When the link tokens are weighted in this fashion, the weights attached to each word will sum to at most one. With the link weights in place, we can compute precision, recall, and D as defined above. This solution is somewhat deficient, because when the lowest common multiple of *fanout*(u) and *fanout*(v) is neither *fanout*(u) nor *fanout*(v), then neither u nor v will carry full weight. However, such cases are so rare that they can be ignored for the sake of a simple evaluation method. Some of the evaluations in the following chapters are based on equation (6.3), weighted by equation (6.4).

For the purposes of evaluating the gold standard itself, I used a slightly more complicated but non-deficient weighting scheme. First, links were treated as directed arcs from the French side of the bitext to the English side. Weights were normalized so that the weights of the arcs emitted by any single French word token summed to 1. However, no limit was placed on the total weight of arcs that could point to an English word token. With the arcs weighted in this fashion, an agreement rate $D_{F \to E}$ was computed between each pair of annotators using equation (6.3). Then the arcs were reversed and reweighted so that the weights of the arcs emitted by any one English word summed to 1, but the weight of arcs pointing to a French word was unrestricted. A second agreement rate $D_{E \to F}$ was computed between each pair of annotators with the arcs normalized in this direction. The final agreement rate was the mean of $D_{F \to E}$ and $D_{E \to F}$. The rates for each pair of annotators, for each part of the gold standard, along with the mean for each annotator and the grand mean, are shown in table 6.2.

Regardless of how literal the translation is in a given bitext, some words will not correspond well to words on the other side. In particular, the translations of function words often depend more strongly on the content words around them

Table 6.2
Percent inter-annotator agreement, $\pm$ standard deviation.

Part 1: Verse pairs 1–100

A2	A3	A4	A5	annotator	mean
81.81 ± 4.61	89.64 ± 5.38	82.91 ± 4.73	86.06 ± 4.21	A1	85.11 ± 5.67
	81.71 ± 3.10	79.27 ± 3.14	81.73 ± 2.75	A2	81.13 ± 3.71
		82.53 ± 5.23	85.96 ± 3.11	A3	84.96 ± 5.38
			79.54 ± 3.84	A4	81.06 ± 4.68
				A5	83.32 ± 4.53
				grand mean	*83.12 ± 5.16*

Part 2: Verse pairs 101–250

A2	A3	A6	A7	annotator	mean
81.92 ± 3.97	87.85 ± 2.79	77.04 ± 2.99	85.82 ± 2.02	A1	83.15 ± 5.12
	81.45 ± 3.91	74.20 ± 4.11	80.50 ± 3.55	A2	79.52 ± 4.99
		76.81 ± 2.89	85.00 ± 2.12	A3	82.78 ± 5.11
			75.63 ± 2.51	A6	75.92 ± 3.38
				A7	81.74 ± 4.84
				grand mean	*80.62 ± 5.44*

than on the function words themselves. Function words are the first to change when a translator decides to paraphrase. Most of the annotation style guide was devoted to annotation conventions for function words. These observations suggest that the inter-annotator agreement may be higher for content words than for function words.

Since function words are not important for some applications of translation models, it is useful to measure the inter-annotator agreement rates for content words only. I compiled a stoplist of 287 function words for English and 375 function words for French. These lists consist of all words that are not nouns, verbs, adverbs or adjectives, in addition to all inflections of all auxiliary verbs (do, go, be, etc. and their French equivalents). The gold standard contained 2871 English word tokens and 2768 French word tokens that were not on the stoplist. From the complete set of annotations, I removed all the links that had a stoplisted word on either side. Then, I re-evaluated inter-annotator agreement, using the same method, but only on the remaining links. Table 6.3 shows the results. The effect of ignoring function words is well illustrated by the 10% rise in the grand mean of table 6.3 over the grand mean of table 6.2.

The inter-annotator agreement rates in tables 6.2 and 6.3 indicate that the annotators were doing mostly the same thing most of the time, and that the

Table 6.3
Percent inter-annotator agreement on content words only, ± standard deviation.

Part 1: Verse pairs 1–100

A2	A3	A4	A5	annotator	mean
90.60 ± 4.62	94.37 ± 4.99	91.75 ± 3.38	94.20 ± 3.28	A1	92.73 ± 4.45
	90.20 ± 3.20	90.52 ± 2.94	90.54 ± 2.24	A2	90.46 ± 3.38
		91.85 ± 4.69	94.33 ± 3.74	A3	92.69 ± 4.58
			92.17 ± 2.48	A4	91.57 ± 3.55
				A5	92.81 ± 3.40
				grand mean	*92.05 ± 4.01*

Part 2: Verse pairs 101–250

A2	A3	A6	A7	annotator	mean
90.91 ± 3.81	94.17 ± 2.69	88.38 ± 3.56	94.37 ± 2.57	A1	91.96 ± 4.06
	90.92 ± 3.43	87.80 ± 4.20	90.79 ± 3.24	A2	90.11 ± 3.93
		88.88 ± 4.23	93.52 ± 2.56	A3	91.87 ± 3.92
			88.04 ± 3.36	A6	88.28 ± 3.90
				A7	91.68 ± 3.87
				grand mean	*90.78 ± 4.18*

task is reasonably well-defined and reasonably easy to replicate. This claim is strengthened by the observation that annotator A6 was a low outlier regardless of whether function word links are considered, which is why the grand means are lower for part 2 than for part 1. Nevertheless, the agreement rates are not as high as one might like. Although much more research is required to draw any conclusions with certainty, I can suggest three reasons why the inter-annotator agreement rates are not any higher.

First, despite the care taken with Biblical translations, many aligned Bible verses carry significantly different meanings. For example:

English: They also brought to the proper place their quotas of barley and straw for the chariot horses and the other horses.

French: Ils faisaient aussi venir de l'orge et de la paille pour les chevaux et les coursiers dans le lieu où se trouvait le roi, chacun selon les ordres qu'il avait reçus.

One possible explanation for the divergence is that neither of my Bible versions is a translation of the other; rather, both are probably translations of a third original, if not two different originals. Furthermore, careful translation often requires non-literal translation. This practice is particularly apparent in the case of the Bible.

Second, the style guide was based on only a small sample of annotated bitext, and it was inevitable that new sources of variation in the annotations would occur in previously unseen bitext. In order to further standardize the annotation style, it would have been necessary to update the style guide iteratively, checking each new batch of annotated verses for new sources of inter-annotator variation. Such a procedure was beyond my time and budget constraints.

Third, as with all first versions of such tools, the Blinker annotation tool left much to be desired. For example, when one of a pair of verses was significantly longer than the other, the lines representing some of the links were nearly vertical and blended together. One annotator admitted by email, "I do at times throw up my hands in frustration at how hard it is . . . to link a word at the top to a word at the veeeeeeeery bottom. I reckon you just may get extra 'not-linked's because of this." A better Blinker design, perhaps akin to the Cairo tool (Smith & Jahr, 2000), might have made it easier for the annotators to follow the style guide.

6.6   Conclusion

This chapter describes a method for manually constructing explicit representations of translational equivalence. After a detailed style guide was written, a special annotation tool was used to annotate corresponding words in a large part of a widely available bitext. Among other uses, the annotations are intended for use as a gold-standard for comparing automatically constructed models of translational equivalence, and thus also for comparing the methods used to construct such models. Inter-annotator agreement rates on the gold standard are roughly 82%, or roughly 92% if function words are ignored. These rates indicate that the gold standard is reasonably reliable and that the task is reasonably easy to replicate. The gold standard annotations are freely available from `http://www.cis.upenn.edu/~melamed`.

III TRANSLATIONAL EQUIVALENCE AMONG WORD TYPES

7 Word-to-Word Models of Translational Equivalence

Bitexts have properties that distinguish them from other kinds of parallel data. First, most words in a bitext translate to only one other word. Second, bitext correspondence is typically only partial—many words in each text have no clear equivalent in the other text. This chapter presents methods for biasing statistical translation models to reflect these properties. Analysis of the expected behavior of these biases in the presence of sparse data predicts that they will result in more accurate models. The prediction is confirmed by evaluation with respect to independent human judgments—models biased in this fashion are significantly more accurate than a baseline knowledge-free model. This chapter also shows how a statistical translation model can take advantage of pre-existing knowledge that might be available about particular language pairs. Even the simplest kinds of language-specific knowledge, such as the distinction between content words and function words, are shown to reliably boost translation model performance on some tasks. Statistical models that reflect knowledge about the model domain combine the best of both the rationalist and empiricist paradigms.

7.1 Introduction

The idea of a computer system for translating from one language to another is almost as old as the idea of computer systems. Warren Weaver (1955) wrote about "mechanical translation" as early as 1949. More recently, Brown et al. (1988) suggested that it may be possible to construct machine translation systems automatically. Instead of codifying the human translation process from introspection, Brown et al. proposed machine learning techniques to induce models of the process from examples of its input and output. The proposal generated much excitement, because it held the promise of automating a task that forty years of research have proven very labor-intensive and error-prone. Yet very few other researchers have taken up the cause, partly because Brown et al.'s approach was quite a departure from the paradigm in vogue at the time.

Brown et al.'s most important insight was that translational equivalence is a relation that can be learned from data. Like all mathematical models, the best translation models are those whose parameters correspond best with the sources of variance in the data. Probabilistic translation models whose parameters reflect universal properties of translational equivalence and/or existing knowledge about particular languages and language pairs benefit from the best of both the empiricist and rationalist traditions.

This chapter presents three such models, along with methods for efficiently estimating their parameters. Each new method is designed to take into account an additional universal property of translational equivalence in bitexts:

1. Most word tokens translate to only one word token. I approximate this tendency with a one-to-one assumption.

2. Most text segments are not translated word for word. I build an explicit noise model.

3. Different linguistic objects have statistically different behavior in translation. I show a way to condition translation models on different word classes to help take the variety into account.

Quantitative evaluation with respect to the gold standard developed in chapter 6 has shown that each of the three biases significantly improves translation model accuracy over a baseline knowledge-free model.

A review of some previously published translation models follows an introduction to translation model taxonomy. The core of the chapter is a presentation of the model estimation biases described above. Section 7.7 describes the results of a variety of experiments designed to evaluate these innovations. The last section suggests ways to employ this chapter's techniques for accelerated development of lexicons for machine translation systems.

7.2   Translation Model Decomposition

There are two kinds of applications of translation models: those where word order plays a crucial role and those where it doesn't. Empirically estimated models of translational equivalence among word types can play a central role in both kinds of applications.

Applications in which word order is not essential include

- cross-language information retrieval (e.g. McCarley, 1999)

- multilingual document filtering (e.g. Oard, 1997)

- computer-assisted language learning (e.g. Nerbonne et al., 1997)

- certain machine-assisted translation tools (e.g. ADOMIT in chapter 4 or Macklovitch, 1994)

- concordancing for bilingual lexicography (e.g. Catizone et al., 1989; Gale & Church, 1991b)

- corpus linguistics (e.g. Svartvik, 1992)

- "crummy" machine translation (e.g. Church & Hovy, 1993; Resnik, 1997)

For these applications, empirically estimated models have a number of advantages over hand-crafted models such as on-line versions of bilingual dictionaries. Two of the advantages are the possibility of better coverage and the possibility of frequent updates by non-expert users to keep up with rapidly evolving vocabularies.

A third advantage is that statistical models can provide more accurate information about the relative importance of different translations. Such information is crucial for applications such as cross-language information retrieval (CLIR). In the vector space approach to CLIR, the query vector Q' is in a different language (a different vector space) from the document vectors D. A word-to-word translation model T can map Q' into a vector Q in the vector space of D. In order for the mapping to be accurate, T must be able to encode many levels of relative importance among the possible translations of each element of Q'. A typical bilingual dictionary says only what the possible translations are, which is equivalent to positing a uniform translational distribution. The performance of cross-language information retrieval with a uniform T is likely to be limited in the same way as the performance of conventional information retrieval without term frequency information, i.e., where the system knows which terms occur in which documents, but not how often (Buckley, 1993).

Applications in which word order is crucial include speech recognition for translation (Brousseau et al., 1995), bootstrapping of OCR systems for new languages (Resnik & Kanungo, 1999), interactive translation (Foster et al., 1996), and fully automatic high-quality machine translation (e.g. Al-Onaizan et al., 1999). In such applications, a word-to-word translation model can serve as an independent module in a more complex sequence-to-sequence[1] translation model. The independence of such a module is desirable for two reasons, one practical and one philosophical. The practical reason is illustrated in this chapter: Order-independent translation models can be accurately estimated more efficiently in isolation. The philosophical reason is that words are an important epistemological category in our naive mental representations of language. We have many intuitions (and even some testable theories) about what words are and how they behave. It is useful to bring these intuitions to bear on our translation models without being distracted by other facets of language, such as phrase structure. For example, the translation models in chapter 8 are motivated by the observation that spaces in text do not necessarily delimit words; the models presented in chapter 9 are motivated by the common belief that words can have multiple senses.

The independence of a word-to-word translation module in a sequence-to-sequence translation model can be effected by a two-stage decomposition. The first stage is based on the observation that every sequence $\mathbf{L}$ is just an ordered bag, and that the bag $\mathbf{B}$ can be modeled independently of its order $\mathbf{O}$. For example, the sequence $\langle abc \rangle$ consists of the bag $\{c, a, b\}$ and the ordering relation $\{(b, 2), (a, 1), (c, 3)\}$. If we represent each sequence $\mathbf{L}$ as a pair $(\mathbf{B}, \mathbf{O})$, then

$$\Pr(\mathbf{L}) \equiv \Pr(\mathbf{B}, \mathbf{O}) \tag{7.1}$$

$$= \Pr(\mathbf{B}) \cdot \Pr(\mathbf{O}|\mathbf{B}). \tag{7.2}$$

Now, let $\mathbf{L}_1$ and $\mathbf{L}_2$ be two sequences and let $\mathbf{A}$ be a one-to-one mapping between the elements of $\mathbf{L}_1$ and the elements of $\mathbf{L}_2$. Borrowing a term from the operations research literature, I shall refer to such mappings as assignments.[2] Let $\mathcal{A}$ be the set of all possible assignments between $\mathbf{L}_1$ and $\mathbf{L}_2$. Using assignments, we can decompose conditional and joint probabilities over sequences:

$$\Pr(\mathbf{L}_1|\mathbf{L}_2) = \sum_{A \in \mathcal{A}} \Pr(\mathbf{L}_1, \mathbf{A}|\mathbf{L}_2), \tag{7.3}$$

$$\Pr(\mathbf{L}_1, \mathbf{L}_2) = \sum_{A \in \mathcal{A}} \Pr(\mathbf{L}_1, \mathbf{A}, \mathbf{L}_2) \tag{7.4}$$

where

$$\Pr(\mathbf{L}_1, \mathbf{A}|\mathbf{L}_2) \equiv \Pr(\mathbf{B}_1, \mathbf{O}_1, \mathbf{A}|\mathbf{L}_2) \tag{7.5}$$

$$= \Pr(\mathbf{B}_1, \mathbf{A}|\mathbf{L}_2) \cdot \Pr(\mathbf{O}_1|\mathbf{B}_1, \mathbf{A}, \mathbf{L}_2), \tag{7.6}$$

$$\Pr(\mathbf{L}_1, \mathbf{A}, \mathbf{L}_2) \equiv \Pr(\mathbf{B}_1, \mathbf{O}_1, \mathbf{A}, \mathbf{B}_2, \mathbf{O}_2) \tag{7.7}$$

$$= \Pr(\mathbf{B}_1, \mathbf{A}, \mathbf{B}_2) \cdot \Pr(\mathbf{O}_1, \mathbf{O}_2|\mathbf{B}_1, \mathbf{A}, \mathbf{B}_2). \tag{7.8}$$

Summing bag pair probabilities over all possible assignments, we obtain a *bag-to-bag translation model*:

$$\Pr(\mathbf{B}_1, \mathbf{B}_2) = \sum_{A \in \mathcal{A}} \Pr(\mathbf{B}_1, \mathbf{A}, \mathbf{B}_2). \tag{7.9}$$

The second stage of decomposition takes us from bags of words to the words they contain. The following bag-pair generation process illustrates how a word-to-word translation model can be embedded in a bag-to-bag translation model for languages $\mathcal{L}_1$ and $\mathcal{L}_2$:

1. Generate a bag size l.[3] l is also the assignment size.

2. Generate l language-independent concepts $C_1, \ldots, C_l$.

3. From each concept C_i, $1 \leq i \leq l$, generate a pair of word sequences $(\vec{u}_i, \vec{v}_i)$ from $\mathcal{L}_1^* \times \mathcal{L}_2^*$, according to the distribution $trans(\vec{u}, \vec{v})$, to lexicalize the concept in the two languages.[4] Some concepts are not lexicalized in some languages, so one of $\vec{u}_i$ and $\vec{v}_i$ may be empty.

A pair of bags containing m and n non-empty word sequences can be generated by a process in which l is anywhere between 1 and $m + n$.

For notational convenience, the elements of the two bags can be labeled so that $\mathbf{B}_1 \equiv \{\vec{\mathbf{u}}_1, \ldots, \vec{\mathbf{u}}_l\}$ and $\mathbf{B}_2 \equiv \{\vec{\mathbf{v}}_1, \ldots, \vec{\mathbf{v}}_l\}$, where some of the $\vec{\mathbf{u}}$s and $\vec{\mathbf{v}}$s may be empty. The elements of an assignment, then, are pairs of bag element labels $\mathbf{A} \equiv \{(i_1, j_1), \ldots, (i_l, j_l)\}$, where each i ranges over $\{\vec{\mathbf{u}}_1, \ldots, \vec{\mathbf{u}}_l\}$, each j ranges over $\{\vec{\mathbf{v}}_1, \ldots, \vec{\mathbf{v}}_l\}$, each i is distinct and each j is distinct. The label pairs in a given assignment can be generated in any order, so there are $l!$ ways to generate an assignment of size l.[5] It follows that the probability of generating a pair of bags $(\mathbf{B}_1, \mathbf{B}_2)$ with a particular assignment $\mathbf{A}$ of size l is

$$\Pr(\mathbf{B}_1, \mathbf{A}, \mathbf{B}_2 | l, \mathcal{C}, trans) = \Pr(l) \cdot l! \prod_{(i,j) \in \mathbf{A}} \sum_{C \in \mathcal{C}} \Pr(C) trans(\vec{\mathbf{u}}_i, \vec{\mathbf{v}}_i | C). \quad (7.10)$$

The above equation holds regardless of how we represent concepts. There are many plausible representations, such as pairs of trees from synchronous tree adjoining grammars (Abeillé et al., 1990; Shieber, 1994; Candito, 1998), lexical conceptual structures (Dorr, 1992) and WordNet synsets (Miller, 1990; Vossen, 1998). Of course, for a representation to be used, a method must exist for estimating its distribution in data. A useful representation will reduce the entropy of the $trans$ distribution, which is conditioned on the concept distribution as shown in equation (7.10). This topic is beyond the scope of this chapter, however. I mention it only to show how the models presented here may be used as building blocks for models that are more psycholinguistically sophisticated.

To make the translation model estimation methods presented here as general as possible, I assume a totally uninformative concept representation—the $trans$ distribution itself. In other words, I assume that each different pair of word sequence types is deterministically generated from a different concept, so that $trans(\vec{\mathbf{u}}_i, \vec{\mathbf{v}}_i | C)$ is zero for all concepts except one. Now, a bag-to-bag translation model can be fully specified by the distributions of l and $trans$:

$$\Pr(\mathbf{B}_1, \mathbf{A}, \mathbf{B}_2 | l, \mathit{trans}) = \Pr(l) \cdot l! \prod_{(i,j) \in \mathbf{A}} \mathit{trans}(\vec{\mathbf{u}}_i, \vec{\mathbf{v}}_j). \tag{7.11}$$

The probability distribution $\mathit{trans}(\vec{\mathbf{u}}, \vec{\mathbf{v}})$ is a *word-to-word translation model*. Unlike the models proposed by Brown et al. (1993b), this model is *symmetric*, because both word bags are generated together from a joint probability distribution. Brown et al.'s models, reviewed in section 7.4.2, generate one half of the bitext given the other half, so they are represented by conditional probability distributions. A sequence-to-sequence translation model can be obtained from a word-to-word translation model by combining equation (7.11) with order information, as in equation (7.8).

7.3 The One-to-One Assumption

The most general word-to-word translation model $\mathit{trans}(\vec{\mathbf{u}}, \vec{\mathbf{v}})$, where $\vec{\mathbf{u}}$ and $\vec{\mathbf{v}}$ range over sequences in $\mathcal{L}_1$ and $\mathcal{L}_2$, has an infinite number of parameters. This model can be constrained in various ways to make it more practical. The models presented in this chapter are based on the *one-to-one assumption*: Each word is translated to at most one other word. In these models, $\vec{\mathbf{u}}$ and $\vec{\mathbf{v}}$ may consist of at most one word each. As before, one of the two sequences (but not both) may be empty. I describe empty sequences as consisting of a special NULL word, so that each word sequence contains exactly one word and can be treated as a scalar. Henceforth, I shall write $\mathbf{u}$ and $\mathbf{v}$ instead of $\vec{\mathbf{u}}$ and $\vec{\mathbf{v}}$. Under the one-to-one assumption, a pair of bags containing m and n non-empty words can be generated by a process where the bag size l is anywhere between $\max(m, n)$ and $m + n$.

The one-to-one assumption is not as restrictive as it may appear. The explanatory power of a model based on this assumption may be raised to an arbitrary level by extending Western notions of what words are to include words that contain spaces (e.g., in English) or several characters (e.g., in Chinese). For example, in chapter 8, I show how to estimate word-to-word translation models where a word can be a non-compositional compound consisting of several space-delimited tokens. For the purposes of this chapter, however, *words* are the tokens generated by my tokenizers and stemmers for the languages in question. Therefore, the models in this chapter are only a first approximation to the vast complexities of translational equivalence between natural languages. They are intended mainly as stepping stones towards better models.

7.4 Previous Work

7.4.1 Non-Probabilistic Translation Lexicons

Many researchers have proposed greedy algorithms for estimating non-probabilistic word-to-word translation models, also known as translation lexicons (e.g. Catizone et al., 1989; Gale & Church, 1991b; Fung, 1995b; Kumano & Hirakawa, 1994; Melamed, 1995; Wu & Xia, 1994). Most of these algorithms can be summarized as follows:

1. Choose a similarity function S between word types in $\mathcal{L}_1$ and word types in $\mathcal{L}_2$.

2. Compute association scores $S(\mathbf{u}, \mathbf{v})$ for a set of word type pairs $(\mathbf{u}, \mathbf{v}) \in (\mathcal{L}_1 \times \mathcal{L}_2)$ that occur in training data.

3. Sort the word pairs in descending order of their association scores.

4. Discard all word pairs for which $S(\mathbf{u}, \mathbf{v})$ is less than a chosen threshold. The remaining word pairs become the entries in the translation lexicon.

The various proposals differ mainly in their choice of similarity function. A minor variant can be found in work by Daille et al. (1994), who discard all but the most highly associated entry for each word on one side of the bitext.

The biggest innovation since the first of these algorithms appeared is the "context heterogeneity" similarity function (Fung, 1995a). It is well known that all words have a characteristic signature in the frequency distribution of the words around them. For example, in English, the frequency of Her is unusually high in the vicinity of Majesty. Fung discovered that certain parts of these signatures are preserved in translation.[6] In particular, the highest peaks in the frequency distribution remain high. These peaks are what Fung collectively calls "context heterogeneity." If two words in two different languages have contexts that are heterogeneous in a similar way, then it is likely that the similarity arose from words in their respective contexts that are mutual translations. Fung showed how the similarity between the heterogeneity of two words' contexts can be measured by approximate spectrum matching techniques borrowed from the speech recognition literature. These techniques are robust to noise in the translation, such as large omissions. A drawback of the context heterogeneity similarity function is that it is reliable only for frequent words. However, it is much better than nothing when parallel texts are not available. It is also

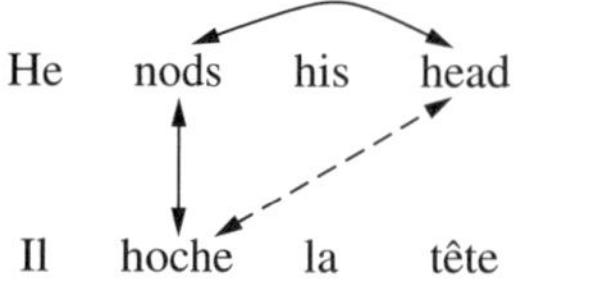

Figure 7.1
nods and hoche often co-occur, as do nods and head. The direct association between nods and
hoche, and the direct association between nods and head give rise to an indirect association
between hoche and head.

useful for constructing a seed translation lexicon for SIMR when no suitable
MRBD or bilingual lexicographer is available (Dagan, 1997).

Given a reasonable similarity function, the greedy algorithm works remarkably well, considering how simple it is. However, the association scores in
step 2 are typically computed independently of each other. The problem with
this independence assumption is illustrated in figure 7.1. The two word sequences represent corresponding regions of an English/French bitext. If nods
and hoche co-occur much more often than expected by chance, then any reasonable similarity metric will deem them likely to be mutual translations. nods
and hoche are indeed mutual translations, so their tendency to co-occur is
called a *direct association*. Now, suppose that nods and head often co-occur
in English. Then hoche and head will also co-occur more often than expected
by chance. The dashed arrow between hoche and head in figure 7.1 represents
an *indirect association*, since the association between hoche and head arises
only by virtue of the association between each of them and nods. Models of
translational equivalence that are ignorant of indirect associations have "a tendency . . . to be confused by collocates" (Dagan et al., 1993b).

Paradoxically, the irregularities (noise) in text and in translation mitigate
the problem. If noise in the data reduces the strength of a direct association,
then the same noise will reduce the strengths of any indirect associations that
are based on this direct association. On the other hand, noise can reduce the
strength of an indirect association without affecting any direct associations.
Therefore, direct associations are usually stronger than indirect associations.
If all the entries in a translation lexicon are sorted by their association scores,
the direct associations will be very dense near the top of the list and sparser
towards the bottom.

Gale & Church (1991b) have shown that entries at the very top of the list can
be over 98% correct. Their algorithm gleaned lexicon entries for about 61% of

the word tokens in a sample of 800 English sentences. To obtain 98% precision, their algorithm selected only entries for which it had high confidence that the association score was high. These would be the word pairs that co-occur most frequently. A random sample of 800 sentences from the same corpus showed that 61% of the word tokens, where the tokens are of the most frequent types, represent 4.5% of all the word types.

A similar strategy was employed by Wu & Xia (1994) and by Fung (1995b). Fung skimmed off the top 23.8% of the noun-noun entries in her lexicon to achieve a precision of 71.6%. Wu & Xia reported automatic acquisition of 6517 lexicon entries from a 3.3-million-word corpus, with a precision of 86%. The first 3.3 million word tokens in an English corpus from a similar genre contained 33490 different word types, suggesting a recall of roughly 19%. Note, however, that Wu & Xia chose to weight their precision estimates by the probabilities attached to each entry:

For example, if the translation set for English word *detect* has the two correct Chinese candidates with 0.533 probability and with 0.277 probability, and the incorrect translation with 0.190 probability, then we count this as 0.810 correct translations and 0.190 incorrect translations. (Wu & Xia, 1994, p. 211)

This is a reasonable evaluation method, but it is not comparable to methods that simply count each lexicon entry as either right or wrong (e.g. Daille et al., 1994; Melamed, 1996a). A weighted precision estimate pays more attention to entries that are more frequent and hence easier to estimate. Therefore, weighted precision estimates are generally higher than unweighted ones.

7.4.2 Re-estimated Sequence-to-Sequence Translation Models

Most probabilistic translation model re-estimation algorithms published to date are variations on the theme proposed by Brown et al. (1993b). These models involve conditional probabilities, but they can be compared to symmetric models if the latter are normalized by the appropriate marginal distribution. I review these models using the notation in table 7.1.

Table 7.1
Variables used to describe translation models.

$(\mathcal{U}, \mathcal{V})$	$=$	the two halves of the bitext
(U, V)	$=$	a pair of aligned text segments in $(\mathcal{U}, \mathcal{V})$
$e(\mathbf{u})$	$=$	the unigram frequency of $\mathbf{u}$ in U
$f(\mathbf{v})$	$=$	the unigram frequency of $\mathbf{v}$ in V
$cooc(\mathbf{u}, \mathbf{v})$	$=$	the number of times that $\mathbf{u}$ and $\mathbf{v}$ co-occur
$trans(\mathbf{v}|\mathbf{u})$	$=$	the probability that a token of $\mathbf{u}$ will be translated as a token of $\mathbf{v}$

Models Using Co-occurrence Information Only Brown et al. (1993) employ the Expectation-Maximization (EM) algorithm (Dempster et al., 1977) to estimate the parameters of their Model 1. On iteration i, the EM algorithm re-estimates the model parameters $trans_i(\mathbf{v}|\mathbf{u})$ based on their estimates from iteration $i - 1$. In Model 1, the relationship between the new parameter estimates and the old ones is

$$trans_i(\mathbf{v}|\mathbf{u}) = z \sum_{(U,V)\in(\mathcal{U},\mathcal{V})} \frac{trans_{i-1}(\mathbf{v}|\mathbf{u}) \cdot e(\mathbf{u}) \cdot f(\mathbf{v})}{\sum_{u'\in U} trans_{i-1}(\mathbf{v}|\mathbf{u}')} \tag{7.12}$$

where z is a normalizing factor.[7]

It is instructive to consider the form of equation (7.12) when all the translation probabilities $trans(\mathbf{v}|\mathbf{u})$ for a particular $\mathbf{u}$ are initialized to the same constant p, as Brown et al. (1993b p. 273) actually do:

$$trans_1(\mathbf{v}|\mathbf{u}) = z \sum_{(U,V)\in(\mathcal{U},\mathcal{V})} \frac{p \cdot e(\mathbf{u}) \cdot f(\mathbf{v})}{p \cdot |U|} \tag{7.13}$$

$$= z \sum_{(U,V)\in(\mathcal{U},\mathcal{V})} \frac{e(\mathbf{u}) \cdot f(\mathbf{v})}{|U|}. \tag{7.14}$$

The initial translation probability $trans_1(\mathbf{v}|\mathbf{u})$ is set proportional to the co-occurrence count of $\mathbf{u}$ and $\mathbf{v}$ and inversely proportional to the length of each segment U in which $\mathbf{u}$ occurs. The intuition behind the numerator is central to most bitext-based translation models: The more often two words co-occur, the more likely they are to be mutual translations. The intuition behind the denominator is that the co-occurrence count of $\mathbf{u}$ and $\mathbf{v}$ should be discounted to the degree that $\mathbf{v}$ also co-occurs with other words in the same segment pair.

Now consider how equation (7.14) would behave if all the text segments on each side were of the same length,[8] so that each token of $\mathbf{v}$ co-occurs with exactly c words (where c is constant):

$$trans_1(\mathbf{v}|\mathbf{u}) = z \sum_{(U,V)\in(\mathcal{U},\mathcal{V})} \frac{e(\mathbf{u}) \cdot f(\mathbf{v})}{c} \tag{7.15}$$

$$= \frac{z}{c} \sum_{(U,V)\in(\mathcal{U},\mathcal{V})} e(\mathbf{u}) \cdot f(\mathbf{v}). \tag{7.16}$$

The normalizing coefficient z/c is constant over all words. The only difference between equations (7.14) and (7.16) is that the former discounts co-occurrences proportionally to the segment lengths. When information about segment lengths is not available, the only information available to initialize Model 1 is the co-occurrence counts. This property makes Model 1 an appropriate baseline for comparison to more sophisticated models that use other information sources, both in the work of Brown et al. and in the work described here.

Word Order Correlation Biases   In any bitext, the positions of words relative to the true bitext map correlate with the positions of their translations. The correlation is stronger for language pairs with more similar word orders. Brown et al. (1988) introduced the idea that this correlation can be encoded in translation model parameters. Under the boundary-based model of co-occurrence, their Model 2 defines alignment probabilities $a(i|j, m, n)$, where i and j denote absolute word positions in a pair of aligned segments and m and n are the segment lengths. In order to estimate Model 2, the alignment probabilities are initialized to be all equally likely: $a(i|j, m, n) = 1/m$; the translation parameters are initialized using Model 1. Both sets of parameters are then re-estimated using the EM algorithm.

In Model 2, the relationships between the new parameter estimates and the old ones are:

$$a_i(i|j, m, n) = y \sum_{(U,V)\in(\mathcal{U},\mathcal{V})} \frac{trans_{i-1}(\mathbf{v}_j|\mathbf{u}_i)a_{i-1}(i|j, m, n)}{\sum_{i'=1}^{n} trans_{i-1}(\mathbf{v}_j|\mathbf{u}_{i'})a_{i-1}(i'|j, m, n)}, \tag{7.17}$$

$$trans_i(\mathbf{v}|\mathbf{u}) =$$

$$z \sum_{(U,V)\in(\mathcal{U},\mathcal{V})} \sum_{i=1}^{n} \sum_{j=1}^{m} \frac{trans_{i-1}(\mathbf{v}|\mathbf{u})a_{i-1}(i|j, m, n)\kappa(u_i, \mathbf{u})\kappa(v_j, \mathbf{v})}{\sum_{i'=1}^{n} trans_{i-1}(\mathbf{v}|\mathbf{u}_{i'})a_{i-1}(i'|j, m, n)}. \tag{7.18}$$

y and z are normalizing factors and κ is the Kronecker function, equal to one when its arguments are the same and zero otherwise. The introduction of the $a(i|j, m, n)$ parameters in the above equations makes the word translation probabilities dependent on the positions of the words in their respective segments. Brown et al. (1993b, p. 283) report that Model 2 has far less perplexity on training data than their Model 1. This is not surprising, since Model 2 has more parameters, and Model 1 makes no attempt to model word order.

Dagan et al. (1993b) observed that the Model 2 parameters "are highly redundant. For example, it is likely that $a(i|j, m, n)$ will be very close to $a(i + 1|j + 1, m, n)$ and $a(i|j, m + 1, n + 1)$" (p. 4). Dagan et al. replaced Brown *et al.*'s alignment parameters, which were based on absolute word positions in aligned segments, with a much smaller set of offset probabilities $o(d)$. $o(d)$ represents the probability that the distance between the coordinate of a pair of words that are mutual translations and the bitext map is d. The number of different parameters $o(d)$ is constrained by δ, the maximum distance from the bitext map at which words may be considered to co-occur (see section 5.2). Dagan et al. measure distances in the bitext space vertically and in words, rather than perpendicular to the bitext map and in characters. Under this metric, they typically limit δ to 20 words. The much smaller number of parameters allowed this model to be effectively trained on much smaller bitexts. Vogel et al. (1996) have shown how some additional independence assumptions can turn this model into an HMM, enabling more efficient parameter estimation. The relative word positions represented by the parameters allow this model to work with the distance-based model of co-occurrence, in which absolute word positions do not exist.

The offset probabilities in Dagan et al.'s model are estimated by the EM algorithm, similarly to the way the alignment probabilities are estimated in Brown et al.'s Model 2. However, Dagan et al. do not use the maximum likelihood parameter estimates. Instead, they make even stronger use of the word order correlation bias to "model the dependence between [alignments for] words that are near one another" (Dagan et al., 1993b, p. 5). First, they determine a "set of relevant connections" by discarding all alignments whose probabilities fall below a certain threshold t. Then, they estimate alignments for words that are not aligned by interpolating between the alignments of preceding and following words. The most probable alignment is then found by a dynamic programming algorithm similar to that described by Gale & Church (1991b). Dagan et al. do not specify how to set the threshold t automatically for previously unseen bitexts.

It cannot be overemphasized that the word order correlation bias is just knowledge about the problem domain, which can be used to guide the search for the optimum model parameters. Translational equivalence can be empirically modeled for any pair of languages, but some models and model biases work better for some language pairs than for others. The word order correlation bias is most useful when it has high predictive power, i.e., when the distribution of alignments or offsets has low entropy. The entropy of this distribution is indeed relatively low for the language pair that both Brown et al. and Dagan et al. were working with—French and English have very similar word order. A word order correlation bias, as well as the phrase-structure biases in Brown et al. (1993b)'s Models 4 and 5, would be less beneficial with noisier training bitexts or for language pairs with less similar word order. Nevertheless, one should use all available information sources if one wants to build the best possible translation model. Section 7.5.3 suggests a way to add word order correlation bias to the models presented in this chapter.

Brown et al.'s Models 3, 4, and 5 Model 3 introduces fertility parameters to model the number of target word tokens that each source word token may arise from. However, the fertility parameters are estimated independently of the translation parameters, so it is not possible to reconstruct a word type's most likely phrasal translations just by convolving the relevant distributions. Models 4 and 5 attempt to take into account phrase structure. Although Brown et al.'s Models 1 and 2 have been widely replicated, I am not aware of any replications of their higher models, except for Al-Onaizan et al.'s (1999) replication of model 3. I can offer two possible explanations for this apparent lack of interest. First, the higher models involve an enormous number of parameters, which can be estimated reasonably well only given vast quantities of training data. Second, these models lack intuitive appeal. For these reasons, I shall give no further consideration to Brown et al.'s Models 3, 4, and 5, except to offer some qualitative comments about Model 3 in section 8.9.

7.4.3 Re-estimated Bag-to-Bag Translation Models

At about the same time that I developed the models in this chapter, Hiemstra (1996) independently developed his own bag-to-bag model of translational equivalence. His model is also based on a one-to-one assumption, but it differs from my models in that it allows empty words in only one of the two bags, the one representing the shorter sentence. Thus, Hiemstra's model is similar to the first model in section 7.5, but it has a little less explanatory power.

Hiemstra's approach also differs from mine in his use of the Iterative Proportional Fitting Procedure (IPFP) (Deming & Stephan, 1940) for parameter estimation.

The IPFP is a method for fitting the cells in a contingency table to the known marginals. In (Hiemstra)'s model, the two-dimensional contingency table is a probability distribution over all possible events in a word-to-word translation model. The row and column totals are fixed at the marginal word probabilities in the two halves of the bitext. After the cells are initialized, the IPFP iteratively adjusts the cells in the table, under the constraint that the whole table must sum to one. On each iteration, the sum of the probabilities in each row approaches the marginal probability for that row, and likewise for the columns. The rate of approach is inversely proportional to the log-ratio of the sum of the values in a given row or column and the relevant marginal total. The IPFP is guaranteed to converge (Rüschendorf, 1995).

The IPFP is quite sensitive to initial conditions, so (Hiemstra) investigated a number of initialization options. Choosing the most advantageous, (Hiemstra) has published parts of the translational distributions of certain words, induced using both his method and Brown et al. (1993b)'s Model 1 from the same training bitext. Subjective comparison of these examples suggests that (Hiemstra)'s method is more accurate. Hiemstra (1998) has also evaluated the recall and precision of his method and of Model 1 on a small hand-constructed set of link tokens in a particular bitext. Model 1 fared worse, on average.

7.5 Parameter Estimation

This section describes my methods for estimating the parameters of a symmetric word-to-word translation model from a bitext. For most applications, we are interested in estimating the probability $trans(\mathbf{u}, \mathbf{v})$ of jointly generating the pair of words $(\mathbf{u}, \mathbf{v})$. Unfortunately, these parameters cannot be directly inferred from a training bitext, because we don't know which words in one half of the bitext were generated together with which words in the other half. The observable features of the bitext are only the co-occurrence counts $cooc(\mathbf{u}, \mathbf{v})$ (see chapter 5).

Methods for estimating translation parameters from co-occurrence counts typically involve *link counts*—$links(\mathbf{u}, \mathbf{v})$—that represent hypotheses about the number of times that $\mathbf{u}$ and $\mathbf{v}$ were generated together, for each $\mathbf{u}$ and $\mathbf{v}$ in the bitext. A *link token* is an ordered pair of word tokens, one from each half of the bitext. A *link type* is an ordered pair of word types. The link counts *links*$(\mathbf{u}, \mathbf{v})$ range over link types. We can always estimate *trans*$(\mathbf{u}, \mathbf{v})$ by normalizing link counts so that $\sum_{\mathbf{u},\mathbf{v}}$ *trans*$(\mathbf{u}, \mathbf{v}) = 1$:

$$trans(\mathbf{u}, \mathbf{v}) = \frac{\text{links}(\mathbf{u}, \mathbf{v})}{\sum_{\mathbf{u}',\mathbf{v}'} \text{links}(\mathbf{u}', \mathbf{v}')}. \tag{7.19}$$

For estimation purposes, it is convenient to employ also a separate set of non-probabilistic parameters *score*$(\mathbf{u}, \mathbf{v})$, which represent the chances that $\mathbf{u}$ and $\mathbf{v}$ can ever be mutual translations, i.e., that there exists some context in which tokens u and v are generated from the same concept. The relationship between *score*$(\mathbf{u}, \mathbf{v})$ and *trans*$(\mathbf{u}, \mathbf{v})$ can be more or less direct, depending on the model and its estimation method. Each of the models presented below uses a different *score* formulation.

All my methods for estimating the translation parameters *trans*$(\mathbf{u}, \mathbf{v})$ share the following general outline:

1. Initialize the *score* parameters to a first approximation, based only on co-occurrence counts.

2. Approximate the expected link counts *links*$(\mathbf{u}, \mathbf{v})$, as a function of the *score* parameters and the co-occurrence counts.

3. Estimate *trans*$(\mathbf{u}, \mathbf{v})$, by normalizing the link counts as in equation (7.19). If less than .0001 of the *trans*$(\mathbf{u}, \mathbf{v})$ distribution changed from the previous iteration, then stop.

4. Re-estimate the parameters *score*$(\mathbf{u}, \mathbf{v})$, as a function of the link counts and the co-occurrence counts.

5. Repeat from step 2.

Under certain conditions, a parameter estimation process of this sort is an instance of the Expectation-Maximization (EM) algorithm (Dempster et al., 1977). As explained below, meeting these conditions is computationally too expensive for my models.[9] Therefore I employ some approximations, which lack the EM algorithm's convergence guarantee.

The maximum likelihood approach to estimating the unknown parameters is to find the set of parameters $\widehat{\Theta}$ that maximize the probability of the training bitext $(\mathcal{U}, \mathcal{V})$:

$$\widehat{\Theta} = \arg \max_{\Theta} \Pr(\mathcal{U}, \mathcal{V} | \Theta). \tag{7.20}$$

The probability of the bitext is a sum over the distribution $\mathcal{A}$ of possible assignments:

$$\Pr(\mathcal{U}, \mathcal{V}|\Theta) = \sum_{A \in \mathcal{A}} \Pr(\mathcal{U}, A, \mathcal{V}|\Theta). \tag{7.21}$$

The number of possible assignments grows exponentially with the size of aligned text segments in the bitext. Due to the parameter interdependencies introduced by the one-to-one assumption, we are unlikely to find a method for decomposing the assignments into parameters that can be estimated independently of each other (as in Brown et al., 1993b, equation 26). Barring such a decomposition method, the MLE approach is infeasible. This is why we must make do with approximations to the EM algorithm.

In this situation, Brown et al. (1993b, p. 293) recommend "evaluating the expectations using only a single, probable alignment." The single most probable assignment A_{max} is the *maximum a posteriori (MAP) assignment*:

$$A_{max} = \arg\max_{A \in \mathcal{A}} \Pr(\mathcal{U}, A, \mathcal{V}|\Theta) \tag{7.22}$$

$$= \arg\max_{A \in \mathcal{A}} \Pr(l) \cdot l! \prod_{(i,j) \in A} trans(\mathbf{u}_i, \mathbf{v}_j) \tag{7.23}$$

$$= \arg\max_{A \in \mathcal{A}} \log \left[\Pr(l) \cdot l! \prod_{(i,j) \in A} trans(\mathbf{u}_i, \mathbf{v}_j) \right] \tag{7.24}$$

$$= \arg\max_{A \in \mathcal{A}} \left\{ \log[\Pr(l) \cdot l!] + \sum_{(i,j) \in A} \log trans(\mathbf{u}_i, \mathbf{v}_j) \right\}. \tag{7.25}$$

To simplify things further, let us assume that $\Pr(l) \cdot l!$ is constant, so that

$$A_{\max} = \arg\max_{A \in \mathcal{A}} \sum_{(i,j) \in A} \log trans(\mathbf{u}_i, \mathbf{v}_j). \tag{7.26}$$

If we represent the bitext as a bipartite graph and weight the edges by log $trans(\mathbf{u}, \mathbf{v})$, then the right-hand side of equation (7.26) is an instance of the *weighted maximum matching problem* and $A_{\max}$ is its solution. For a bipartite graph $G = (V_1 \cup V_2, E)$, with $v = |V_1 \cup V_2|$ and $e = |E|$, the lowest currently known upper bound on the computational complexity of this problem is $O(ve + v^2 \log v)$ (Ahuja et al., 1993, p. 500). Although this upper bound is

Table 7.2
A co-occurrence contingency table.

	u	**¬u**	Total
v	$\boxed{cooc(\mathbf{u}, \mathbf{v})}$	$cooc(\neg\mathbf{u}, \mathbf{v})$	$\boxed{cooc(\cdot, \mathbf{v})}$
¬v	$cooc(\mathbf{u}, \neg\mathbf{v})$	$cooc(\neg\mathbf{u}, \neg\mathbf{v})$	$cooc(\cdot, \neg\mathbf{v})$
Total	$\boxed{cooc(\mathbf{u}, \cdot)}$	$cooc(\neg\mathbf{u}, \cdot)$	$cooc(\cdot, \cdot)$

polynomial, it is still too expensive for typical bitexts.[10] Section 7.5.1 describes a greedy approximation to the MAP approximation.

7.5.1 Method A: The Competitive Linking Algorithm

Step 1: Initialization Almost every translation model estimation algorithm exploits the well-known correlation between translation probabilities and co-occurrence counts. Many algorithms also normalize the co occurrence counts $cooc(\mathbf{u}, \mathbf{v})$ by the marginal frequencies of **u** and **v**. However, these quantities account for only the three outlined cells in table 7.2. The statistical interdependence between two word types can be estimated more robustly by considering the whole table. For example, Gale & Church (1991b) suggest that "ϕ^2, a χ^2-like statistic, seems to be a particularly good choice because it makes good use of the off-diagonal cells" in the contingency table.

In informal experiments described elsewhere (Melamed, 1995), I found that the G^2 statistic suggested by Dunning (1993) slightly outperforms ϕ^2. Let the cells of the contingency table be named as follows:

	u	**¬u**
v	a	b
¬v	c	d

Now,

$$G^2(\mathbf{u}, \mathbf{v}) = 2 \log \frac{B(a|a + b, p_1)B(c|c + d, p_2)}{B(a|a + b, p)B(c|c + d, p)}, \qquad (7.27)$$

where $B(k|n, p) = \binom{n}{k} p^k (1 - p)^{n-k}$ are binomial probabilities. The statistic uses maximum likelihood estimates for the probability parameters: $p_1 = \frac{a}{a+b}$, $p_2 = \frac{c}{c+d}$, $p = \frac{a+c}{a+b+c+d}$. G^2 is easy to compute because the binomial coefficients in the numerator and in the denominator cancel each other out. All my methods initialize the parameters $score(\mathbf{u}, \mathbf{v})$ to $G^2(\mathbf{u}, \mathbf{v})$, except that any pairing with NULL is initialized to an infinitesimal value. I have also found it useful to smooth the co-occurrence counts, e.g., using the Simple Good-Turing smoothing method (Gale & Sampson, 1995), before computing G^2.

Step 2: Estimation of Link Counts To further reduce the complexity of estimating link counts, I employ the *competitive linking algorithm*, which is a greedy approximation to the MAP approximation:

1. Sort all the $score(\mathbf{u}, \mathbf{v})$ from highest to lowest.

2. For each $score(\mathbf{u}, \mathbf{v})$, in order:

(a) If $\mathbf{u}$ (resp., $\mathbf{v}$) is NULL, consider all tokens of $\mathbf{v}$ (resp., $\mathbf{u}$) in the bitext linked to NULL. Otherwise, link all co-occurring token pairs (u, v) in the bitext.

(b) The one-to-one assumption implies that linked words cannot be linked again. Therefore, remove all linked word tokens from their respective halves of the bitext.

The competitive linking algorithm can be viewed as a heuristic search for the most likely assignment in the space of all possible assignments. The heuristic is that the most likely assignments contain links that are individually the most likely. The search proceeds by a process of elimination. In the first search iteration, all the assignments that do not contain the most likely link are discarded. In the second iteration, all the assignments that do not contain the second most likely link are discarded, and so on until only one assignment remains.[11] The algorithm greedily selects the most likely links first, and then selects less likely links only if they don't conflict with previous selections. The probability of a link being rejected increases with the number of links that are selected before it, and thus decreases with the link's *score*. In this problem domain, the competitive linking algorithm usually finds one of the most likely assignments, as I show in section 7.7. Under an appropriate hashing scheme, the expected running time of the competitive linking algorithm is linear in the size of the input bitext.

Step 4: Re-estimation of the Model Parameters Method A re-estimates the *score* parameters as the logarithm of the *trans* parameters. The competitive linking algorithm cares only about the *relative* magnitudes of the various $score(\mathbf{u}, \mathbf{v})$. However, equation (7.26) is a sum rather than a product, so I scale the *trans* parameters logarithmically, to be consistent with its probabilistic interpretation:

$$score_A(\mathbf{u}, \mathbf{v}) = \log trans(\mathbf{u}, \mathbf{v}). \tag{7.28}$$

7.5.2   Method B: Improved Estimation Using an Explicit Noise Model

Yarowsky (1993) has shown that "for several definitions of sense and collocation, an ambiguous word has only one sense in a given collocation with a probability of 90–99%." In other words, a single contextual clue can be a highly reliable indicator of a word's sense. One of the definitions of "sense" studied by Yarowsky was a word token's translation in the other half of a bitext. For example, the English word sentence may be considered to have two senses, corresponding to its French translations peine (judicial sentence) and phrase (grammatical sentence). If a token of sentence occurs in the vicinity of a word like jury or prison, then it is far more likely to be translated as peine than as phrase. "In the vicinity of" is one kind of collocation. Co-occurrence in bitext space is another kind of collocation. If each word's translation is treated as a sense tag (Resnik & Yarowsky, 1997), then "translational" collocations have the unique property that the collocate and the word sense are one and the same!

Method B exploits this property under the hypothesis that "one sense per collocation" holds for translational collocations. This hypothesis implies that if $\mathbf{u}$ and $\mathbf{v}$ are *possible* mutual translations and a token u co-occurs with a token v in the bitext, then with very high probability the pair (u, v) was generated from the same concept and should be linked. To test this hypothesis, I ran one iteration of Method A on 300000 aligned sentence pairs from the Canadian Hansards bitext. I then plotted the ratio $\frac{links(\mathbf{u},\mathbf{v})}{cooc(\mathbf{u},\mathbf{v})}$ for several values of $cooc(\mathbf{u}, \mathbf{v})$ as in figure 7.2. The curves show that the ratio $\frac{links(\mathbf{u},\mathbf{v})}{cooc(\mathbf{u},\mathbf{v})}$ tends to be either very high or very low. This bimodality is not an artifact of the competitive linking process, because in the first iteration, linking decisions are based only on the initial similarity metric.

Information about how often words co-occur without being linked can be used to bias the estimation of translation model parameters. The smaller the ratio $\frac{links(\mathbf{u},\mathbf{v})}{cooc(\mathbf{u},\mathbf{v})}$, the more likely it is that $\mathbf{u}$ and $\mathbf{v}$ are *not* mutual translations, and that links posited between tokens of $\mathbf{u}$ and $\mathbf{v}$ are noise. The bias can be implemented via auxiliary parameters that model the curve illustrated in figure 7.2. The competitive linking algorithm creates all the links of a given type independently of each other.[12] So, the distribution of the number $links(\mathbf{u}, \mathbf{v})$ of links connecting word types $\mathbf{u}$ and $\mathbf{v}$ can be modeled by a binomial distribution with parameters $cooc(\mathbf{u}, \mathbf{v})$ and $p(\mathbf{u}, \mathbf{v})$. $p(\mathbf{u}, \mathbf{v})$ is the probability that $\mathbf{u}$ and $\mathbf{v}$ will be linked when they co-occur. There is never enough data to robustly estimate each p parameter separately. Instead, I model all the ps with

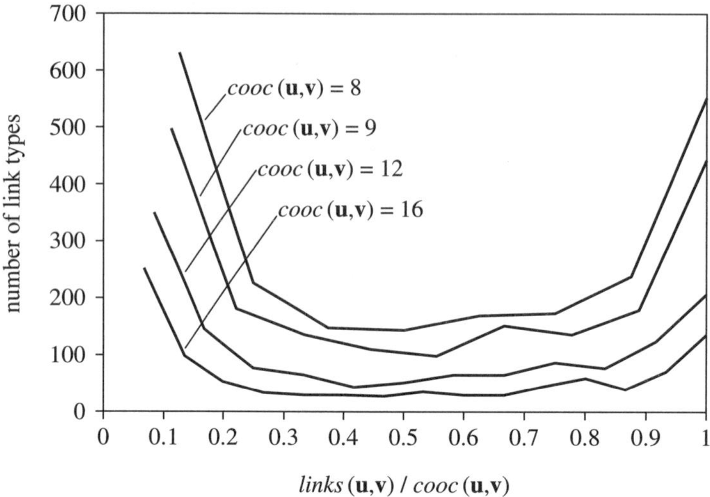

Figure 7.2
The ratio $links(\mathbf{u}, \mathbf{v})/cooc(\mathbf{u}, \mathbf{v})$, for several values of $cooc(\mathbf{u}, \mathbf{v})$.

just two parameters. For $\mathbf{u}$ and $\mathbf{v}$ that are mutual translations, $p(\mathbf{u}, \mathbf{v})$ will average to a relatively high probability, which I call λ^+. For $\mathbf{u}$ and $\mathbf{v}$ that are not mutual translations, $p(\mathbf{u}, \mathbf{v})$ will average to a relatively low probability, which I call λ^-. λ^+ and λ^- correspond to the two peaks of the distribution $\frac{links(\mathbf{u},\mathbf{v})}{cooc(\mathbf{u},\mathbf{v})}$ illustrated in figure 7.2. The two parameters can also be interpreted as the rates of true and false positives. If the translation in the bitext is consistent and the translation model is accurate, then λ^+ will be close to one and λ^- will be close to zero.

To find the most likely values of the auxiliary parameters λ^+ and λ^-, I adopt the standard method of maximum likelihood estimation and find the values that maximize the probability of the link frequency distribution under the usual independence assumptions:

$$\Pr(links|\text{model}) = \prod_{\mathbf{u},\mathbf{v}} \Pr(links(\mathbf{u}, \mathbf{v})|cooc(\mathbf{u}, \mathbf{v}), \lambda^+, \lambda^-). \qquad (7.29)$$

Table 7.3 summarizes the variables involved in this auxiliary estimation process.

The factors on the right-hand side of equation (7.29) can be written explicitly with the help of a mixture coefficient. Let τ be the probability that an arbitrary

Table 7.3
Variables used to describe Method B.

$links(\mathbf{u}, \mathbf{v})$	$=$	the number of times that $\mathbf{u}$ and $\mathbf{v}$ are hypothesized to co-occur as mutual translations
$B(k\|n, p)$	$=$	probability of k being generated from a binomial distribution with parameters n and p
λ^{+}	$=$	probability of a link given mutual translations
λ^{-}	$=$	probability of a link given not mutual translations
λ	$=$	probability of a link
τ	$=$	probability of mutual translations
K	$=$	total number of links in the bitext
N	$=$	total number of co-occurrences in the bitext

co-occurring pair of word types are mutual translations. Let $B(k|n, p)$ denote the probability that k links are observed out of n co-occurrences, where k has a binomial distribution with parameters n and p. Then the probability that word types $\mathbf{u}$ and $\mathbf{v}$ will be linked $links(\mathbf{u}, \mathbf{v})$ times out of $cooc(\mathbf{u}, \mathbf{v})$ co-occurrences is a mixture of two binomials:

$$\Pr(links(\mathbf{u}, \mathbf{v})|cooc(\mathbf{u}, \mathbf{v}), \lambda^{+}, \lambda^{-})$$

$$= \tau B(links(\mathbf{u}, \mathbf{v})|cooc(\mathbf{u}, \mathbf{v}), \lambda^{+}) + (1 - \tau)B(links(\mathbf{u}, \mathbf{v})|cooc(\mathbf{u}, \mathbf{v}), \lambda^{-})$$

$$(7.30)$$

One more variable allows us to express τ in terms of λ^{+} and λ^{-}: Let λ be the probability that an arbitrary co-occuring pair of word tokens will be linked, regardless of whether or not they are mutual translations. Since τ is constant over all word types, it also represents the probability that an arbitrary co-occurring pair of word *tokens* are mutual translations. Therefore,

$$\lambda = \tau\lambda^{+} + (1 - \tau)\lambda^{-}. \qquad (7.31)$$

λ can also be estimated empirically. Let K be the total number of links in the bitext and let N be the total number of word token pair co-occurrences:

$$K = \sum_{\mathbf{u},\mathbf{v}} links(\mathbf{u}, \mathbf{v}), \qquad (7.32)$$

$$N = \sum_{\mathbf{u},\mathbf{v}} cooc(\mathbf{u}, \mathbf{v}). \qquad (7.33)$$

By definition,

$$\lambda = K/N. \qquad (7.34)$$

Equating the right-hand sides of equations (7.31) and (7.34) and rearranging the terms, we get:

$$\tau = \frac{K/N - \lambda^-}{\lambda^+ - \lambda^-}. \tag{7.35}$$

Since τ is now a function of λ^+ and λ^-, only the latter two variables represent degrees of freedom in the model.

In the preceding equations, either $\mathbf{u}$ or $\mathbf{v}$ can be NULL. However, the number of times that a word co-occurs with NULL is not an observable feature of bitexts. To make sense of co-occurrences with NULL, we can view co-occurrences as *potential* links and $cooc(\mathbf{u}, \mathbf{v})$ as the maximum number of times that tokens of $\mathbf{u}$ and $\mathbf{v}$ might be linked. From this point of view, $cooc(\mathbf{u}, \text{NULL})$ should be set to the unigram frequency of $\mathbf{u}$, since each token of $\mathbf{u}$ represents one potential link to NULL, and similarly for $cooc(\text{NULL}, \mathbf{v})$. These co-occurrence counts should be summed together with all the others in equation (7.33).

The probability function expressed by equations (7.29) and (7.30) may have many local maxima. In practice, these local maxima are like pebbles on a mountain, invisible at low resolution. I computed equation (7.29) over various combinations of λ^+ and λ^- after one iteration of Method A over 300000 aligned sentence pairs from the Canadian Hansard bitext. Figure 7.3 illustrates

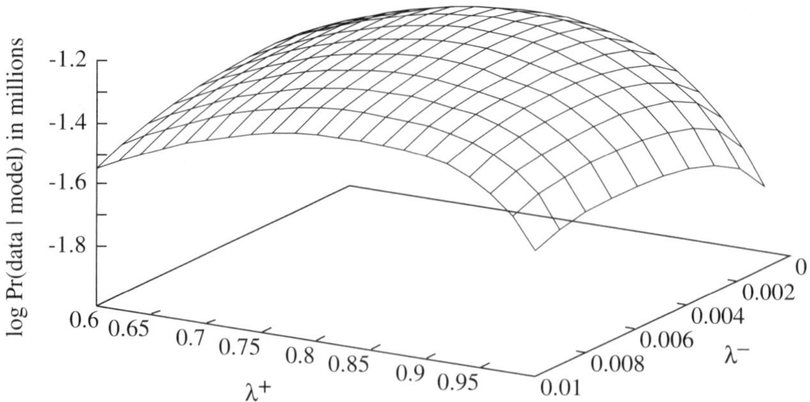

Figure 7.3
Pr(*links|model*), as given in equation (7.29), has only one global maximum in the region of interest, where $1 > \lambda^+ > \lambda > \lambda^- > 0$.

that the region of interest in the parameter space, where $1 > \lambda^+ > \lambda > \lambda^- > 0$, has only one dominant global maximum. This global maximum can be found by standard hill-climbing methods, as long as the step size is large enough to avoid getting stuck on the pebbles.

Given estimates for λ^+ and λ^-, we can compute $B(links(\mathbf{u}, \mathbf{v})|cooc(\mathbf{u}, \mathbf{v}), \lambda^+)$ and $B(links(\mathbf{u}, \mathbf{v})|cooc(\mathbf{u}, \mathbf{v}), \lambda^-)$ for each occurring combination of $links$ and $cooc$ values. These are the probabilities that $links(\mathbf{u}, \mathbf{v})$ links were generated out of $cooc(\mathbf{u}, \mathbf{v})$ possible links by a process that generates correct links and by a process that generates incorrect links, respectively. The ratio of these probabilities is the likelihood ratio in favor of the types $\mathbf{u}$ and $\mathbf{v}$ being possible mutual translations, for all $\mathbf{u}$ and $\mathbf{v}$:

$$score_B(\mathbf{u}, \mathbf{v}) = \log \frac{B(links(\mathbf{u}, \mathbf{v})|cooc(\mathbf{u}, \mathbf{v}), \lambda^+)}{B(links(\mathbf{u}, \mathbf{v})|cooc(\mathbf{u}, \mathbf{v}), \lambda^-)}. \tag{7.36}$$

Method B differs from Method A only in its redefinition of the $score$ function in equation (7.36). The auxiliary parameters λ^+ and λ^- and the noise model that they represent can be employed the same way in translation models that are not based on the one-to-one assumption.

7.5.3 Method C: Improved Estimation Using Pre-Existing Word Classes

In Method B, the estimation of the auxiliary parameters λ^+ and λ^- depends only on the overall distribution of co-occurrence counts and link frequencies. All word pairs that co-occur the same number of times and are linked the same number of times are assigned the same $score$. More accurate models can be induced by taking into account various features of the linked tokens. For example, frequent words are translated less consistently than rare words (Catizone et al., 1989). To take these differences into account, we can estimate separate values of λ^+ and λ^- for different ranges of $cooc(\mathbf{u}, \mathbf{v})$. Similarly, the auxiliary parameters can be conditioned on the linked parts of speech. A kind of word order correlation bias can be effected by conditioning the auxiliary parameters on the relative positions of linked word tokens in their respective texts. Just as easily, we can model link types that coincide with entries in an on-line bilingual dictionary separately from those that do not (cf. Brown et al., 1993a). When the auxiliary parameters are conditioned on different link classes, their optimization is carried out separately for each class:

$$score_C(\mathbf{u}, \mathbf{v} | Z = \text{class}(\mathbf{u}, \mathbf{v})) = \log \frac{B(links(\mathbf{u}, \mathbf{v}) | cooc(\mathbf{u}, \mathbf{v}), \lambda_Z^+)}{B(links(\mathbf{u}, \mathbf{v}) | cooc(\mathbf{u}, \mathbf{v}), \lambda_Z^-)}. \qquad (7.37)$$

Section 7.7.1 describes the link classes used in the experiments below.

7.6 Effects of Sparse Data

The one-to-one assumption is a potent weapon against the ever-present sparse data problem. The assumption makes possible accurate estimation of translational distributions even for words that occur only once, as long as the surrounding words are more frequent. In most translation models, link scores are correlated with co-occurrence frequency. So, the links between tokens u and v for which $score(\mathbf{u}, \mathbf{v})$ is highest are the ones for which there is the most evidence, and thus also the ones that are easiest to predict correctly. Winner-take-all link assignment methods, such as the competitive linking algorithm, can leverage their accuracy on the more confident links to raise the accuracy of the less confident links, thereby preventing links based on indirect associations (see section 7.4.1). For example, suppose that u_1 and u_2 co-occur with v_1 and v_2 in the training data, and the model estimates $score(\mathbf{u_1}, \mathbf{v_1}) = .05$, $score(\mathbf{u_1}, \mathbf{v_2}) = .02$, and $score(\mathbf{u_2}, \mathbf{v_2}) = .01$. According to the one-to-one assumption, (u_1, v_2) is an indirect association and the correct translation of v_2 is u_2. To the extent that the one-to-one assumption is valid, it reduces the probability of spurious links for the rarer words. The more incorrect candidate translations can be eliminated for a given rare word, the more likely the correct translation is to be found. So, the probability of a correct match for a rare word is proportional to the fraction of words around it that can be linked with higher confidence. This fraction is largely determined by two bitext properties: the distribution of word frequencies and the distribution of co-occurrence counts. I explore each of these properties in turn.

The distribution of word frequencies is a function of corpus size. The words in any text corpus are drawn from a large but finite vocabulary. As the corpus gets larger, fewer new words appear, and the average frequency of words already in the corpus rises. I took random samples of varying sizes from large text corpora in French and in English. The corpora comprised news text (*Le Monde* and *Wall Street Journal*), parliamentary debate transcripts (Hansards) and Sun Microsystems software documentation (AnswerBooks). Figure 7.4 shows the log-log relationship between sample size and the fraction

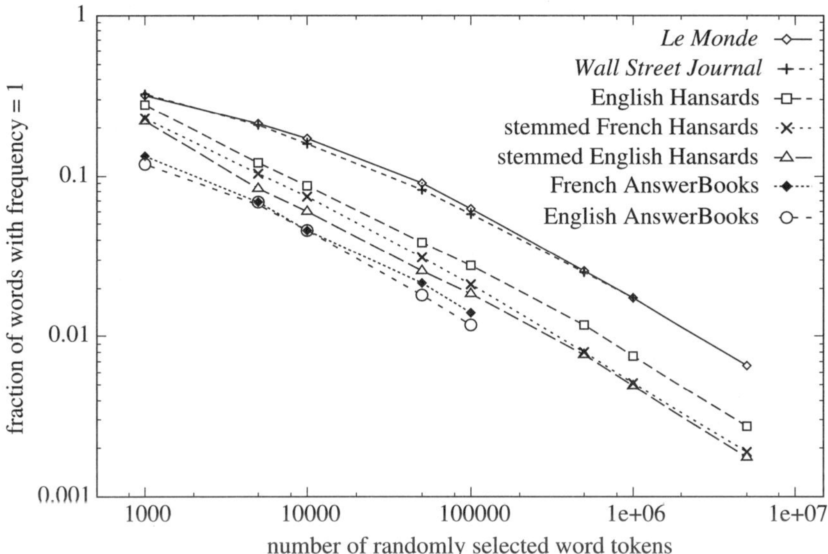

Figure 7.4
The log-log relationship between corpus size and the proportion of singletons.

of words (by token) that appear in the sample only once. For example, suppose we draw a random sample of one million words from *Le Monde* and then select a random word type **w** from this random sample. According to figure 7.4, the chances are roughly 0.017 that **w** appears only once in that one million words. If the sample were only one thousand words, however, our chances of drawing a singleton rise to 0.317. The nearly linear shape of the log-log curve seems largely invariant across languages and text genres, as predicted by Zipf (1936). Some curves in the graph are higher than others, because the language genres from which the corpora were drawn have richer vocabularies. For example, the fraction of singleton words is consistently smaller in the stemmed English Hansards than in the same text when it is not stemmed, which is the whole motivation for stemming. Figure 7.5, based on *Le Monde* text, shows that the log-log relationship holds for higher frequencies too. In a larger corpus, a larger fraction of the word types appear more frequently. Thus, corpus size determines the probability that a randomly chosen word will have a particular frequency.

The likelihood of a correct link for a rare word token w also depends on one other variable. If w co-occurs with only one rare word (in the opposite half of

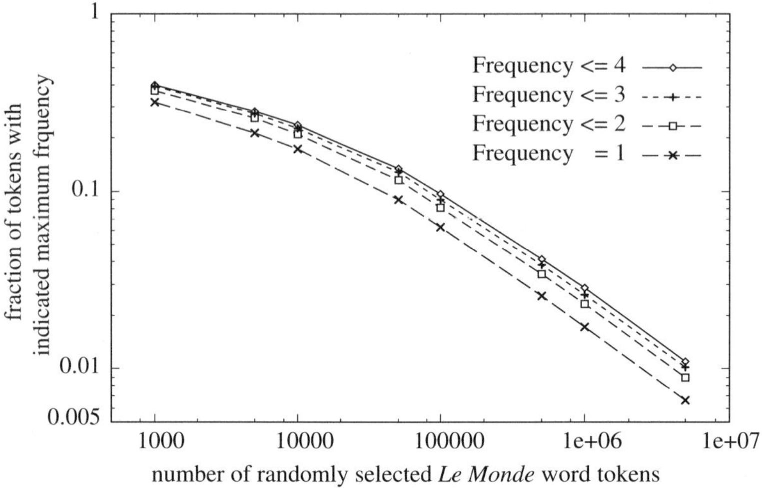

Figure 7.5
The log-log relationship for higher frequencies. The bottom curve in this graph is the same as the top curve in figure 7.4

the bitext), then the competitive linking algorithm is likely to eliminate all of w's indirect associations before it attempts to link w. Problems arise only when more than one candidate remains for linking to w. What is the probability that w co-occurs with more than one rare word? Suppose that w co-occurs with γ words in the opposite half of the bitext, where γ is either the vertical or horizontal component of δ.[13] Let p be the probability that a word co-occurring with w is rare. Then the probability of exactly k rare words co-occuring with w can be approximated by a binomial distribution with parameters γ and p. It follows that the probability of more than one rare word co-occurring with w is

$$\text{Pr}(\text{more than 1 rare word co-occuring}) = 1 - B(0|\gamma, p) - B(1|\gamma, p). \quad (7.38)$$

Figure 7.6 plots equation (7.38) over different values of γ and p. The range of p corresponds roughly to the range of the y-axis in figures 7.4 and 7.5. The figure illustrates how the power of the one-to-one assumption varies with corpus size. It also illustrates why δ should not be set too high in the distance-based model of co-occurrence. For example, at $p = .03$ and $\gamma = 10$, the probability of a second rare word co-occurring is .034, but if γ is doubled to 20, the probability of a second rare word more than triples to .12.

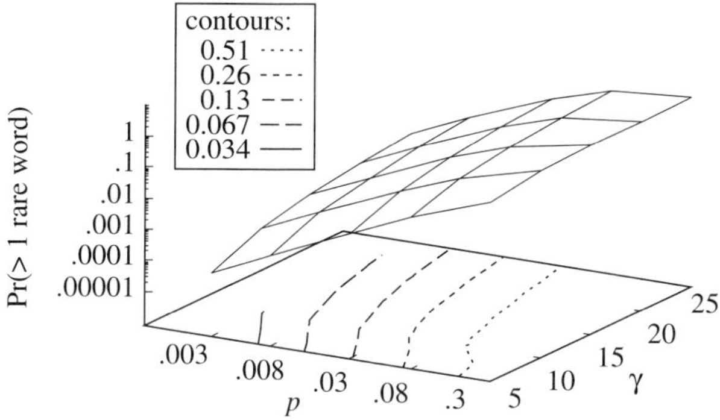

Figure 7.6
Probability of more than one rare word co-occurring.

7.7 Evaluation

7.7.1 Evaluation at the Token Level

This section compares translation model estimation methods A, B, and C to one another and to Brown et al. (1993b)'s Model 1. To reiterate, Model 1 is based on co-occurrence information only; Method A is based on the one-to-one assumption; Method B adds the "one sense per collocation" hypothesis to Method A; Method C conditions the auxiliary parameters of Method B on various word classes. Whereas Methods A and B and Model 1 were fully specified in section 7.4.2 and section 7.5, the latter section described a variety of features on which Method C might classify links. For the purposes of the experiments described in this chapter, Method C employed the simple classification in table 7.4 for both languages in the bitext. All classification was performed by table lookup; no context-aware part-of-speech tagger was used. In particular, words that were ambiguous between open classes and closed classes were always deemed to be in the closed class. The only language-specific knowledge involved in this classification method is the list of function words in class F. Certainly, more sophisticated word classification methods could produce better models, but even the simple classification in Table 7.4 should suffice to demonstrate the method's potential.

Rates of Convergence   Before diving into the main results, it is interesting to compare the convergence rates of the four different models. Figure 7.7 shows that, although the EM algorithm guarantees monotonic convergence

Table 7.4
Word classes used by Method C for the experiments described in this chapter. Link classes were constructed by taking the cross-product of the word classes.

Class code	Description
EOS	End-Of-Sentence punctuation
EOP	End-Of-Phrase punctuation, such as commas and colons
SCM	Subordinate Clause Markers, such as " and (
SYM	Symbols, such as ˜ and *
NU	the NULL word, in a class by itself
C	Content words: nouns, adjectives, adverbs, non-auxiliary verbs
F	all other words, i.e., function words

for Model 1, it requires more iterations to converge on these training data than Models A, B, and C. To be fair, we must remember that Method B and Method C take time to estimate their auxiliary parameters on each iteration, so figure 7.7 does not say which method is fastest in real time. Such a comparison is very dependent on the details of each method's implementation. In the current (very inefficient) implementations, Model A converged in about six hours, Model B in about 20 hours, Model C in about 24 hours, and Model 1 in about 27 hours.

Experimental Method Each of the four methods was used to estimate a word-to-word translation model from the 29614 verse pairs in the Bible bitext described in chapter 6. All methods were deemed to have converged when less than .0001 of the translational probability distribution changed from one iteration to the next. The links assigned by each of Methods A, B, and C in the last iteration were normalized into joint probability distributions using equation (7.19). I shall refer to these joint distributions as Model A, Model B and Model C, respectively. Each of the joint probability distributions was further normalized into two conditional probability distributions, one in each direction. Since Model 1 is inherently directional, its conditional probability distributions were estimated separately in each direction, instead of being derived from a joint distribution.

The four models' predictions were compared to the gold-standard annotations described in chapter 6. Each model guessed one translation (either stochastically or deterministically, depending on the task) for each word on one side of the gold-standard bitext. Therefore, precision = recall here, and I refer to the results simply as "percent correct." The accuracy of each model was av-

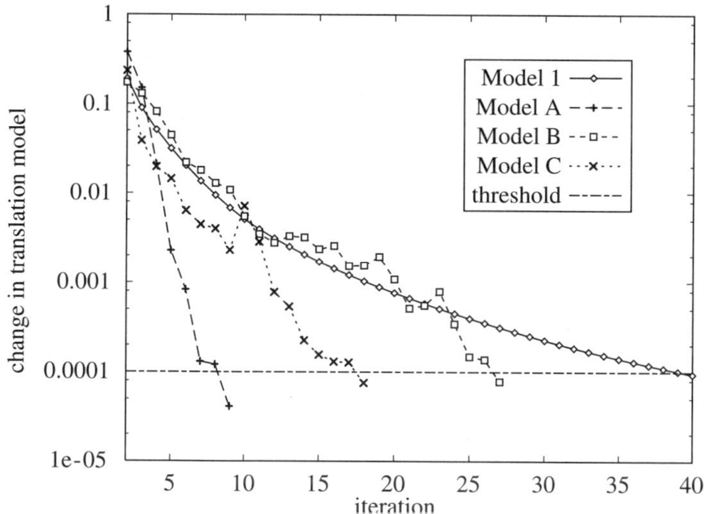

Figure 7.7
Convergence rates for Model 1 and Methods A, B, and C. Changes from each iteration to the next were measured in terms of the set-theoretic Dice coefficient.

eraged over the two directions of translation: English to French and French to English. The five-fold replication of annotations in the test data made possible computation of the statistical significance of the differences in model accuracy. The statistical significance of all results in this section was measured at the $\alpha = .05$ level, using the Wilcoxon signed ranks test. Although the models were evaluated on part of the same bitext on which they were trained, the evaluations were with respect to the translational equivalence relation hidden in this bitext, not with respect to any of the bitext's visible features. Such testing on training data is standard practice for unsupervised learning algorithms, where the objective is to compare several methods. Of course, performance would degrade on previously unseen data.

In addition to the different translation models, there were two other independent variables in the experiment: method of translation and whether function words were included. Some applications, such as query translation for CLIR, don't care about function words. To get a sense of the relative effectiveness of the different translation model estimation methods when function words are taken out of the equation, I removed from the gold standard all link tokens where one or both of the linked words were closed-class words. Then, I removed all closed-class words (including non-alphabetic symbols) from the models and renormalized the conditional probabilities.

The method of translation was either "single-best" or "whole distribution." "Single-best" translation is the kind that somebody might use to get the gist of a foreign-language document. The input to the task was one side of the gold standard bitext. The output was the model's single best guess about the translation of each word in the input, together with the input word. In other words, each model produced link tokens consisting of input words and their translations.

For some applications, however, it is insufficient to guess only the single most likely translation of each word in the input. The model is expected to output the "whole distribution" of possible translations for each input word. This distribution is then combined with other distributions that are relevant to the application. For example, for cross-language information retrieval, the translational distribution can be combined with the distribution of term frequencies. For statistical machine translation, the translational distribution can be decoded with a source language model (Brown et al., 1988; Al-Onaizan et al., 1999). To predict how the different models might perform in such applications, the "whole distribution" task was to generate a whole set of links from each input word, weighted according to the probability assigned by the model to each of the input word's translations.

The mean results are plotted in figures 7.8 and 7.9 with 95% confidence intervals. All four graphs in these figures are on the same scale to facilitate comparison. On both tasks involving the entire vocabulary, each of the biases presented in this chapter improves the efficiency of modeling the available training data. When closed-class words were ignored, Model 1 performed better than Method A, because open-class words are more likely to violate the one-to-one assumption. However, the explicit noise model in Methods B and C boosted their scores significantly higher than Model 1 and Method A. Method B was better than Method C at choosing the single best open-class links, and the situation was reversed for the whole distribution of open-class links. However, the differences in performance between these two methods were tiny on the open-class tasks, because they left only two classes for Method C to distinguish: content words and NULLS. Most of the scores on the whole distribution task were lower than their counterparts on the single-best translation task, because it is more difficult for any statistical method to correctly model the less common translations. The "best" translations are usually the most common.

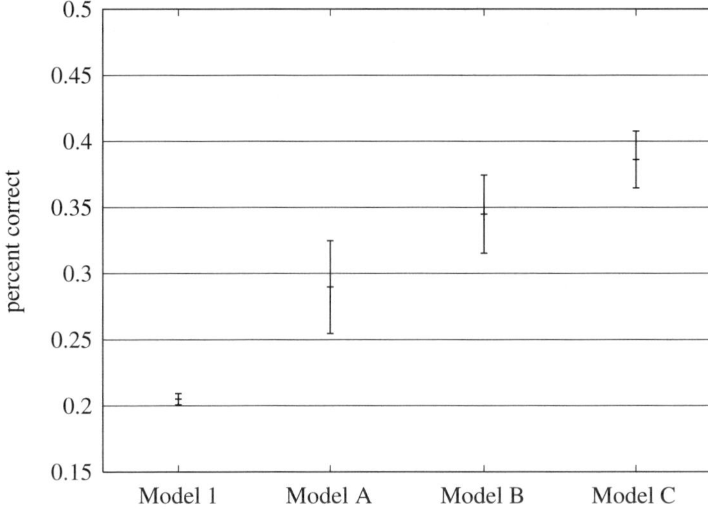

(a)

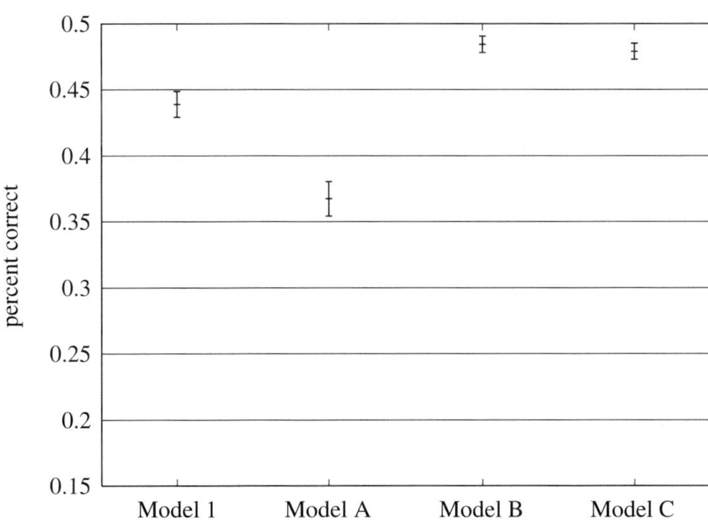

(b)

Figure 7.8
Comparison of model performance on "single-best" translation task. (a) All links; (b) open-class links only.

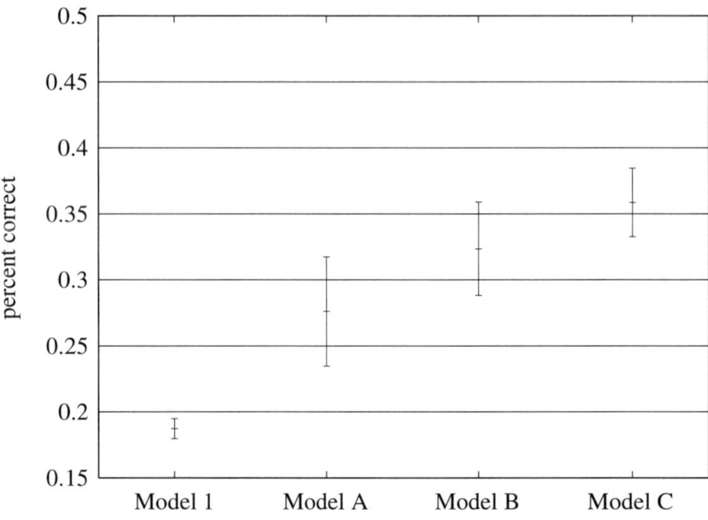

(a)

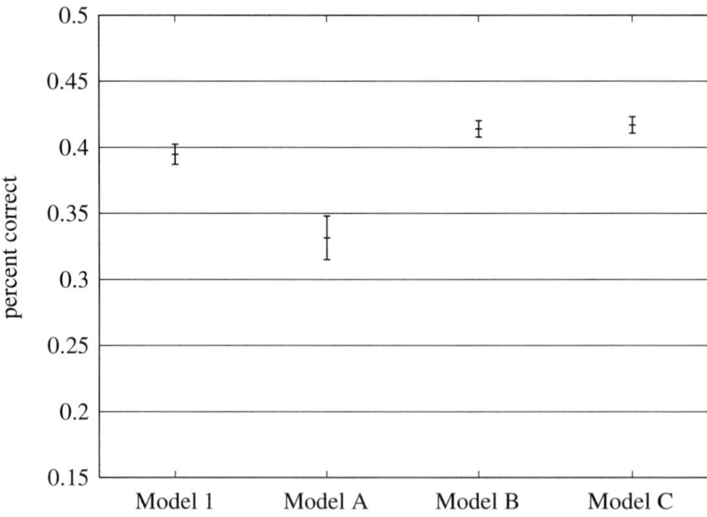

(b)

Figure 7.9
Comparison of model performance on "whole-distribution" task. (a) All links; (b) open-class links only.

To study how the benefits of the various biases vary with training corpus size, I evaluated Models A, B, C, and 1 on the "whole distribution" translation task, after training them on three different-size subsets of the Bible bitext. The first subset consisted of only the 250 verse pairs in the gold-standard. The second subset included these 250 plus another random sample of 2250 for a total of 2500, an order of magnitude larger than the first subset. The third subset contained all 29614 verse pairs in the Bible bitext, roughly an order of magnitude larger than the second subset. All models were compared to the five gold standard annotations, and the scores were averaged over the two directions of translation, as before. Again, because the total probability assigned to all translations for each source word was one, precision = recall = percent correct on this task.

The mean scores over the five gold standard annotations are graphed in figure 7.10, where the right edge of the figure corresponds to the means of figure 7.9(a). Figure 7.10 supports the hypothesis in section 7.6 that the biases presented in this chapter are even more valuable when the training data are more sparse. The one-to-one assumption is useful, even though it forces us to use a greedy approximation to maximum likelihood. In relative terms, the advantage of the one-to-one assumption is much more pronounced on smaller training sets. For example, Model A is 102% more accurate than Model 1 when

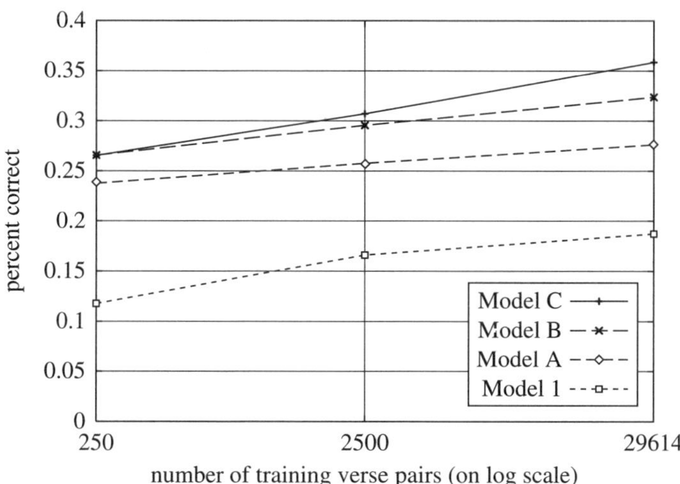

Figure 7.10
Effects of training set size on model accuracy on the "whole distribution" task.

trained on only 250 verse pairs. The explicit noise model buys a considerable gain in accuracy across all sizes of training data, as do the link classes of Model C. In concert, when trained and tested only on the gold-standard test set, the three biases outperformed Model 1 by up to 125%. This difference is even more significant given the absolute performance ceiling of 82% established by the inter-annotator agreement rates on the gold standard.

7.7.2 Evaluation at the Type Level

An important application of statistical translation models is to help lexicographers compile bilingual dictionaries. Dictionaries are written to answer the question, "What are the possible translations of X?" This is a question about link types, rather than about link tokens.

Evaluation by link type is a thorny issue. Human judges often disagree about the degree to which context should play a role in judgments of translational equivalence. For example, the Harper-Collins French Dictionary (Cousin et al., 1990) gives the following French translations for English appoint: nommer, engager, fixer, désigner. Likewise, most lay judges would not consider instituer a correct French translation of appoint. In actual translations, however, when the object of the verb is commission, task force, panel, etc., English appoint is usually translated into French as instituer. To take into account this kind of context-dependent translational equivalence, link types must be evaluated with respect to the bitext whence they were induced.

It is with this kind of evaluation in mind that I designed the verse-pair sampling strategy described in section 6.2. The gold standard consists of verse pairs that include all of the Bible bitext's instances of a focus set of 100 randomly sampled English word types. The set of French word types with which an annotator linked tokens of each English word type constitutes the set of valid translations in this bitext for that English word type in the Bible. These translation sets can be compared by type to the translations of the focus types predicted by each translation model.

The evaluation of translation models at the word-type level is complicated by the possibility of phrasal translations. The gold-standard annotators were free to link each word to as many other words as they wished (e.g., "take their stand" in figure 6.3). In contrast, all the methods being evaluated here produce models of translational equivalence between individual words only. How can we decide whether a single-word translation "matches" a phrasal translation? The answer lies in the observation that corpus-based lexicography usually involves a lexicographer. Bilingual lexicographers can use bilingual concor-

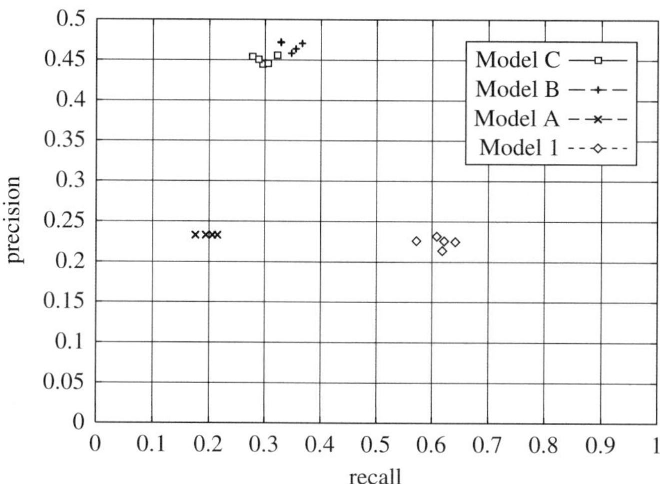

Figure 7.11
Model accuracy on the gold-standard focus types, averaged by type.

dancing software to find instances of any link type induced from a bitext and
to display these instances sorted by their contexts (e.g. Simard et al., 1993;
Langlois, 1996). Given a partially correct link type, the lexicographer can usually reconstruct the complete link type from the contexts in the concordance.
For example, if the model proposes an equivalence between immédiatement
and right, a bilingual concordance can show the lexicographer that the model
was really trying to capture the equivalence between immédiatement and right
away or between immédiatement and right now. Since link type evaluation is
intended to gauge performance on a task that has a person in the loop, I shall
treat partially correct link types as correct.

Another way in which the lexicographer can complement the translation
model is to weed out links between content words and function words. The
focus set contains only content words. To make the evaluation more true to the
task, I ignored all links involving any function words, both in the gold standard
and in the translation models.[14]

Figure 7.11 compares the recall and precision of the focus types in Models 1,
A, B, and C with respect to each of the five gold-standard annotations. As
expected, Model 1's long tail of low probabilities gives it high recall but low
precision. In contrast, most bilingual dictionaries have nearly perfect precision
at low recall. Lexicographers are likely to prefer tools with a similar bias in
their output.

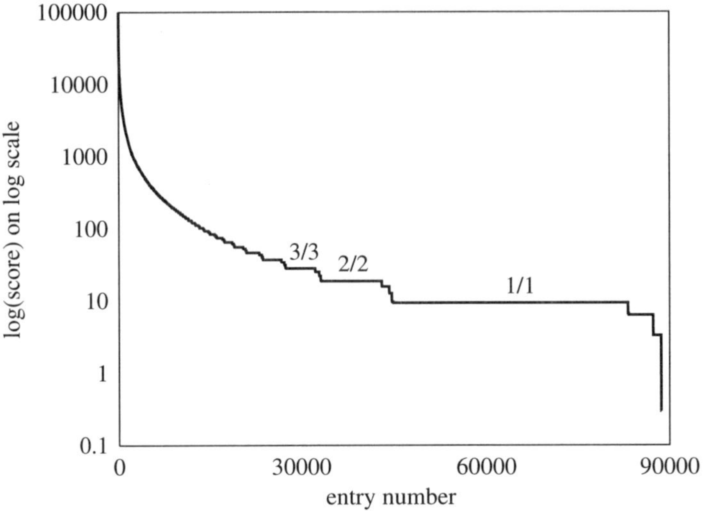

Figure 7.12
Distribution of link type scores. The long plateaus correspond to the most common combinations
of $\frac{links(\mathbf{u},\mathbf{v})}{cooc(\mathbf{u},\mathbf{v})}$: $1/1, 2/2$ and $3/3$.

In earlier work (Melamed, 1996a), I performed a less rigorous post-hoc evaluation of the link types produced by an earlier version of Method B.[15] The
bitext used for this evaluation was the same aligned Hansards bitext used by
Gale & Church (1991b), except that I used only 300,000 aligned segment pairs
to save time. The bitext was automatically pre-tokenized to delimit punctuation, English possessive pronouns and French elisions. Morphological variants
in both halves of the bitext were stemmed to a canonical form.

The link types assigned by the converged model were sorted by the scores
in equation (7.36). Figure 7.12 shows the distribution of these scores on a log
scale. The log scale helps to illustrate the plateaus in the curve. The longest
plateau represents the set of word pairs that were linked once out of one co-
occurrence (1/1) in the bitext. All these word pairs were equally likely to be
correct. The second-longest plateau resulted from word pairs that were linked
twice out of two co-occurrences (2/2), and the third longest plateau is from
word pairs that were linked three times out of three co-occurrences (3/3).
As usual, the entries with higher scores were more likely to be correct. By
discarding entries with lower scores, coverage could be traded for accuracy.
This trade-off was measured at three points, representing cutoffs at the end of
each of the three longest plateaus.

Table 7.5
Lexicon coverage at three different minimum score thresholds. The bitext contained 41028 different English words and 36314 different French words, for a total of 77342.

Cutoff plateau	Minimum score	Total lexicon entries	English words represented	%	French words represented	%
3/3	28	32274	14299	35	13409	37
2/2	18	43075	18533	45	17133	47
1/1	9	88633	36371	89	33017	91

The traditional method of measuring coverage requires knowledge of the correct link types, which is impossible to determine without a gold standard. An approximate coverage measure can be based on the number of different words in the corpus. For lexicons extracted from corpora, perfect coverage implies at least one entry containing each word in the corpus. One-sided variants, which consider only source words, have also been used (Gale & Church, 1991b). Table 7.5 shows both the marginal (one-sided) and the combined coverage at each of the three cutoff points. It also shows the absolute number of (non-NULL) entries in each of the three lexicons. Of course, the size of automatically induced lexicons depends on the size of the training bitext. Table 7.5 shows that, given a sufficiently large bitext, the method can automatically construct translation lexicons with as many entries as published bilingual dictionaries.

The next task was to measure accuracy. It would have taken too long to evaluate every lexicon entry manually. Instead, I took five random samples (with replacement) of 100 entries each from each of the three lexicons. Each of the samples was first compared to a translation lexicon extracted from a machine-readable bilingual dictionary (Cousin et al., 1991). All the entries in the sample that appeared in the dictionary were assumed to be correct. I checked the remaining entries in all the samples by hand. To take context-dependent translational equivalence into account, I evaluated the accuracy of the translation lexicons in the context of the bitext whence they were extracted, using a simple bilingual concordancer. A lexicon entry $(\mathbf{u},\mathbf{v})$ was considered correct if u and v ever appeared as direct translations of each other in an aligned segment pair. That is, a link type was considered correct if any of its tokens were correct.

Direct translations come in different flavors. Most entries that I checked by hand were of the plain vanilla variety that you might find in a bilingual

Table 7.6
Distribution of different types of correct lexicon entries at varying levels of coverage
(mean ± standard deviation).

Cutoff	Coverage	% type V	% type P	% type I	Total % accuracy
3/3	36%	89 ± 2.2	3.4 ± 0.5	7.6 ± 3.2	99.2 ± 0.8
2/2	46%	81 ± 3.0	8.0 ± 2.1	9.8 ± 1.8	99.0 ± 1.4
1/1	90%	82 ± 2.5	4.4 ± 0.5	6.0 ± 1.9	92.8 ± 1.1

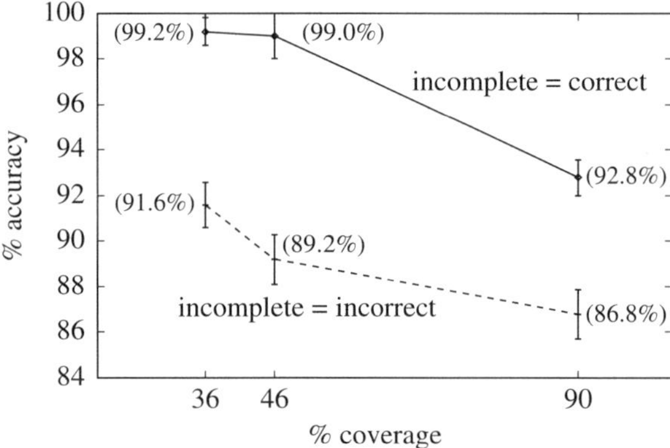

Figure 7.13
Translation lexicon accuracy with 95% confidence intervals at varying levels of coverage.

dictionary (entry type V). However, a significant number of words translated into a different part of speech (entry type P). For instance, in the entry
(protection, protégé), the English word is a noun but the French word is an
adjective. This entry appeared because to have protection is often translated
as être protégé (to be protected) in the bitext. The entry will never occur in
a bilingual dictionary, but users of translation lexicons, be they human or
machine, will want to know that translations often happen this way. Incomplete entries, described above, were counted in a third category (entry type
I). Whether incomplete entries should be considered correct depends on the
application.

Table 7.6 shows the distribution of correct lexicon entries among the types
V, P, and I. Figure 7.13 graphs the accuracy of the method against coverage,
with 95% confidence intervals. The upper curve represents accuracy when incomplete links are considered correct, and the lower when they are considered

incorrect. On the former metric, the method can generate translation lexicons with accuracy and coverage both exceeding 90%, as well as dictionary-sized translation lexicons that are over 99% correct.

7.8 Application to MT Lexicon Development

Translation lexicons are a vital component of any machine translation (MT) system. The high cost of lexicon development and maintenance is a major entry barrier for potential new vendors in the MT market, and a hindrance to growth for existing vendors. Many have tried to accelerate the MT lexicon development process by incorporating automatic methods for finding translation candidates in text corpora. Typically, these candidates are presented to a human expert for validation. Automatic methods must be accurate to be effective; otherwise, the experts in the loop would spend most of their time filtering errors, instead of adding information to the MT system. Dagan & Church (1994) were the first to report sufficiently accurate methods, and the state of the art has advanced considerably since then.

The integration of automatic methods into the MT lexicon development process has the potential to improve not only cost-efficiency but also accuracy. This is especially true when an existing lexicon is being retargeted or specialized for a new domain or sublanguage. In most cases, the MT developer is not a domain expert, and will be unable to predict accurately which entries need to be added or modified. Discrepancies between an existing translation lexicon and translation patterns in a bitext are easy to detect automatically. In the same way, automatic methods can help MT developers keep up with rapidly evolving vocabulary.

Translation lexicons that are probabilistic offer additional advantages. If there isn't enough time or money to enhance the lexicon by hand, then the most frequent translation in the automatically constructed lexicon is better than no translation at all. Even with a manually enhanced lexicon, frequency information can be used as a default target word selection strategy in unfamiliar linguistic contexts (Turcato, 1998). The same information can also be used to produce more natural-looking language, by generating synonyms in proportion to their frequency. Perhaps most importantly, only probabilistic translation lexicons contain sufficient information to make possible automatic methods for accurate identification of non-compositional compounds, such as the one described in chapter 8.

To understand the optimal division of labor between MT developers and existing automatic methods for translation lexicon construction, it helps to think of the MT lexicon construction process as answering two questions:

1. What are the possible translations for each source word?

2. In what contexts are the various translations used?

Automatic methods are not yet good enough to answer question 2 reliably. They can, however, answer question 1, as demonstrated in this chapter. They can answer it even better when used in a semi-automatic mode with a human in the loop. Once a set of possible translations has been semi-automatically identified, it can be filtered and supplemented by hand and enhanced with context-dependent selectional preferences.

If we assume that the cost of computer time is negligible compared to the cost of human labor, then the most efficient lexicon construction process is one that does as much of the work as possible. To be helpful, automation must help the lexicon developer to construct lexicon entries more quickly. In addition, the time saved by accelerated entry construction must not be wasted in rejecting false candidates. Much of this chapter described how to improve automatic translation lexicon construction methods by taking advantage of pre-existing knowledge. Such knowledge is just as valuable if it is not previously encoded, but is supplied on the fly by the MT developer.

These observations suggest an iterative semi-automatic MT lexicon development strategy:

1. Run the best available automatic translation lexicon construction algorithm on all available bitexts in the relevant language pair.

2. Sort the entries in the output by their association score, as in figure 7.12.

3. Present the human developer with the sorted lexicon entries for validation, along with their bilingual contexts in a bilingual concordance (Langlois, 1996).

4. The developer should continue validating entries in order down the list, until the ratio of true and false entries drops below some reasonable threshold.

5. Fix the association scores of the rejected entries at negative infinity. This will prevent their co-occurrences in the bitext from ever being linked. Since links are very interdependent, this negative information should improve the average quality of entries that have not yet been presented for validation.

6. Repeat from step 1 until valid entries become too rare to worry about.

I am not aware of any empirical evaluations of the above strategy. Yet the experiments summarized in section 7.7.2 suggest that automatic methods are now sufficiently accurate to have a significant positive impact on the efficiency of MT lexicon development. In addition, these methods may be able to increase coverage and accuracy, and to provide better information about noncompositional compounds. These considerations will become more important as MT consumers become more demanding and vocabulary evolution accelerates.

7.9 Conclusion

There are many ways to model translational equivalence and many ways to estimate translation models. "The mathematics of statistical machine translation" proposed by Brown et al. (1993b) is just one kind of mathematics for onc kind of statistical translation. In this chaptcr, I havc proposcd and cvaluated new kinds of translation model biases, alternative parameter estimation strategies, and techniques for exploiting pre-existing knowledge that may be available about particular languages and language pairs. On a variety of evaluation metrics, each infusion of knowledge about the problem domain yielded better translation models.

Each innovation presented here opens the way for more research. Model biases can be mixed and matched with one another, with previously published biases like the word order correlation bias, and with other biases yet to be invented. The competitive linking algorithm can be generalized in various ways. New kinds of pre-existing knowledge can be exploited to improve accuracy for particular language pairs or even just for particular bitexts. It is difficult to say where the greatest advances will come from. Yet one thing is clear from our current vantage point: Research on empirical methods for modeling translational equivalence has not run out of steam, as some have claimed, but has only just begun.

8 Automatic Discovery of Non-Compositional Compounds

Automatic segmentation of text into minimal content-bearing units is an unsolved problem even for languages like English. Spaces between words offer an easy first approximation, but this approximation is not good enough for machine translation, because many word sequences are not translated word for word. This chapter presents an efficient automatic method for discovering sequences of words that are translated as a unit. The method can discover hundreds of non-compositional compounds on each iteration, and it can construct longer compounds out of shorter ones. Objective evaluation on a word-for-word translation task has shown the method's potential to improve the accuracy of statistical models of translational equivalence.

8.1   Introduction

The optimal way to analyze linguistic data into its primitive elements is rarely obvious but often crucial. Identifying phones and words in speech has been a major focus of research. Automatically finding words in text, the problem addressed here, is largely unsolved for languages such as Chinese and Thai, which are written without spaces (but see Wu & Fung, 1994; Sproat et al., 1996. Spaces in texts of languages like English offer an easy first approximation to minimal content-bearing units. However, this approximation misanalyzes non-compositional compound (NCC) words such as kick the bucket and hot dog. The interesting property of such word sequences for our purposes is that they are not translated word for word. Therefore, translation models that treat NCCs as atomic units are likely to perform better.

Non-compositionality with respect to translational equivalence is the only kind of non-compositionality that a translation model needs to take into account, and it is the only kind that the methods in this chapter are designed to discover. In particular, these methods pay no attention to phrases that are translated word for word despite non-compositional semantics, such as the English metaphors ivory tower and banana republic, which translate literally into French. On the other hand, these methods will detect word sequences that are often paraphrased in translation but have compositional meanings in the monolingual sense. For example, tax system is most often translated into French as régime fiscal. In this chapter, a *non-compositional compound (NCC)* is a (not necessarily contiguous) sequence of words whose translation is not typically composed of the translations of its parts. The classification of a given word sequence with respect to translational compositionality depends on the language to which it is being translated.

If NCCs are not translated word for word, then one way to discover NCCs is to induce and analyze a translation model. This chapter is about an information-theoretic approach to this kind of epistemological discovery. The method is based on the insight that treatment of NCCs as atomic units increases the predictive power of translation models. Therefore, whether a given sequence of words is an NCC can be determined by comparing the predictive power of two translation models that differ on whether or not they treat the word sequence as an NCC.

Searching a space of data models in this manner has been proposed before, e.g., by Brown et al. (1992) and Wang et al. (1996) (reviewed in section 8.9), but these proposals have been limited by the computational expense of model induction and the typically vast number of potential NCCs that need to be tested. The method presented here overcomes this limitation by making independence assumptions that allow hundreds of NCCs to be discovered from each pair of induced translation models. It is further accelerated by heuristics for gauging the *a priori* likelihood of validation for each candidate NCC.

The predictive power of a translation model depends on what the model is meant to predict. This chapter considers two different applications of translation models and two corresponding objective functions. The different objective functions lead to different mathematical formulations of predictive power, different heuristics for estimating predictive power, and different classifications of word sequences with respect to compositionality. Each new batch of validated NCCs raises the value of the objective function for the given application, as demonstrated in section 8.8. You can skip ahead to table 8.3 for a random sample of the NCCs that the method validated for use in a machine translation task.

8.2   Objective Functions

The decision whether a given sequence of words is usually translated as a unit can be made automatically if it can be expressed in terms of an explicit objective function for the given application. The first application I consider is statistical machine translation involving a directed word-to-word translation model and a target language model. Recall that if S and T represent the distributions of linked words in the source and target[1] texts, then a *word-to-word translation model* is a joint probability distribution $\Pr(s, t)$, that indicates the

Segment #	English half	French half
1	balance	équilibre
2	sheet	feuille
3	balance sheet	bilan

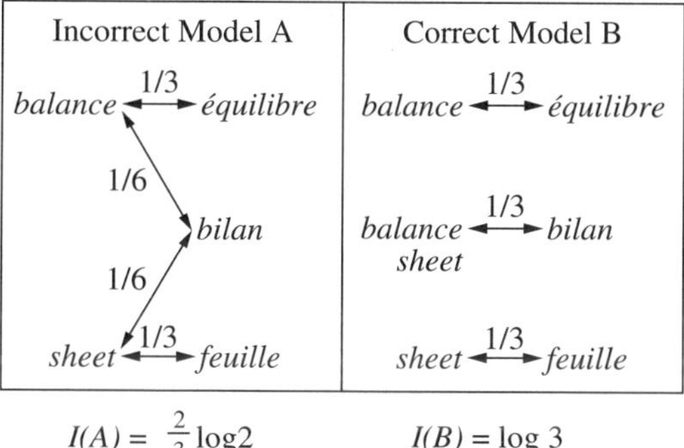

Figure 8.1
Two translation models that may be induced from the trivial bitext at the top of the figure. Translation models that know about NCCs have higher mutual information than those that do not.

probability that a randomly selected link in the bitext links $s \in S$ with $t \in \mathcal{T}$.[2] If only the translation model may be varied, then the objective function for this application should be based on how well the translation model predicts the distribution of words in the target language. One such objective function is called mutual information. *Mutual information* measures how well one random variable predicts another:[3]

$$I(S; \mathcal{T}) = \sum_{s \in S} \sum_{t \in \mathcal{T}} \Pr(s, t) \log \frac{\Pr(s, t)}{\Pr(s) \Pr(t)}. \tag{8.1}$$

When $\Pr(s, t)$ is a word-to-word translation model, mutual information indicates how well the model can predict the distribution of words in the target text given the distribution of words in the source text, and vice versa.

Figure 8.1 shows a simple example of how recognition of NCCs increases the mutual information of translation models. The English word balance is most often translated into French as équilibre and sheet usually becomes feuille. However, a balance sheet is a bilan. A translation model that doesn't recognize balance sheet as an NCC would distribute the translation probabilities of bilan over multiple English words, as shown in the Incorrect Model. The Incorrect Model is uncertain about how bilan should be translated. On the other hand, the Correct Model, which recognizes balance sheet as an NCC, is completely certain about its translation. As a result, the mutual information of the Incorrect Model is

$$2 \cdot \frac{1}{3} \log \frac{\frac{1}{3}}{\frac{1}{2} \cdot \frac{1}{3}} + 2 \cdot \frac{1}{6} \log \frac{\frac{1}{6}}{\frac{1}{2} \cdot \frac{1}{3}} = \frac{2}{3} \log 2,$$

whereas the mutual information of the Correct Model is $\log 3$.

8.3   Search

An explicit objective function immediately leads to a simple NCC discovery method:

1. Pick a random sequence of words in the source text.

2. Induce two translation models, a *trial translation model* that treats the candidate word sequence as an NCC and a *base translation model* that does not.

3. Compute the value of the objective function for both translation models.

4. If the value of the objective function is higher in the trial model than in the base model, then the candidate NCC is, in fact, an NCC; otherwise it is not.

5. Repeat.

Whenever an NCC is discovered in this manner, both the base and trial translation models in subsequent search iterations can take it into account.

The NCC discovery algorithm can be viewed as a search through a lattice of compound lexicons, like the one in figure 8.2. Each compound lexicon is identified by the NCCs that it recognizes. The lexicons are ordered by inclusion. The search begins at the bottom of the lattice, with a lexicon that does not recognize any NCCs. Selecting a random NCC to test is equivalent to selecting a random parent node, one level higher. Each time an NCC is discovered, the next search iteration begins one level higher. Thus, the level at which a search iteration begins indicates the number of NCCs discovered so far.

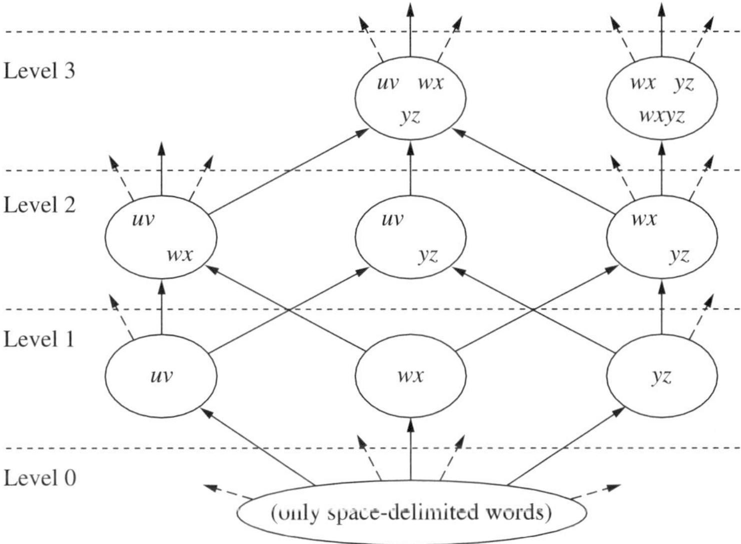

Figure 8.2
A fragment of the lattice of compound lexicons for the text $\langle u\ v\ w\ x\ y\ z\rangle$. Each compound lexicon is identified by the NCCs that it recognizes. The lexicons are ordered by inclusion.

8.4 Predictive Value Functions

Texts contain an enormous number of word sequences, only a tiny fraction of which are NCCs, and it takes considerable computational effort to induce each translation model. Therefore, the simple NCC discovery method described above is impractical. It is necessary to test many NCCs on each pair of translation models. Suppose we induce a trial translation model from texts E and F that simultaneously involves a number of NCCs in the language S of E, and compare it to a base translation model without any of those NCCs. We would like to keep the NCCs that caused a net increase in the objective function I and discard those that caused a net decrease. We need some method of assigning credit for the difference in the value of I between the two models.

The most straightforward method for credit assignment is to define a *predictive value function* $i^{\mathcal{I}}(s)$ that distributes the model's objective function over the words $s \in S$:

$$I(\mathcal{S}; \mathcal{T}) = \sum_{s \in \mathcal{S}} i^{\mathcal{T}}(s). \tag{8.2}$$

Since the objective function in equation (8.1) is already a summation over the source words, a corresponding predictive value function can be derived by canceling that summation:

$$i^{\mathcal{T}}(s) = \sum_{t \in \mathcal{T}} \Pr(s, t) \log \frac{\Pr(s, t)}{\Pr(s) \Pr(t)}. \tag{8.3}$$

The predictive value function $i^{\mathcal{T}}(s)$ represents the contribution of s to the objective function of the whole translation model. I write simply $i(s)$ when $\mathcal{T}$ is clear from the context.

If i and i' are the predictive value functions for source words in the base translation model and trial translation model, respectively, then the net change in the objective function effected by each candidate NCC xy is

$$\Delta_{xy} = i'(x) + i'(y) + i'(xy) - i(x) - i(y). \tag{8.4}$$

The terms $i'(x)$ and $i'(y)$ are necessary to take into account the predictive value of x and y in the trial translation model when they occur without each other. If $\Delta_{xy} > 0$, then xy is a valid NCC with respect to the objective function from which i and i' were derived.

Comparison of predictive value functions across translation models can be done only under

ASSUMPTION 8.1   Treating the bigram $\langle x, y \rangle$ as an NCC does not affect the predictive value function of any $s \in \mathcal{S}$ other than x and y.

Assumption 8.1 would be likely to be false if either x or y were part of any candidate NCC other than xy. Therefore, NCCs that are tested at the same time must satisfy the *mutual exclusion condition*: No word $s \in \mathcal{S}$ may participate in more than one candidate NCC at the same time. Assumption 8.1 may not be completely safe even under this condition, due to the imprecise nature of translation model estimation algorithms.

8.5   Iteration

The mutual exclusion condition implies that multiple tests are still necessary. Furthermore, equation (8.4) allows testing of only two-word NCCs, but longer

NCCs certainly exist. Given parallel texts E and F, the following algorithm runs multiple NCC tests and allows for recognition of progressively longer NCCs:

1. Initialize the stop-list and the NCC list to be empty.

2. Induce a base translation model between E and F.

3. For all contiguous bigrams $\langle x, y \rangle$ in E that are not on the stop-list and whose frequency is at least ϕ,[4] compute $\widehat{\Delta}_{xy}$, the estimate of Δ_{xy}, using the equations in section 8.6.

4. Make a list of candidate NCCs, consisting of all the bigrams $\langle x, y \rangle$ for which $\widehat{\Delta}_{xy} > 0$. Sort the list in decreasing order of $\widehat{\Delta}_{xy}$.

5. To enforce the mutual exclusion condition, remove from the list all candidates $\langle x, y \rangle$ in which either x or y is part of another bigram higher in the list.

6. Copy E to E'. For each bigram $\langle x, y \rangle$ remaining on the candidate NCC list, fuse each instance of $\langle x, y \rangle$ in E' into a single token xy.

7. Induce a trial translation model between E' and F.

8. Compute the actual Δ_{xy} values for all candidate NCCs, using equations (8.3) and (8.4).

9. For each candidate NCC xy, if $\Delta_{xy} > 0$, then add xy to the NCC list; otherwise add $\langle x, y \rangle$ to the stop-list.

10. In E, find all occurrences of all NCCs on the NCC list and replace them with single "fused" tokens, which the translation model construction algorithm will treat as atomic units.

11. Repeat from step 2.

This iterative NCC discovery algorithm can also be viewed as a search through a lattice of compound lexicons. Refer again to figure 8.2. On the first search iteration, as before, the base translation model is based on the lexicon at level 0, which does not recognize any NCCs. On subsequent iterations, the base translation model is based on the lexicon that recognizes all the previously validated NCCs. As in the simpler search algorithm in section 8.3, the trial translation model on each iteration is based on the lowest lexicon in the lattice that recognizes all of the candidate NCCs (as well as the NCCs validated on previous iterations). Unlike in the simpler search algorithm, however, the trial model's lexicon need not be an immediate parent of the base model's lexicon.

For example, if the NCCs remaining on the list of candidates after step 5 of the first iteration are uv, wx, and yz, then the trial translation model will be based on the lexicon in the center of level 3. Now, suppose that the NCCs wx and yz are validated, but the NCC uv is rejected. Then the next iteration of the search will begin at the lowest lexicon that recognizes only the newly validated NCCs and the NCCs that were recognized previously. In this case, it is the rightmost lexicon on level 2. Note that, on the next iteration, the newly discovered NCCs wx and yz can be put together into the longer candidate NCC $wxyz$, as shown in the rightmost lexicon on level 3. Also note that the difference in the lattice levels between the base lexicons of successive search iterations corresponds to the number of validated NCCs on those iterations. As will be shown in section 8.8, this NCC discovery algorithm can jump up hundreds of levels on each iteration.

In its simplest form, the algorithm considers only contiguous word sequences as candidate NCCs. However, function words are translated very inconsistently, and it is difficult to model their translational distributions accurately. Ahrenberg et al. (1998) have suggested that it may be more practical to construct lists of non-compositional closed-class words by hand, and to remove them from consideration by the NCC recognition system. Certainly, pre-existing knowledge from a human expert can improve efficiency. However, this kind of preprocessing does not help us discover non-compositional open-class NCCs that happen to contain function words. In some cases, adding linguistic knowledge by hand is not even an option. To make discovery of NCCs involving function words more likely, I consider content words that are separated by one or two function words to be contiguous. Thus, NCCs like blow . . . whistle and icing . . . cake may contain gaps. Fusing NCCs with gaps may fuse some words incorrectly, when the NCC is a frozen expression. For example, we would want to recognize that icing . . . cake is an NCC when we see it in new text, but not if it occurs in a sentence like "Mary ate the icing off the cake." To distinguish such cases, it is necessary to determine, for each NCC containing a gap, whether that NCC is part of a frozen expression. The price for the flexibility afforded by NCC gaps is three extra steps in each search iteration, after step 5.

5.1 Fill gaps in proposed NCCs by looking through the text. Some NCCs have multiple possible gap fillers, as in make up {my, your, his, their, etc.} mind. When the gap-filling procedure finds two or three possible fillers, the most frequent filler is used, and the rest are ignored in the hope that they will be discovered on the next iteration. When there are more than three possible fillers, the NCC is probably not part of a frozen expression, so the gap remains unfilled.

5.2 The gap fillers may be identical to elements of other NCCs either higher or lower on the list of candidate NCCs, violating the mutual exclusion condition. If the gap is an element in a candidate NCC higher on the list, then remove the current candidate from the list. If the gap is an element in a candidate NCC lower on the list, then remove that other candidate from the list.

6.1 (after step 6) Move all words in the fused NCC to the location of the leftmost word in E'. E.g., an instance of the previous example in the text might be fused as make_up_$\langle GAP \rangle$_mind his.

The algorithm can also be run in "two-sided" mode so that it looks for NCCs in E and in F on alternate iterations. This mode enables the translation model to link NCCs in one language to NCCs in the other. A separate lattice of compound lexicons would be required for each half of the bitext, to represent the search space of the two-sided NCC discovery algorithm.

In principle, the NCC discovery algorithm could iterate until $\widehat{\Delta}_{xy} \leq 0$ for all bigrams. This would be a classic case of over-fitting the model to the training data. NCC discovery is most useful if it is stopped at the point where the validated NCCs maximize the application's objective function on *new* data. A domain-independent method to find this point is to use held-out data or, more generally, to cross-validate between different subsets of the training data. Alternatively, when the application involves human inspection, e.g., for bilingual lexicography, a suitable stopping point can be found by manually inspecting validated NCCs.

8.6 Credit Estimation

Section 8.4 described how to carry out NCC validity tests, but not how to choose which NCCs to test. Making this choice at random would make the NCC discovery process too slow, because the vast majority of word sequences are not valid NCCs. The discovery process can be greatly accelerated by testing only candidate NCCs for which equation (8.4) is likely to be positive. This section presents a way to guess, *before* inducing a trial translation model, whether Δ_{xy} will be positive for a given candidate NCC xy. To do so, it is necessary to estimate $i'(x)$, $i'(y)$, and $i'(xy)$, using only the base translation model.

First, a bit of notation. Let $(x|\_y)$ be the set of tokens of x whose right context is y, and let $(y|x\_)$ be the set of tokens of y whose left context is x. Now, $i'(x)$ and $i'(y)$, can be estimated under

ASSUMPTION 8.2   When x occurs *without* y in its context, it will be linked to the same target words by the trial translation model as by the base translation model, and likewise for y without x.

Assumption 8.2 says that

$$i'(x) = i(x|\_\neg y), \tag{8.5}$$
$$i'(y) = i(y|\neg x\_). \tag{8.6}$$

Estimating $i'(xy)$ is more difficult because it requires knowledge of the entire translational distributions of both x and y, conditioned on all the contexts of x and y. Since we wish to consider hundreds of candidate NCCs simultaneously, and contexts from many megabytes of text, all this information would not fit on disk, let alone in memory. The best we can do with today's resources is approximate with lower-order distributions that are easier to compute.

The approximation begins with

ASSUMPTION 8.3   If xy is a valid NCC, then at most one of x and y is linked to a target word whenever x and y co-occur.

Assumption 8.3 follows from the one-to-one assumption explained in section 7.3. It implies that for all $t \in \mathcal{T}$

$$\mathrm{Pr}'(xy, t) = \mathrm{Pr}(x|\_y, t) + \mathrm{Pr}(y|x\_, t), \tag{8.7}$$

where $\mathrm{Pr}'()$ refers to the trial translation model. The approximation continues with

ASSUMPTION 8.4   If xy is a valid NCC, then for all $t \in \mathcal{T}$, either $\mathrm{Pr}(x, t) = 0$ or $\mathrm{Pr}(y, t) = 0$.

Assumption 8.4 expresses the "one sense per collocation" hypothesis for translational collocations explained in section 7.5.2. It implies that for all $t \in \mathcal{T}$, either

$$\mathrm{Pr}(x|\_y, t) = 0 \tag{8.8}$$

or

$$\Pr(y|x\_, t) = 0. \tag{8.9}$$

Under assumptions 8.3 and 8.4, we can estimate $i'(xy)$ as follows:

$$i'(xy) = \sum_{t \in \mathcal{T}} \Pr'(xy, t) \log \frac{\Pr'(xy, t)}{\Pr(xy) \Pr(t)} \tag{8.10}$$

$$(\text{by Eq. 8.7}) = \sum_{t \in \mathcal{T}} [\Pr(x|\_y, t) + \Pr(y|x\_, t)] \log \frac{[\Pr(x|\_y, t) + \Pr(y|x\_, t)]}{\Pr(xy) \Pr(t)}$$

$$(\text{by Eq. 8.8}) = \sum_{t \in \mathcal{T}} \Pr(x|\_y, t) \log \frac{\Pr(x|\_y, t)}{\Pr(x|\_y) \Pr(t)}$$

$$(\text{by Eq. 8.9}) \quad + \sum_{t \in \mathcal{T}} \Pr(y|x\_, t) \log \frac{\Pr(y|x\_, t)}{\Pr(y|x\_) \Pr(t)}.$$

Note that, by definition, $\Pr(x|\_y) = \Pr(y|x\_) = \Pr(xy)$.

The final form of equation (8.10) allows us to partition the terms in equation (8.4) into two sets, one for each of the components of the candidate NCC:

$$\widehat{\Delta}_{xy} = \widehat{\Delta}_{x \to y} + \widehat{\Delta}_{x \leftarrow y} \tag{8.11}$$

where

$$\widehat{\Delta}_{x \to y} = \quad - i(x) \tag{8.12}$$

$$+ \sum_{t \in \mathcal{T}} \Pr(x|\_\neg y, t) \log \frac{\Pr(x|\_\neg y, t)}{\Pr(x|\_\neg y) \Pr(t)}$$

$$+ \sum_{t \in \mathcal{T}} \Pr(x|\_y, t) \log \frac{\Pr(x|\_y, t)}{\Pr(x|\_y) \Pr(t)}$$

and

$$\widehat{\Delta}_{x \leftarrow y} = \quad - i(y) \tag{8.13}$$

$$+ \sum_{t \in \mathcal{T}} \Pr(y|\neg x\_, t) \log \frac{\Pr(y|\neg x\_, t)}{\Pr(y|\neg x\_) \Pr(t)}$$

$$+ \sum_{t \in \mathcal{T}} \Pr(y|x\_, t) \log \frac{\Pr(y|x\_, t)}{\Pr(y|x\_) \Pr(t)}.$$

All the terms in equation (8.12) depend only on the probability distributions $\Pr(x, t)$, $\Pr(x|\_y, t)$ and $\Pr(x|\_\neg y, t)$. All the terms in equation (8.13) depend only on $\Pr(y, t)$, $\Pr(y|x\_, t)$ and $\Pr(y|\neg x\_, t)$. These distributions can be computed reasonably efficiently by memory-external sorting and streamed accumulation.

8.7 Single-Best Translation

Single-best translation is the kind of translation that somebody might use to get the gist of a foreign-language document, without a target language model. For this application, it is sufficient to predict only the most likely translation of each source word. The rest of the translational distribution can be ignored. Let $m^{\mathcal{T}}(s)$ be the most likely translation of each source word s, according to the translation model:

$$m^{\mathcal{T}}(s) = \arg \max_{t \in T} \Pr(s, t). \tag{8.14}$$

Again, I write simply $m(s)$ when $\mathcal{T}$ is clear from the context. The objective function V for this application follows by analogy with the mutual information function I in equation (8.1):

$$V(\mathcal{S}; \mathcal{T}) = \sum_{s \in \mathcal{S}} \sum_{t \in \mathcal{T}} \delta(t, m(s)) \Pr(s, t) \log \frac{\Pr(s, t)}{\Pr(s) \Pr(t)}$$

$$= \sum_{s \in \mathcal{S}} \Pr(s, m(s)) \log \frac{\Pr(s, m(s))}{\Pr(s) \Pr(m(s))}. \tag{8.15}$$

δ is the Kronecker delta function, equal to one when its arguments are identical and zero otherwise. The form of the objective function again permits easy distribution of its value over the $s \in \mathcal{S}$:

$$v^{\mathcal{T}}(s) = \Pr(s, m(s)) \log \frac{\Pr(s, m(s))}{\Pr(s) \Pr(m(s))}. \tag{8.16}$$

The formula for assigning credit among the candidate NCCs for the net change in the objective function remains the same as in equation (8.4):

$$\Delta_{xy} = v'(x) + v'(y) + v'(xy) - v(x) - v(y). \tag{8.17}$$

It is easier to estimate the values of v', using only the base translation model, than to estimate the values of i', since only the most likely translations need to be considered, rather than entire translational distributions. $v'(x)$ and $v'(y)$ are again estimated under assumption 8.2:

$$v'(x) = v(x|\_\neg y) \tag{8.18}$$

$$v'(y) = v(y|\neg x\_). \tag{8.19}$$

$v'(xy)$ can be estimated without making the strong assumptions 8.3 and 8.4. Instead, I use the weaker

ASSUMPTION 8.5   Let $m(x|\_y)$ and $m(y|x\_)$ be the most frequent translations of x and y in each other's presence, in the base translation model. Then in the trial translation model that recognizes xy as an NCC, the most frequent translation of xy will be the more frequent of $m(x|\_y)$ and $m(y|x\_)$.

Assumption 8.5 implies that

$$v'(xy) = \max[v(x|\_y), v(y|x\_)]. \tag{8.20}$$

This quantity can be computed exactly at a reasonable computational expense.

8.8   Experiments

I carried out two experiments on transcripts of Canadian parliamentary debates, known as the Hansards. French and English versions of these texts had been previously aligned by sentence (Gale & Church, 1991a).[5] Morphological variants in both languages were stemmed to a canonical form. Thirteen million words (in both languages combined) were used for training and another two and a half million were used for testing. The training data contained 31663 distinct French word types and 29635 distinct English word types. All translation models were induced using the method of Melamed (1997c).[6] Six iterations of the NCC discovery algorithm were run in "two-sided" mode, using the objective function I, and ten iterations were run using the objective function V.

Tables 8.1 and 8.2 chart the NCC discovery process. The NCCs proposed for the V objective function were much more likely to be validated than those proposed for I, because the predictive value function v' is much easier to estimate *a priori* than the predictive value function i'. In the first three iterations on the English side of the bitext, 192 NCCs were validated for I and 1493 were validated for V. Of the 1493 NCCs validated for V, 98 NCCs consisted of three words, three consisted of four words and one consisted of five words.

Table 8.1
NCCs proposed and validated, using the mutual information objective function I.

Iteration number	Bitext side	Number of candidate NCCs	Number of validated NCCs	Validation rate
1	English	647	105	16%
2	French	618	121	20%
3	English	253	49	19%
4	French	245	41	17%
5	English	161	38	24%
6	French	205	33	16%

Table 8.2
NCCs proposed and validated, using the simpler objective function V.

Iteration number	Bitext side	Number of candidate NCCs	Number of validated NCCs	Validation rate
1	English	761	747	98%
2	French	480	471	98%
3	English	428	412	96%
4	French	217	213	98%
5	English	342	334	98%
6	French	206	201	98%
7	English	323	311	96%
8	French	386	370	96%
9	English	267	256	96%
10	French	475	461	97%

The French NCCs were longer on average, due to the frequent "N de N" construction for noun compounds.

The first experiment involved the mutual information objective function I and its associated predictive value function in equation (8.3). The first step in the experiment was the construction of five new versions of the test data, in addition to the original version. Version k of the test data was constructed by fusing all NCCs validated up to iteration k on the training data. The second step was to induce a translation model from each version of the test data. Figure 8.3 shows that the mutual information of successive test translation models rose as desired.

The impact of NCC recognition on the single-best translation task was measured using *unsupervised evaluation,* illustrated in figure 8.4. Unsupervised evaluation can be used to compare different translation methods objectively

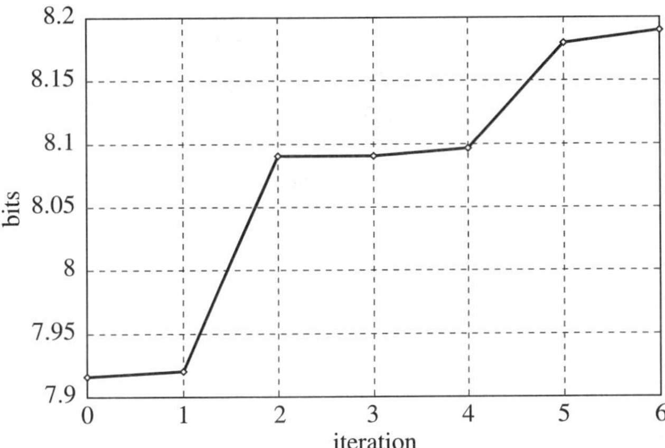

Figure 8.3
Mutual information of successive translation models induced on held-out test data. Translation models that know about NCCs have higher mutual information than those that do not

and automatically without a gold-standard. The algorithms are based on the observation that if translation model X is better than translation model Y, and each model generates a bag of words from one half of a held-out test bitext, then the bag of words in the other half of that bitext will be more similar to the translation produced by X than to the translation produced by Y. Evaluation supervised by a gold standard can test whether a translation model generated the correct target word from each source word. In the absence of a gold standard, we can still test whether the target words generated by the model match the target words in the corresponding segment of the bitext, without considering which source word generated which target word. This test is insensitive to errors involving NULL words. It also ignores the errors of a translation model that generates the right target words from the wrong source words. However, such a model is usually penalized for not generating the target word that should have been generated from those source words. The only case where a model might "cheat" on unsupervised evaluation is when there is insufficient evidence for the correct translation of a source word s_1 in the training data, but the model generates the correct translation of s_1 from another source word s_2. Unsupervised evaluation can be done the same way on a "whole distribution" translation task, where the model is expected to generate the entire translational distribution for each source word, rather than just the single most likely translation. Either way, the performance metric is based on intersections of fuzzy

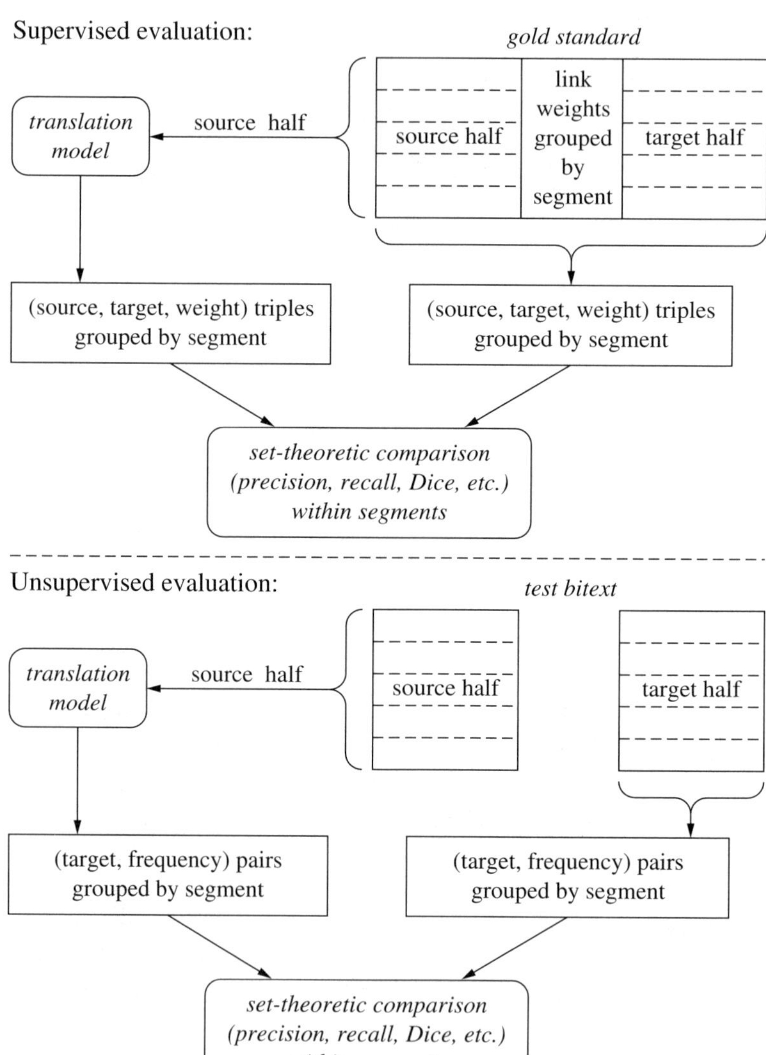

Figure 8.4
Comparison of translation model evaluation methods, with and without a gold standard.

sets, as described in section 6.5. The reliability of unsupervised evaluation will be investigated in section 9.7.1.

For the models in this chapter, unsupervised evaluation is actually more appropriate than comparison to a gold standard, because the objective functions I and V are designed to optimize predictions about which words appear in the target text, not predictions about which source words generate which target words. For example, suppose that in the bitext (E, F), words w and v often co-occur in E, and that v is usually translated to u in F, but w is a function word that is usually not translated. An annotator might consistently link u to v but link w to "Not Translated", i.e., to NULL. However, a model of translational equivalence between E to F would have higher predictive power if it recognized vw as an NCC and generated both v and w from each token of u.

The second experiment was based on the simpler objective function V and its associated predictive value function in equation (8.16). The single best translations generated by different translation models were compared with the words in the target half of a held-out test bitext. The comparison was made in terms of word precision and word recall in aligned sentence pairs, ignoring word order. I compared the 11 base translation models induced in 10 iterations of the algorithm in section 8.5. The first model is numbered 0, to indicate that it did not recognize any NCCs. Each of the 11 translation models generated a trial target text from the test source text as follows, one sentence at a time:

1. Fuse all word sequences in the source text that correspond to NCCs recognized by the translation model.

2. For each word in the source text, add its most likely translation to the trial target text.

3. If the most likely translation is an NCC, then break it up into its components.

I computed precision, recall, and the set-theoretic Dice coefficient, by sentence, for each of the models' trial target texts, with respect to the target half of the test bitext, in both directions of translation. Figure 8.5 shows that NCC recognition generally increased recall while decreasing precision on successive iterations. The Dice coefficients show that the increase in recall generally outweighed the loss in precision.[7] The number of NCCs validated on each iteration was never more than 2.5% of the vocabulary size. Thus, the curves in figure 8.5 have a very small range, but the trends are clear.

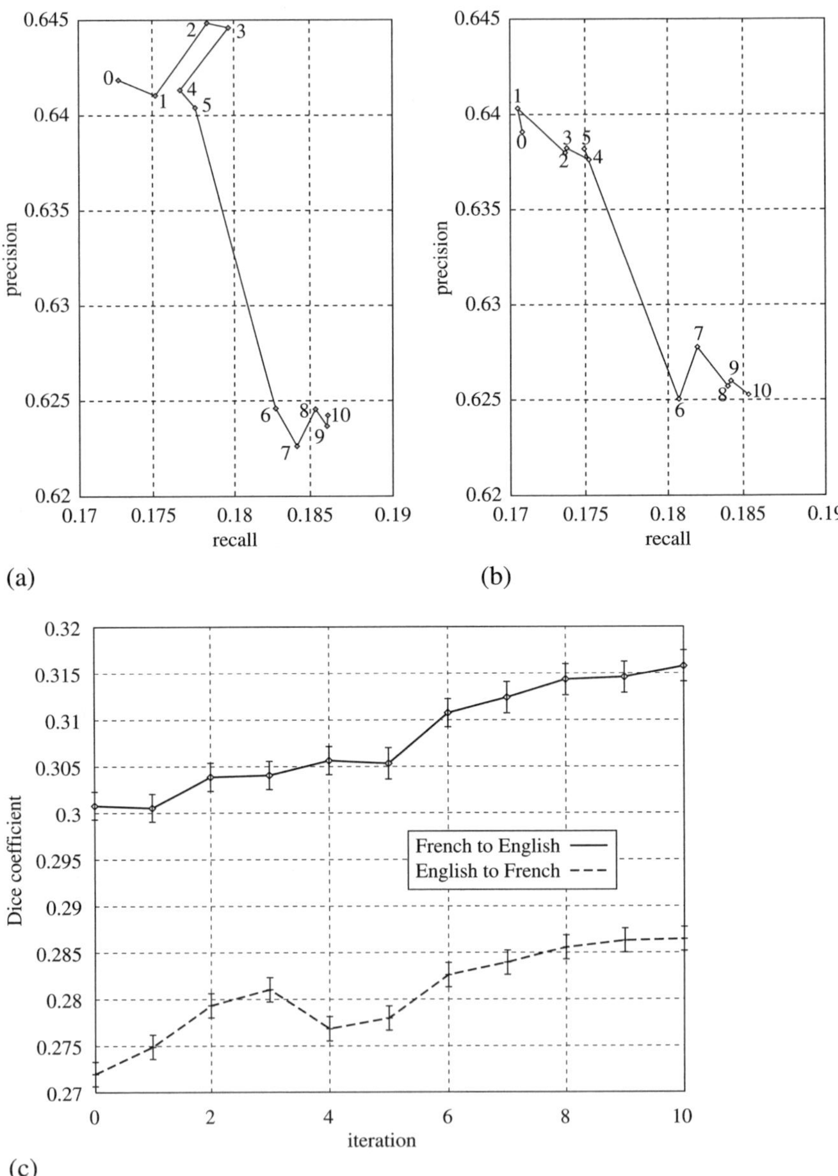

(a)

(b)

(c)

Figure 8.5
Unsupervised evaluation scores for 11 translation models. Labels 0 to 10 indicate iteration number. Left: English → French; Right: French → English. Below: Dice coefficients with 95% confidence intervals.

A qualitative assessment of the NCC discovery method can be made by looking at table 8.3. It contains a random sample of 50 of the English NCCs accumulated in the first five iterations of the algorithm in section 8.5, using the simpler objective function V. All of the NCCs in the table are non-compositional with respect to the objective function V. Many of the NCCs, like red tape and blaze the trail, are true idioms. Some NCCs are incomplete. E.g., flow- has not yet been recognized as a non-compositional part of flow-through share, and likewise for head in rear its ugly head. These NCCs would probably be completed if the algorithm were allowed to run for more iterations.

Some of the other entries deserve more explanation. First, Della Noce is the last name of a former Canadian Member of Parliament. Every occurrence of this name in the French training text was tokenized as Della noce with a lowercase "n," because noce is a common noun in French meaning marriage, and the tokenization algorithm lowercased all capitalized words that were found in the lexicon. When this word occurred in the French text without Della, its English translation was marriage, but when it occurred as part of the name, its translation was Noce. So, the algorithm decided that the French bigram Della Noce is non-compositional with respect to the objective function V and validated it as an NCC. On a subsequent iteration, the algorithm found that only half of the English bigram Della Noce was ever linked to a French word (the French NCC Della_noce) so it decided that the English Della Noce must also be an NCC. This is one of the few personal names in the Hansards that are NCCs with respect to translational equivalence.

Another interesting entry in the table is the last one. The capitalized English words Generic and Association are translated with perfect consistency to Generic and association, respectively, in the training text. The translation of the middle two words, however, is non-compositional. When Pharmaceutical and Industry occur together, they are rendered in the French text without translation as Pharmaceutical Industry. When they occur separately, they are translated into pharmaceutique and industrie. Thus, the English bigram Pharmaceutical Industry is an NCC, but the words that always occur around it are not part of the NCC. Similar reasoning applies to ship unprocessed uranium. The bigram ⟨ship, unprocessed⟩ is an NCC because its components are translated non-compositionally whenever they co-occur. However, uranium is always translated as uranium in this bitext, so it is not part of the NCC. This NCC demonstrates that valid NCCs may span the boundaries of grammatical constituents.

Table 8.3
Random sample of 50 of the 1493 NCCs validated in the first three iterations of the NCC discovery algorithm on the English half of the bitext, using the objective function V.

Count	NCC (in italics) in typical context	Non-compositional translation in French text
786	*could have*	pourrait
183	flow-*through shares*	actions accréditives
79	*I repeat*	je tiens à dire
63	the case I *just mentioned*	le cas que je viens de mentionner
36	*tax base*	assiette fiscale
34	*single parent* family	famille monoparentale
24	*perform* ⟨*GAP*⟩ *duty*	assumer . . . fonction
23	*red tape*	la paperasserie
17	*middle of the night*	en pleine nuit
17	*Della Noce*	Della noce (see text for explanation)
16	*heating oil*	mazout
14	*proceeds of crime*	les produits tirés du crime
11	*rat pack*	meute
10	*urban dwellers*	citadins
10	nuclear *generating station*	centrale nucléaire
10	Air *India disaster*	écrasement de l'avion indien
9	*Ottawa River*	Outaouais
8	I *dare hope*	j'ose croire
8	*Ottawa Valley*	vallée de l'Outaouais
7	*plea bargaining*	marchandage
7	*manifestly unfounded* claims	avoir revendiqué á tort le statut
7	a group called *Rural Dignity*	une groupe appelé Rural Dignity
6	a *slight bit*	la moindre
6	*cry for help*	appel au secour
5	*video tape*	vidéo
5	*sow the seed*	semer
5	*arrange a meeting*	organiser un entretien
4	*shot-gun wedding*	mariage forcé
4	we *lag behind*	nous traînions de la patte
4	*Great West* Life Company	Great West Life Company
4	Canadian Forces *Base and cease* negotiations	mettre fin et interrompre le négociation
3	*severe sentence*	sévère sanction
3	*rear its ugly* head	manifesté
3	*inability to deal* effectively with	ne sait pas traiter de manière efficace avec
3	*en masse*	en bloc
3	*create a disturbance*	suscite de perturbation
3	*blaze the trail*	ouvre la voie
2	*wrongful conviction*	erreur judiciaire
2	*weak sister*	parent pauvre
2	the *users and providers* of transportation	des utilisateurs et des transporteurs
2	*understand the motivation*	saisir le motif
2	*swimming pool*	piscine
2	*ship unprocessed* uranium	expédier de l'uranium non raffiné
2	by *reason of insanity*	pour cause d'aliénation mentale
2	l'agence de Presse *libre du* Québec	l'agence de Presse libre du Québec
2	do *cold weather* research	étudier l'effet du froid
2	the *bread basket* of the nation	le grenier du Canada
2	turn back the *boatload of European* Jews	renvoyer tout ces juifs européens
2	Generic *Pharmaceutical Industry* Association	Generic Pharmaceutical Industry Association

8.9   Related Work

Brown et al. (1993b)'s Model 3 implicitly accounted for NCCs in the target language by estimating "fertility" distributions for words in the source language. A source word s with fertility n could generate a sequence of n target words, if each word in the sequence was also in the translational distribution of s and the target language model assigned a sufficiently high probability to the sequence. However, (Brown et al.)'s models do not account for NCCs in the source language. Recognition of source-language NCCs would improve the performance of their models, but (Brown et al.) warn that

[O]ne must be discriminating in choosing multi-word [con]cepts. The caution that we have displayed thus far in limiting ourselves to [con]cepts with fewer than two words was motivated primarily by our respect for the featureless desert that multi-word [con]cepts offer a priori. (Brown et al., 1993b, p. 294)

The heuristics in section 8.6 are designed specifically to find the interesting features in that featureless desert. Ahrenberg et al. (1998) have proposed some simpler search methods whose performance may be sufficient for less automated applications. They also recommended some knowledge-based efficiency boosters that can be applied both to their search methods and to the ones described in this chapter.

Another approach is possible when part-of-speech taggers are available for both languages under consideration. Shin et al. (1996) began by inducing a translation model from a small Korean/English bitext using Brown et al. (1993b)'s Model 1. They found that the Korean/English desert is not quite as featureless as the French/English one, because only 34% of the word-token translational equivalences in their bitext were one to one. Still, they were faced with the problem of estimation from sparse data. Instead of analyzing the grains of sand in their desert, they chose to look at the dunes represented by part-of-speech sequences. The backing-off strategy simplified their estimation problem, and they reported respectable precision. However, the information lost by ignoring the words may explain why they did not report how many NCCs the method discovered.

Many authors (e.g. Daille et al., 1994; Smadja, 1992) define "collocations" in terms of monolingual frequency and part-of-speech patterns. Markedly high frequency is a necessary property of NCCs, because otherwise they would fall out of use (Baayen & Lieber, 1997). However, at least for translation-related applications, it is not a sufficient property. Non-compositional translation cannot be detected reliably without looking at translational distributions. The deficiency of criteria that ignore translational distributions is illustrated by their propensity to validate most personal names as "collocations." At least among Western European languages, translations of the vast majority of personal names are perfectly compositional.

Several authors have used mutual information or related statistics as an objective function for word clustering (Dagan et al., 1993a; Brown et al., 1992; Pereira et al., 1993; Wang et al., 1996), for automatic determination of phonemic baseforms (Lucassen & Mercer, 1984), for knowledge acquisition for second language learning (Kita et al., 1993), and for language modeling for speech recognition (Ries et al., 1996). Wang et al. (1996) also employ parallel texts and independence assumptions that are similar to those described in section 8.6. Like Brown et al. (1992), they report a modest improvement in model perplexity and encouraging qualitative results. Although the applications considered in this chapter are different, the strategy is similar: search a space of data models for the one with maximum predictive power.

There has been some research into matching *compositional* phrases across bitexts. For example, Kupiec (1993) presented a method for finding translations of whole noun phrases. Wu (1995) showed how to use an existing translation lexicon to populate a database of "phrasal correspondences" for use in example-based machine translation. Knowledge about such compositional translation patterns will be indispensable as we progress from word-to-word translation models towards more structured sequence-to-sequence models.

8.10 Conclusion

It is well known that two languages are more informative than one (Dagan et al., 1991). I have argued that texts in two languages are not only preferable but necessary for automatic discovery of non-compositional compounds for translation-related applications. Given a method for constructing statistical translation models, NCCs can be discovered by maximizing the models' information-theoretic predictive power over parallel data sets. This chapter presented an efficient algorithm for such epistemological discovery. Recognition of NCCs improved model performance on a simple translation task.

Lists of NCCs derived from parallel data may be useful for NLP applications that do not involve parallel data. Translation-oriented NCC lists can be used directly in applications that have a human in the loop, such as computer-assisted lexicography, computer-assisted language learning, and corpus linguistics. To the extent that translation-oriented definitions of compositionality overlap with other definitions, NCC lists derived from parallel data may benefit other applications where NCCs play a role, such as information retrieval (Evans & Zhai, 1996) and language modeling for speech recognition (Ries et al., 1996). To the extent that different applications have different objective functions, researchers seeking to optimize these functions can benefit from an understanding of how they differ. The present work is a step towards such understanding, because "an explication of a monolingual idiom might best be given after bilingual idioms have been properly understood" (Bar-Hillel, 1964, p. 48).

9 Sense-to-Sense Models of Translational Equivalence

Polysemy is a major confounding variable for empirically estimated models of translational equivalence. Automatic word-sense disambiguation can improve such models, but only if the disambiguation is with respect to word senses that actually occur in the data. This chapter presents an algorithm for deciding the sense inventories of words in bitext, including the number of sense divisions appropriate for each word. The decisions are based on information-theoretic measures of the predictive values of the contexts of the words in question. Evaluation on held-out data has shown that the algorithm can boost the accuracy of word-to-word translation models.

9.1 Introduction

The explanatory power of a statistical model depends on how well its parameters correspond with sources of variation in the data. One of the main sources of variation in translational equivalence is polysemy. Different senses of the same word often have different translations. A good statistical translation model should have independent parameters for all the word senses in the data, not just for all the words.

In order to estimate such a model, we must first distinguish the different word senses in the training bitext. In this chapter, I present an automatic method for deciding the sense inventory for each word that occurs in a given bitext. The sense inventory is based on and used by a word-to-word translation model in an iterative fashion, for the purpose of improving the translation model. This goal should not be confused with the goal of inducing context-aware translation models, which is a vast topic beyond the scope of this book.

Each word's sense inventory is based on the contexts in which that word appears. For clarity, I adopt Brown et al. (1991b)'s term *informant* to denote a single piece of evidence from the context of the word in question; i.e., a single context can contain many informants. Yarowsky (1993) has studied the relative efficacy of different informants for distinguishing word senses. This chapter explores only the orthogonal question of how best to exploit whatever informants happen to be available, for the purpose of improving word-to-word translation models. In keeping with the language-independent tenor of this book, I have not experimented with syntactic context, the use of which presumes the availability of at least a rudimentary syntactic parser. Instead, I have considered only the simplest kind of informants: words anywhere within a fixed-size window around the word to be disambiguated. This kind of informant is one of the few kinds available to information retrieval systems for disambiguating the senses of words in queries, which are often just a few words with no syntactic structure. To save computing time, I limited the window boundaries to ± 5 words. The restriction to very simple informants in a very small window is quite severe, but the aim here is to demonstrate the method's general viability, rather than to post huge performance gains. Much more information from the context can and should be used in practice.

There are many different notions of word sense. Section 9.3 motivates and operationalizes the notion that is relevant to statistical translation models. From this notion I derive an information-theoretic objective function, whose optimization is hypothesized to improve statistical translation models. Section 9.5 describes an efficient optimization method. An application is described in section 9.6, which is followed by experimental results. Most of this chapter discusses word sense disambiguation for only one (arbitrary) word type, with the understanding that the method can be repeated for every word in the vocabulary.

9.2 Previous Work

Many authors have proposed automatic methods for disambiguating polysemous words. However, I know of no published work on automatically determining, in the first place, the number of senses that a given word type has in a given text or text collection. Instead, a popular approach has been to assume that the text's sense inventory coincides with an existing sense inventory extracted from a machine-readable dictionary, from an on-line thesaurus, or from WordNet (Miller, 1990). However, machine-readable bilingual dictionaries are a poor source of word sense inventories. Fewer than 60% of the word types in the relatively non-domain-specific record of the Canadian parliamentary debates (Hansards) can be found in the on-line version of the college-size Collins French/English Dictionary (Cousin et al., 1991). The coverage drops to only 25% for more specialized texts like computer software manuals. Even worse, the entries that do appear in the dictionary may be misleading for technical terms that are derived from common words, such as file and mouse. In general, the vocabulary in any such resource does not overlap very much with the vocabulary in any given text.

The coverage is even worse for word senses than for words. There is little agreement on the correct granularity of sense distinctions between any two dictionaries. So, we should not expect any pre-existing sense inventory to correctly model the distribution of word senses in a given text, unless the inventory is based exclusively on that text. After an extensive survey of the way word senses are used in lexicography and in NLP, Kilgarriff (1997a) concluded:

There is no reason to expect a single set of word senses to be appropriate for different NLP applications. In particular, the sets of word senses presented in different dictionaries and thesauri have been prepared, for various purposes, for various human users: there is no reason to believe those sets are appropriate for any NLP application.

A more sophisticated approach starts by decomposing word sense disambiguation into two subtasks. The first subtask is to cluster word tokens into senses; the second subtask is to label the clusters with one of a predetermined set of sense labels. Schuetze (1998) has named the first subtask *word sense discrimination*, and has observed that the second subtask (labeling) is not necessary for some applications. Word sense discrimination can be accomplished by standard clustering algorithms, if the appropriate number of senses is specified in advance. Instead of relying on a pre-existing sense inventory, Schuetze & Pedersen (1995) suggested that the number of senses of each word should be determined by the word's frequency. One can imagine choosing the number of clusters based on other properties of the word as well, such as on its semantic entropy (Melamed, 1997a). In practice, this approach works better than using a pre-existing sense inventory (cf. Schuetze, 1998; Voorhees, 1993), because the granularity of sense divisions for each word is partially determined by the amount of information available about that word in the text corpus. In particular, the likelihood of finding a reliably discriminating informant for each word sense rises with the word's frequency. A drawback of Schuetze's discrimination method is that the contexts of a given word type may not have sufficient discriminating power to distinguish the preselected number of senses. When this happens, the clustering process is either random or driven by noise.

The word sense discrimination problem is arguably easier in the context of translation models than in the context of Schuetze & Pedersen (1995)'s vector space models, because the number of link types in a translation model is an upper bound on the number of possible word senses. The symbiotic relationship between translation models and word sense discrimination algorithms was first exploited by Brown et al. (1991b). Their strategy was to partition words into word senses so as to maximize the mutual information between word senses and their informants. This mathematically elegant and intuitively plausible objective function turned the task into an immense search problem. Lacking efficient search methods, Brown et al. decided to pursue the less ambitious goal of sense-tagging a predetermined number of words with only two senses each. Even this more modest approach improved the accuracy of their context-aware translation models.

9.3 Formulation of the Problem

The sense distinctions that are most relevant to translation models and their applications are those that are "lexicalized cross-linguistically" (Resnik & Yarowsky, 1997). Conversely, translation models provide a way to characterize cross-linguistic lexicalization patterns. Given a perfect translation model and a noise-free bitext, we need only look at the link types generated by the model in the bitext to determine the inventory of senses for each word in that bitext and the contexts in which each sense occurs. Of course, perfect translation models do not exist, so we must deal with noise. In addition to noise, we must deal with synonymy. Suppose that word s_1 in one half of a bitext is sometimes translated as t_1 and sometimes as t_2 in the other half. It's possible that t_1 and t_2 are translations of two different senses of s_1, but it's also possible that t_1 and t_2 are synonyms and correspond to one and the same sense of s_1! It is impossible to distinguish the two cases by looking only at the translation model. How can we decide between polysemy and synonymy? The answer is that if a word is polysemous, then its different senses will typically appear in different contexts.

A word sense should be considered distinct if its presence or absence is significantly easier to predict in particular contexts than in general. If the presence or absence of a word sense is governed by the probability distribution s, the difficulty of predicting events in this distribution is an information-theoretic quantity called entropy, denoted $H(s)$. Entropy can also be computed for conditional distributions. For example, we can compute the difficulty of predicting the presence or absence of a word sense given a particular informant c, and call it $H(s|c)$. The greater the difference between $H(s)$ and $H(s|c)$, the more likely it is that s is a distinct word sense. It is a theorem of information theory that $H(s) - H(s|c) = I(s; c)$. Thus, the degree to which the presence or absence of a word sense s is conditioned by the distribution C of informants in which s's word type appears can be expressed by the mutual information between the distribution of that word sense and the distribution of its informants:

$$I(s; C) = \sum_{c \in C} \left[\Pr(s, c) \log \frac{\Pr(s, c)}{\Pr(s)\,\Pr(c)} + \Pr(\neg s, c) \log \frac{\Pr(\neg s, c)}{\Pr(\neg s)\,\Pr(c)} \right]. \quad (9.1)$$

In general, we want to partition each word type into as many senses as can be reliably predicted by the distribution of co-occurring informants. If $I(s; c) > 0$ for a word sense s and an informant c, then c is a *predictive informant* and s can be *reliably predicted*. If we let S be a partitioning of a word's link types into senses, then the word sense discrimination problem can be formulated as follows: Find the partition of link types S and the set of informants C that maximize

$$I(S; C) = \sum_{s \in S} \sum_{c \in C} \Pr(s, c) \log \frac{\Pr(s, c)}{\Pr(s) \Pr(c)}. \tag{9.2}$$

The objective function above is more general that the objective function used by Brown et al. (1991b) because S is not limited to binary partitions. The two main obstacles to maximizing equation (9.2) are estimation error and computational complexity. Section 9.4 addresses the former; section 9.5 addresses the latter.

9.4 Noise Filters

Truly predictive informants are relatively rare. Most words that co-occur do so by chance. So, $I(s; c) > 0$ for almost any (s, c) pair that occurs in the data. If these estimates of mutual information were taken at face value, then almost all link types would be discriminated as distinct senses. I have adopted several measures to distinguish the truly predictive informants from noise. First, I smooth all (sense, informant) co-occurrence counts using the method described by Yarowsky (1996, pp. 66–79). Second, I disallow very rare word senses—a link type must occur at least twice in the bitext to be allowed its own sense partition. Singleton link types are forced to merge. Third, I model the noise with pseudolinks.

A *pseudolink* is a randomly chosen subset of the tokens of one link type. The tokens of the link type not in the chosen subset represent another subset and another pseudolink. Once a link type is partitioned into two pseudolinks p_1 and p_2, it is possible to measure $I(P; c)$ for each informant c, where P is the smoothed probability distribution over $\{p_1, p_2\}$. The procedure can be repeated for all link types in the bitext to generate a distribution of mutual information values. Since pseudolinks represent spurious sense partitions, this distribution is a noise model.

The noise model provides a simple way to distinguish the informants that are truly predictive from the ones that co-occur randomly: The mutual information between a truly predictive informant and the given sense partition will usually exceed most of the values in the noise model. In my experiments, I have set the threshold at the 99th percentile of the noise distribution. This is a very strict criterion, set to demonstrate the method's general viability in the absence of most noise. The optimal noise threshold depends on the application, the languages involved, and the literalness of translation in the bitext.

9.5 The SenseClusters Algorithm

The computational complexity of the word sense discrimination problem stems from two sources. First, the number of possible informants for each word can be as large as the whole vocabulary. Second, the number of possible partitions of t link types is exponential in t. For some words, the number of different link types exceeds 30 even in the relatively compact translation models described in chapter 7, so it is infeasible to search an exponential number of partitions. There are two approaches to reducing the computational complexity, one randomized and one greedy.

The top-down approach, also known as divisive clustering, would start with all link types in the same cluster, then recursively split the cluster to optimize the objective function. For a cluster with t link types, there would be 2^{t-1} ways to partition it into two clusters, which is still exponential. However, Li & Abe (1996) have proposed that the split can be made randomly and then "fixed," e.g., by simulated annealing. Depending on the parameter settings, simulated annealing need not be exponential, but it is typically not very fast. For the present purposes, it would also need to be repeated once to form each new cluster.

The bottom-up approach, also known as agglomerative clustering, admits a greater reduction in complexity via a greedy heuristic.[1] The algorithm starts with each link type in its own cluster. It then greedily merges one pair of clusters at a time. The pair to be merged at each step is the one that, if merged, would effect the biggest gain in the objective function. If S_i and S_j are two sense clusters, then the gain in merging them into $S_{i \cup j}$ is given by:

$$\text{gain}(S_i, S_j) = I(S_{i \cup j}; C_{i \cup j}) - I(S_i; C_i) - I(S_j; C_j). \tag{9.3}$$

The algorithm stops when $gain(S_i, S_j) \leq 0$ for all i and j. If t is the number of different link types for the word being discriminated, then initially there are $O(t^2)$ possible merges. The total number of possible merge operations is bounded by $\log t^2 = 2 \log t$. However, after the initial t^2 computations, $gain(S_i, S_j)$ needs to be recomputed only for the cluster S_i created in the most recent merge together with each of the remaining clusters S_j, $1 \leq j \leq t$, $j \neq i$. Thus, the algorithm runs in $O(t^2 + t \log t) = O(t^2)$.

To reduce the number of informants considered during each computation of the objective function, I make two simplifying assumptions:

ASSUMPTION 9.1   Informants are independently distributed.

ASSUMPTION 9.2   Suppose that

- $S_{i \cup j} = S_i \cup S_j$ is the union of two sense clusters;
- $C_{i \cup j}$ is the set of informants that predict $S_{i \cup j}$ better than any other sense, i.e., $C_{i \cup j} = \{c | I(S_{i \cup j}; c) \geq I(S_k; c), \text{ for } 1 \leq k \leq |S|\}$;
- C_i is the set of informants that predict S_i better than any other sense, i.e., $C_i = \{c | I(S_i; c) \geq I(S_k; c), \text{ for } 1 \leq k \leq |S|\}$;
- C_j is the set of informants that predict S_j better than any other sense, i.e., $C_j = \{c | I(S_j; c) \geq I(S_k; c), \text{ for } 1 \leq k \leq |S|\}$;
- C_0 is the set of informants that are not predictive of any sense cluster, i.e., $C_0 = \{c | I(S_k; c) \leq \theta \text{ for } 1 \leq k \leq |S|\}$, where θ is the noise threshold;

then $C_{i \cup j} \subseteq C_i \cup C_j \cup C_0$.

These assumptions are embodied in the SenseClusters algorithm in figure 9.1.

The output of SenseClusters is a partitioning of the link types into clusters, some with predictive informants attached and some without. According to the principle of maximum entropy, we should not attempt to model more degrees of freedom than are supported by the data. So, in a final clean-up sweep, all the clusters without predictive informants attached are merged with the maximum likelihood (most frequent) cluster. In the context of translation model estimation, this step can be viewed as "backing off" to a less specific but more reliable estimator. If none of a word's link types can be reliably distinguished from the most frequent link type, then, according to the data, that word has only one sense.

Initialization:

1. Put each link type in a separate sense cluster.

2. Assign each informant c to the sense cluster S_i that maximizes $I(S_i; c)$. Let the set of informants assigned to sense cluster S_i be called C_i. A sense cluster may have no informants assigned to it.

3. If an informant is not predictive of any sense cluster, then put it in the "non-predictive" informant set C_0.

4. For each pair of sense clusters S_i and S_j,

(a) Let $S_{i \cup j}$ and $C_{i \cup j}$ be defined as in assumption 9.2.

(b) Estimate $gain(S_i, S_j)$, using equation (9.3).

Iteration: While there is a pair of sense clusters S_i and S_j for which $gain(S_i, S_j) > 0$,

1. Merge the two sense clusters S_i and S_j for which $gain(S_i, S_j)$ is greatest.

2. Let $C_{i \cup j}$, defined in 4(a) above, be the set of informants assigned to the merged cluster.

3. Return the non-predictive informants to $C_0 = C_i \cup C_j \cup C_0 - C_{i \cup j}$.

4. For each remaining cluster S_k, $k \neq i$, $k \neq j$, estimate $gain(S_{i \cup j}, S_k)$ using equation (9.3).

Figure 9.1
Algorithm SenseClusters

9.6 An Application

The most straightforward way to exploit the output of SenseClusters is to construct a decision procedure based on the informants attached to each sense, to sense-tag[2] all polysemous words in the bitext, and then to induce a new translation model that treats each sense as a different word. Sense-tagging increases the vocabulary size, thereby increasing the degrees of freedom in the model. The extra degrees of freedom are the main reason why Brown et al. (1991b) were able to show significantly improved performance. However, if Yarowsky (1993) is right that two senses of the same word are very unlikely to co-occur, then the $score()$s of all link types in the various translation models in chapter 7 are already estimated independently of each other. And if we take a word's translation to be its sense, then each link type involving a given word represents a different sense of that word, so models that account for each different link type independently already have enough parameters to model independent word senses.

Nevertheless, all published probabilistic translation models require an initial similarity metric based only on co-occurrence counts. The metrics that work best scale down their similarity estimates by the marginal probabilities of the words involved, which makes all the parameters for a given word type initially interdependent. Even though the one-to-one assumption can gradually reduce this interdependence, I hypothesized that stronger enforcement of the independence of different senses during computation of the initial similarity metric could improve translation model accuracy. A sense-tagged text gives each word sense its own frequency count, allowing the initial similarity metric to be estimated independently for each word sense.

To test my hypothesis, I implemented the following translation model induction system:

1. Induce a translation model from bitext, using translation Model C described in chapter 7.

2. Use SenseClusters to determine a sense inventory for all words on one side of the bitext.

3. Build a decision list (Yarowsky, 1996, chapter 5), in which the decisions can be based on a word's translations or on the informants in its monolingual context.

4. Use the decision list to sense-tag one side of the bitext.

5. Repeat from Step 2, treating each sense of each word as a different word type.

The cycle can be terminated when SenseClusters discovers no additional sense distinctions in Step 2, or when the translation model's performance on a development test set stops improving. Sense-to-sense translation models can also be co-trained (Blum & Mitchell, 1998) in "two-sided" mode, if SenseClusters distinguishes senses in alternate halves of the bitext on each iteration. It may also be advantageous to process both halves in the same iteration.

9.7 Experiments

I ran six iterations of the above system on two different training bitexts. The translation models resulting from each iteration were then evaluated on a previously unseen test bitext. The first training bitext consisted of the 29364

Table 9.1
Number of additional sense distinctions discovered by SenseClusters on each iteration on the English side of two bitexts.

Iteration	Bible	Hansards
1	774	1206
2	204	356
3	62	88
4	19	25
5	9	8
6	2	3

unannotated verse pairs in the Bible bitext described in chapter 6. The corresponding test bitext was the 250 hand-annotated verses in that bitext. The second bitext was the first 100000 segment pairs from Set-A of the Canadian Hansards CD-ROM (Graff et al., 1997). For testing, I used 10 sets of 5000 segment pairs each from the next 100000 segment pairs in Set-A. In both bitexts, punctuation was ignored for efficiency reasons.

9.7.1 Quantitative Results

Table 9.1 shows the number of new sense distinctions discovered by Sense-Clusters on each iteration in each bitext. The English vocabulary in the Bible training bitext originally contained 14644 word types. The English half of the Hansards training bitext comprised 19650 word types. No lemmatization was performed on the Bible bitext, so the English Bible vocabulary includes a number of morphological variants of some lemmas. On the other hand, all morphological variants in the Hansards bitext were conflated to a canonical form. Lemmatization makes the data less sparse (see section 7.6) and provides insight into how the system would behave given more training data, without incurring more computational expense. Table 9.1 shows that both runs have nearly converged after six iterations.

Table 9.2 shows the final polysemy distribution of English words in each bitext, i.e., the number of words that have the given number of senses after six iterations. Note that the Bible sense distinctions may include distinctions between morphological variants of the same lemma. The average polysemy in the English Hansards is significantly higher than in the English Bible, because lemmatization made the Hansards less sparse, so there was more evidence for more sense distinctions. On the other hand, SenseClusters did not come even close to making all the possible distinctions. After six iterations, 51%

Table 9.2
Number and percentage of English words in each bitext that have the given polysemy, i.e., the given number of senses.

Polysemy	Bible	%	Hansards	%
1	14193	96.92	18815	95.83
2	224	1.53	434	2.257
3	82	0.56	193	0.983
4	45	0.31	75	0.38
5	37	0.25	45	0.23
6	24	0.16	27	0.14
7	15	0.10	21	0.11
8	13		7	
9	6		9	
10	2		4	
11	1		2	
12	2		1	
13	0		1	

of the sense clusters in the English Bible vocabulary and 48% of the sense clusters in the English Hansards vocabulary consisted of more than one link type. Moreover, there were 148 clusters in the English Hansard vocabulary with twenty or more link types each, and there were 57 such large clusters in the English Bible vocabulary.

I evaluated the Bible translation models in two ways. First, I ran the "whole distribution" task described in section 7.7.1. The five-fold replication of annotations in the test data made it possible to compute the statistical significance of the differences in model accuracy. Second, I took this opportunity to test the validity of the unsupervised evaluation method described in section 8.8. To measure statistical significance, I divided the 250 verse pairs in the test bitext into ten samples of 25 verse pairs each. No hand-annotated links were available for the Hansards bitext, so I could evaluate its models only by using unsupervised evaluation.

Since the test bitexts had not been sense-tagged, I removed the sense tags from the words in the translation models and conflated the different senses of each word, before normalizing each translation model into a conditional distributions. No contextual information was used during evaluation, in contrast to the experiments of Brown et al. (1991b) and Kikui (1998). For both supervised and unsupervised evaluation, the translation models distributed a total probability mass of one among the predicted translations for each "source" word,

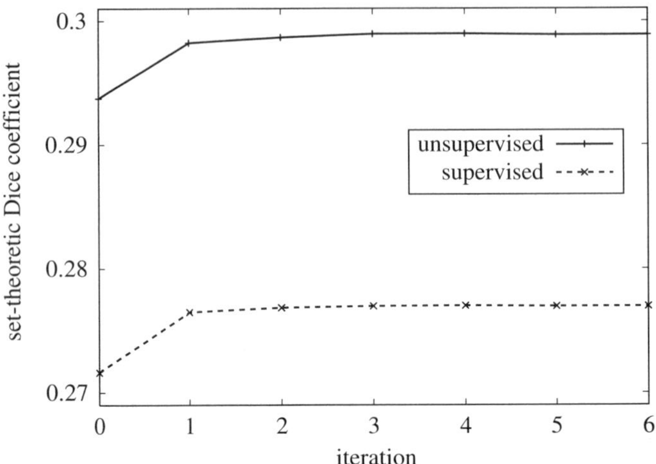

Figure 9.2
Effect of SenseClusters on translation model accuracy on the hand-annotated portion of the Bible
bitext. Iteration 0 is the baseline model.

regardless of the number of words in the held-out "target" text. Under unsupervised evaluation, this translation method usually results in higher precision
than recall if the target text has more words than the source, and vice versa. To
counter this bias, and to make the results comparable across the two evaluation
methods, I measured performance using the set-theoretic Dice coefficient (see
chapter 6), and averaged the scores between the two directions of translation,
as in section 7.7.1.

The performance of SenseClusters on the Bible bitext, using both supervised and unsupervised evaluation, is shown in figure 9.2. In both cases, the
performance improvements after the first and second iterations are statistically
significant at the $\alpha = .05$ level using the Wilcoxon signed ranks test. Subsequent iterations resulted in no significant differences. These scores are not
comparable to those reported in section 7.7.1, because there the training bitext included the test bitext, but here it does not. The correlation of $\rho = .999$
between the supervised and unsupervised scores is empirical evidence that unsupervised evaluation is internally valid.

Figure 9.3 plots the mean unsupervised evaluation scores for the Hansards
test bitexts. By far the biggest change in performance was the improvement
after the first iteration, after which performance dropped slightly on iterations
three and four, rose on iteration five and dropped again on iteration six. On

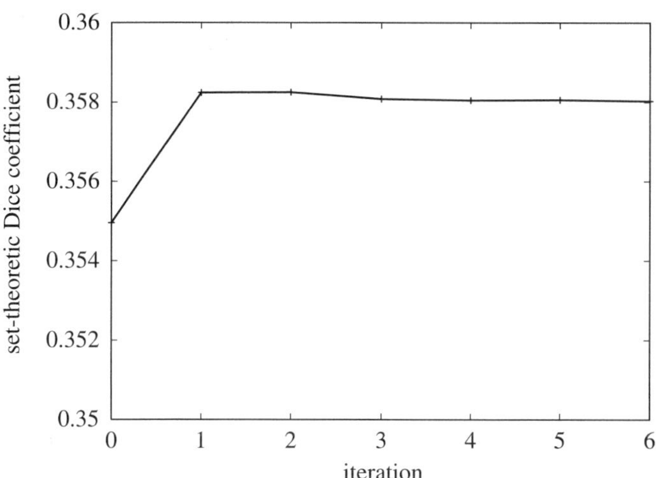

Figure 9.3
Effect of SenseClusters on translation model accuracy on the Hansard test bitext. Iteration 0 is the baseline model.

this bitext, SenseClusters seems to have done most of its useful work on the first iteration. The subsequent tiny performance drops may have resulted from overtraining.

These results show that SenseClusters can improve the accuracy of word-to-word translation models. The demonstrated performance improvements were small, as expected, due to the severe limits on the kinds and amount of information made available to the system (see section 9.1). To understand why SenseClusters improves translation models, recall that model induction is a search for optimal parameters. Even though parameter estimation algorithms such as EM (e.g., Dempster et al., 1977) are guaranteed to find a local maximum in their search space, the peak at which they converge depends on the topology of the search space. This dependence is stronger for algorithms like competitive linking that lack any convergence guarantees. Polysemous words force a single dimension of the search space (a single word) to represent what should ideally be independent dimensions for each word sense. The spurious conflation of independent dimensions confounds the search. Sense-tagging deconflates these separate dimensions, giving the model more degrees of freedom and making it easier for the model induction algorithm to find a good representation of the training data. A better translation model will, in turn, generate more correct link tokens in the bitext, enabling more of them to contribute relevant contextual evidence. When more of the evidence passes the noise filter described in section 9.4, SenseClusters can distinguish more senses. The system converges when it cannot find any more dimensions to deconflate.

9.7.2 Qualitative Results

To illustrate the kinds of sense distinctions discovered by SenseClusters, I selected ten words at random among the polysemous words in the Hansards English vocabulary. For each of these ten words, table 9.3 shows the French translations that account for at least 10% of each sense's translational probability mass, and the predictive informants for each sense.[3] The table reveals some translation modeling errors and several interesting properties of the experimental system described above. The system constructs a hierarchy of senses for each word, where SenseClusters adds another level to the hierarchy on each iteration. Of course, a new level is only added for a given word if it is supported by the data. The hierarchy of sense tags is a decision tree, in which the tagging decision at each node depends on the informants attached to each subnode. At each node, there can be a default "most frequent" decision that has no informants attached. In table 9.3, digits attached to informants represent sense tags; e.g., "be.1.2" is the second subsense of the first sense of "be."

The existence of multiple levels of sense distinctions in the Hansards data shows that some sense distinctions could be made reliably only after the relevant informants were themselves split into distinct senses. For example, the translations of like were initially split into five clusters, where the most frequent translations in each cluster were aimer, <NULL>, comme, ressembler, and question, respectively. On the second iteration, the aimer cluster was further split into an aimer cluster and a vouloir cluster, and a second <NULL> cluster was split off the comme cluster. Finally, the third iteration found that the most frequent translation of the ressembler cluster was also <NULL>, but that the links to ressembler were reliably predictable in the context of the first sense of be. Thus, two of the <NULL> clusters represent the default senses at their nodes in the sense hierarchy of like. This example also illustrates that the system is somewhat vulnerable to fragmentation of training data, especially where the troublesome <NULL> links are concerned. More efficient utilization of contextual information is a rich topic for future work.

Table 9.3
A random sample of ten English words from the Hansards that SenseClusters deemed polysemous.
Digits appended to informants are sense tags.

Word	Sense freq.	Translation(s) in cluster	Informant(s) in monolingual context	Explanatory notes
Act	1667	loi	the	
	46	acte	BNA, British, North, America	"the British North America Act"
	3	agricole	Land.1	
	2	pension	Social	"Social Security Act"
South	178	sud	York	"York-sud"
	37	South, <NULL>	Shore	
	19	Sud	Africa	"Afrique du Sud"
after	881	après	<NUMBER>, <COMMA>	
	427	<NULL>	look	particle in "look after"
	25	ensuite	that	
close	177	<NULL>		
	94	fermer	down	
	90	près, presque	to, <NUMBER>, per, cent	"close to <NUMBER> per cent"
	55	étroit	with, consultation	
	22	terminer	I, like	"In closing, I would like . . . "
	20	fermeture	programme, small, post, office, end	"The programme to close small post offices ends in September."
could	2610	pouvoir	the	
	204	ne, y, faire	not	
	80	alors, sans, possible	be.2	
	53	afin, ainsi	so	
	15	si	truth	
like	1166	aimer	to.1, should.2	"I should like to . . . "
	605	vouloir	would.1	"Je voudrais . . . "
	583	<NULL>	put, a, question	
	422	comme		
	163	<NULL>		
	62	<NULL>	should.2, to.2, to.1	
	26	ressembler	be.1.1	"to be like . . . "
	24	question	ask, supplementary	T.M. error
market	1046	marché	the	
	46	vente, sur, débouché	for	
	24	commercialiser, commercialisation	produce, quantity, article	
	20	marchand	value	
please	722	avoir	<PERIOD>, <COMMA>	T.M. error
	156	heureux	be.1.2	
	87	plaisir, réjouir, volontiers	be.1.1	
	47	<NULL>	<PERIOD>	

Table 9.3 *(continued)*

Word	Sense freq.	Translation(s) in cluster	Informant(s) in monolingual context	Explanatory notes
promote	138	favoriser		
	5	créer	unemployment	
right	977	droit	have, their, human, to, of, strike, the	" . . . have their human right to strike . . . "
	541	<NULL>	now, way	"right now"
	281	très	question, direct, by, gentleman, hon., prime, minister, member, for, Prince, Albert	"the question directed by the gentleman from Prince Albert to the right honorable prime minister"
	94	raison	think, he, be, wrong	"I think he is wrong."
	44	tout	across, country	"right across the country" "dans tout le pays"
	41	droite	my, friend	"my friend to my right"
	20	direction	step, in, direction	"a step in the right direction"

9.8 Conclusion

In this chapter, I have shown how an information-theoretic criterion for sense
distinctions can be used as an objective function for improving translation
model accuracy. Under a couple of simplifying assumptions, this objective
function can be efficiently optimized by the SenseClusters word sense discrimination algorithm. SenseClusters overcomes a serious limitation of previous
attempts: it automatically determines the number of sense divisions that are
appropriate to each word, ranging from one for monosemous words up to as
many senses as there are link types for the word in a word-to-word translation
model. Objective evaluation has shown that these techniques can improve the
accuracy of word-to-word translation models.

The research described in this chapter naturally intersects with a variety
of other research areas, and these intersections deserve more attention than I
have given them so far. For example, it would be useful to adopt the methods
of Yarowsky (1993) to investigate which informant types are most useful for
this kind of lexical ambiguity resolution, and how they can be combined without violating too many independence assumptions. The noise filtering methods
in section 9.4 can benefit from more principled methods of finding optimum
thresholds. In addition to splitting single words into multiple senses, it would

be useful to combine SenseClusters with methods for automatically discovering sets of words that have the same sense, i.e., synonyms. These need not necessarily be synonyms in the classical sense; they can be arbitrary word classes used to back off from sparse data (Brown et al., 1992; Och, 1999). The fine-tuning of equivalence classes of words in bitext can also improve the performance of other algorithms that are based on translation models, such as the algorithms for NCC induction described in chapter 8.

It is likely that SenseClusters can be retargeted towards other applications, especially if it is used with context-aware translation models. The algorithm produces sense-tags and lists of their predictive informants as a side effect. Predictive informants are the key to accurate context-aware translation models. The sense tags might be used as training data for supervised word sense disambiguation (Resnik & Yarowsky, 1997). Kilgarriff (1997b) suggests that sense-tagged corpora are also useful for lexicographers, who often need to find more examples of a particular word sense.

10 Summary and Outlook

Parts I and III of this book presented state-of-the-art solutions to the first two major problems along the path from raw bitext to real-world applications: mapping bitext correspondence and inducing word-to-word translation models. Part II showed how generalized models of co-occurrence can glue together the solutions to these two problems into an integrated system for exploiting *arbitrary* parallel texts.

I. Translational Equivalence among Word Tokens

Chapter 2 began by showing that the language-specific aspects of the bitext mapping problem can be encapsulated and modularized away. What remains is a geometric pattern recognition problem. From this point of view, the best solution is the one that maximizes the signal-to-noise ratio in the search space and employs the fastest and most accurate search algorithm. Chapter 2 continued by demonstrating how to maximize the signal strength for any bitext in any pair of languages, and how to minimize noise using a novel localized filter. In addition to these programmatic insights, the chapter's chief contribution is the Smooth Injective Map Recognizer (SIMR) algorithm. SIMR is the first general bitext mapping algorithm to achieve state-of-the-art accuracy in linear expected space and time. SIMR's accuracy made possible the applications in chapters 3 and 4.

Chapter 3 applied the insights of chapter 2 to the long-standing bitext alignment problem. Since alignment is formally easier that the general bitext mapping problem, a good alignment can be extracted from a good general bitext map. Chapter 3 presented the Geometric Segment Alignment (GSA) algorithm, designed to distill a segment alignment from a bitext map combined with information about segment boundaries. Evaluation on a pre-existing gold standard has shown that alignments extracted by GSA from a good general bitext map are more accurate than those produced directly by other published methods.

Chapter 4 is proof positive that bitext maps are useful for something other than machine translation. Omissions in translations are one of the biggest quality control problems facing translators today. Chapter 4 showed that accurate general bitext maps of the kind produced by SIMR make possible the first published practical solution to this problem. A geometric characterization of omissions in translations and a noise filter designed to overcome characteristic imperfections in bitext maps are the key to Automatic Detection of OMIssions in Translations (ADOMIT). ADOMIT can be used by translators to catch omission errors in translations, in the same way that they might use a spell-checker.

II. The Type-Token Interface

Chapter 5 introduced formal models of co-occurrence. These models dictate how to compute co-occurrence counts, which are the starting point for most statistical translation models. Although counting co-occurrences is a simple idea, its correct implementation turned out to be rather subtle, especially in the absence of information about text segment boundaries. To reduce the reliance of many published translation model estimation methods on clean and order-preserving translations, chapter 5 showed how to compute co-occurrence counts given an arbitrary (not necessarily monotonic) bitext map. Given a tool for harvesting bitexts from the internet, such as the one described by Resnik (1999), these insights have the potential to break the data bottleneck that has stifled research in this field.

Chapter 6 described a project to design and implement a model-independent gold standard for evaluating models of translational equivalence. The design made evaluation possible at both the type and token levels. The project included the design and implementation of the "Blinker" bitext annotation tool, the development of an annotation style guide (appendix A), and the invention of several strategies for raising inter-annotator agreement rates. The agreement rates indicated that the annotations are reasonably reliable and that the task is easy to replicate. The gold-standard annotations are freely downloadable from `http://www.cis.upenn.edu/~melamed` to encourage further research in this field.

III. Translational Equivalence among Word Types

Chapter 7 proved the feasibility of modeling translational equivalence independently of word order. The computational complexity of estimating translation models of this kind led to the introduction of the one-to-one assumption and the invention of the competitive linking algorithm. Chapter 7 also showed why and how more accurate translation models can be estimated using an explicit noise model. Further, chapter 7 showed how the noise model can be conditioned on almost any kind of pre-existing language-specific knowledge that might be available, and that even the simplest linguistic bias can improve translation model accuracy.

Chapters 8 and 9 strove to break free of the word typology imposed on text translation models by the idiosyncratic orthographic conventions of written languages. Translational equivalence between the vocabularies of two languages is easiest to describe in terms of their minimal content-bearing units. One such unit may be represented by a phrase of several words; several units may be represented by the same word type. The set of possible mappings between minimal content-bearing units and strings in text represents a search space. Chapters 8 and 9 developed information-theoretic objective functions for searching two subspaces of this space. In both cases, the goal was to modify the parameter set of a translation model to better match the sources of variance in the data, thereby improving the resulting models. The objective function in chapter 8 was designed to discover word sequences whose translations were not composed of the translations of the individual words, so that these word sequences could be assigned their own translational distribution. The objective function in chapter 9 was designed to increase the number of translation parameters for each word proportionally to the degree of polysemy of that word, so that each distinct word sense would have its own translational distribution. Each of these two chapters presented novel efficient methods for optimizing their respective objective functions. In both cases, optimization of the objective function improved translation model accuracy.

Outlook

It is in the nature of engineering research to improve on existing solutions. Future advances in the state of the art of solving the problems addressed in this book are likely to come from research with the following foci:

- If bitext mapping can be viewed as a pattern recognition problem, then the way to improve its solution is to improve the signal-to-noise ratio in the bitext space. The most valuable improvements in signal generation or in noise filtering will be the language-independent ones, but many language-specific heuristics are also possible.

- Manual annotation of translational equivalence can be done more reliably given a better annotation tool and a more detailed style guide.

- All the translation model biases introduced in this book can be modeled more cleverly and estimated more efficiently. They can also be combined with other biases in the literature, such as the word order correlation bias. However, the most significant improvements in statistical translation models will come from insights into how to model the remaining sources of variation in the data. The next big challenge is to account for word order variation with bilingual bilexical dependency models.

A   Annotation Style Guide for the Blinker Project

A.1   General Guidelines

You will be working with pairs of corresponding Bible verses in English and French. Your task will be to specify how words correspond within the paired verses, using the Blinker. For example, when the Blinker presents you with the pair of verses in figure A.1, you might link them as in figure A.2. As you can see, most words are linked to only one word in the other language. However, this is not always the case, as demonstrated by "toute" and "leur" in this example.

Sometimes you will see the English on the left and the French on the right, sometimes vice versa. You will also notice that we have done some "retokenization" on some of the verses. In both the English and the French, we separate hyphenated words and elisions into separate words. For example, you will see "de le" instead of "du" in French, and "Lord's" will appear as "Lord's"

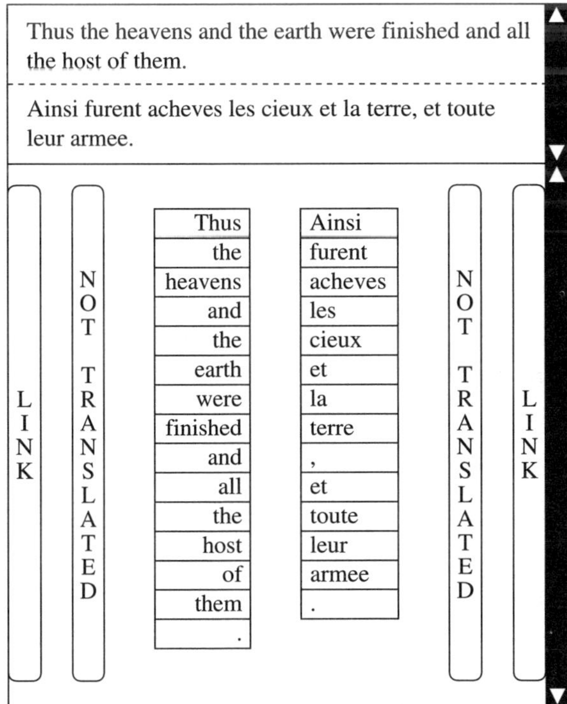

Figure A.1
Example 1.

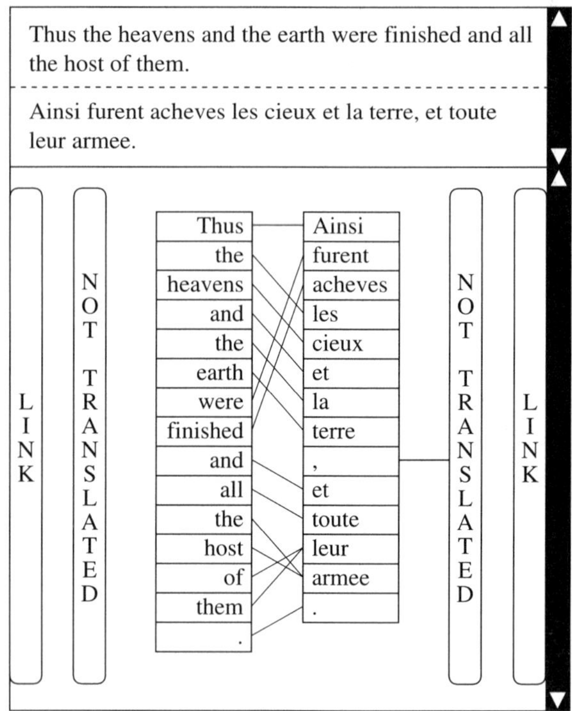

Figure A.2
Example 2.

in English. Although this is an unusual way of writing, it will make it easier for you to link the words correctly.

Two kinds of complications arise when the translation is not very literal.

A.1.1   Omissions in Translation

You may see words in the verse of one language whose meaning is not contained at all in the verse of the other language. Here is another verse pair from Genesis:

French: *fixe moi ton salaire , et je te le donnerai .*

English: *And he said , Appoint me thy wages , and I will give it .*

Although the English verse begins "And he said," there is no corresponding language in the French verse. When this happens, you should link the extrane-

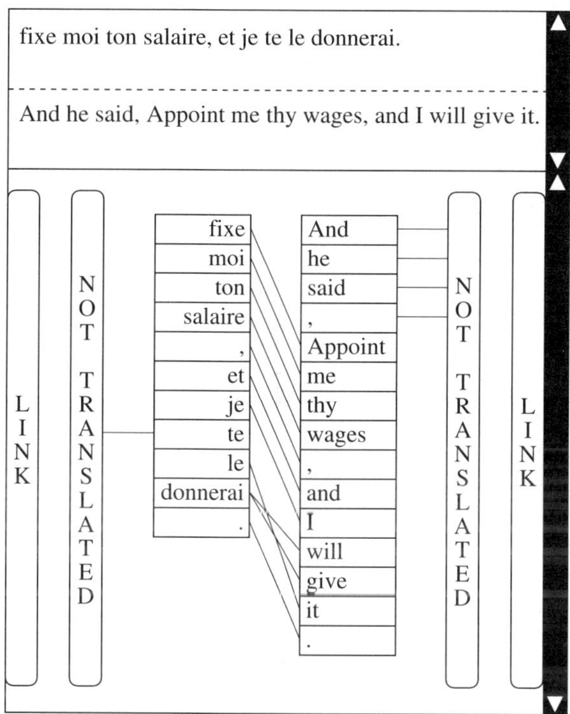

Figure A.3
Example 3.

ous words to the "Not Translated" bar on the corresponding side of the screen, as in figure A.3.

Careful! Many of the translations are very non-literal. However, you should only link words to "Not Translated" when you can answer "Yes" to the following question: If the seemingly extraneous words were simply deleted from their verse, would the two verses become more similar in meaning? If the answer is "No," then some words in the translation share some meaning with some of the words that seem extraneous. So, those words are not really extraneous and should not be marked "Not Translated."

A.1.2   Phrasal Correspondence

The other problem with non-literal translations is that sometimes it is necessary to link entire phrases to each other. Here is another example from Genesis:

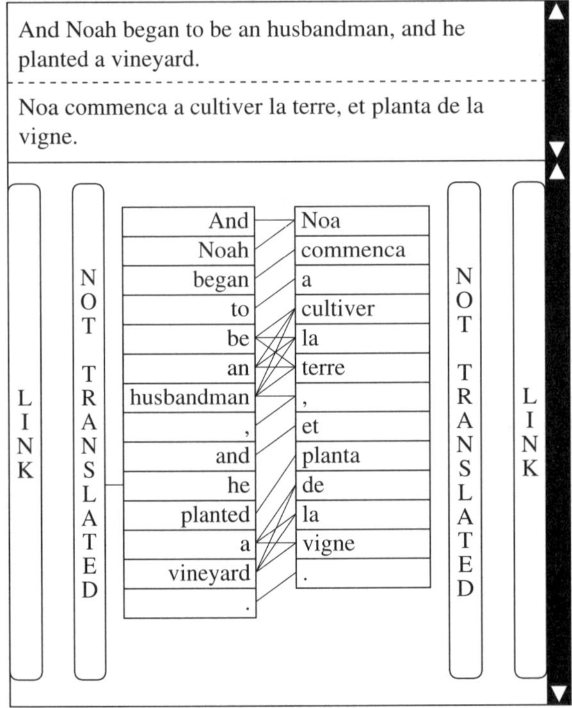

Figure A.4
Example 4.

English: *And Noah began to be an husbandman , and he planted a vineyard :*

French: *Noà commença á cultiver la terre , et planta de la vigne .*

The words in "to be an husbandman" and in "cultiver la terre" do not correspond one to one, although the two phrases mean the same thing in this context. Therefore, the two phrases should be linked as wholes, by linking each word in one to each word in the other, as in figure A.4. Likewise, "de la vigne" means "some vines," not "a vineyard." figure A.4 shows these phrases as completely interlinked.

The divergence in meaning may be so great for some pairs of passages that the best annotation might seem to be to link both passages to "Not Translated" in their entirety. Whenever you have this urge, please remember that neither version of the Bible from which we drew these verses is a translation of the other. Instead, they are both translations of a third version. Each translation introduces some idiosyncrasies, and when two such idiosyncrasies happen in the same place in the text, the two passages may seem to have nothing to do with each other. The decision whether to link or not to link should *not* be based on the question of whether one passage could have arisen as a translation of the other. A more appropriate criterion is whether both passages could have arisen as translations of a third.

A.2 Detailed Guidelines

You should specify as detailed a correspondence as possible, even when non-literal translations make it difficult to find corresponding words. See figures A.5—A.7.

A.2.1 Idioms and Near Idioms

"Frozen" expressions that are unique to one language or the other should be linked as wholes. See figure A.8.

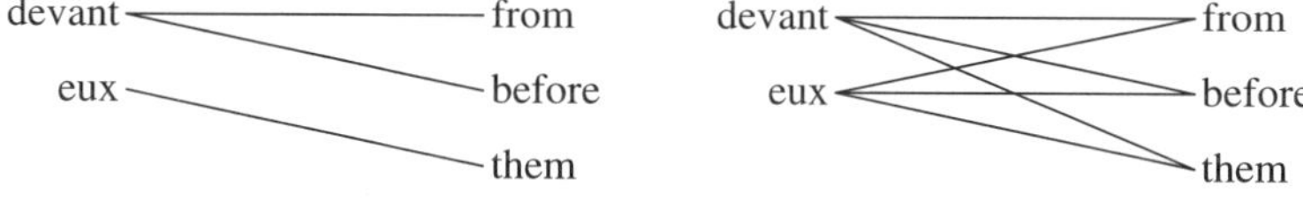

Figure A.5
Example 5: Right.   Example 6: Wrong.

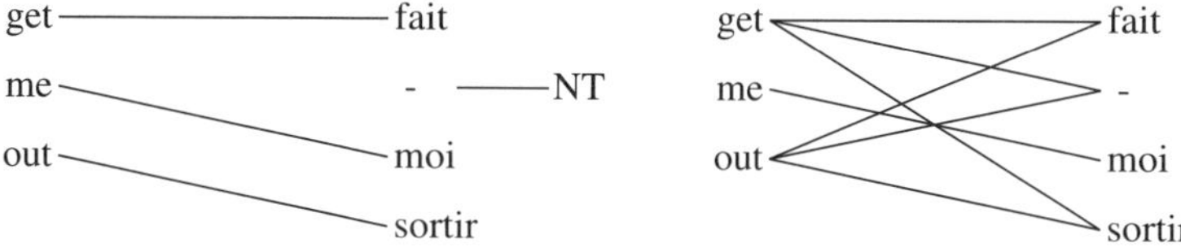

Figure A.6
Example 7: Right.   Example 8: Wrong.

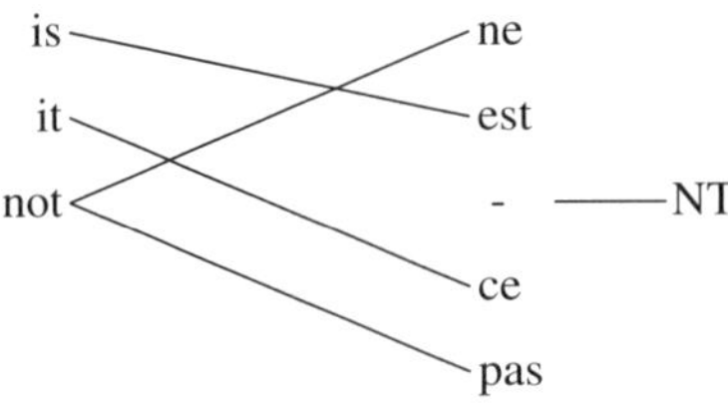

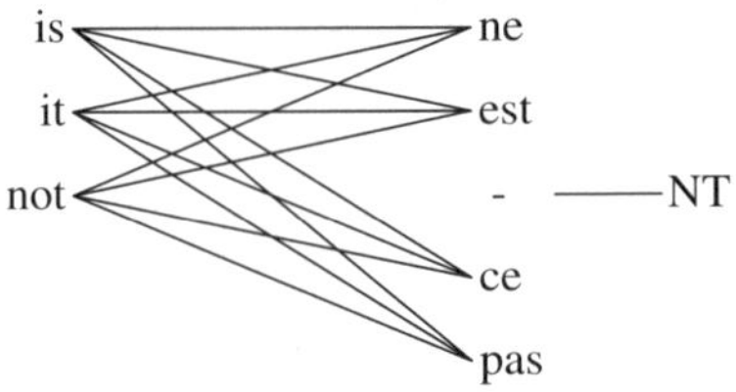

Figure A.7
Example 9: Right.   Example 10: Wrong.

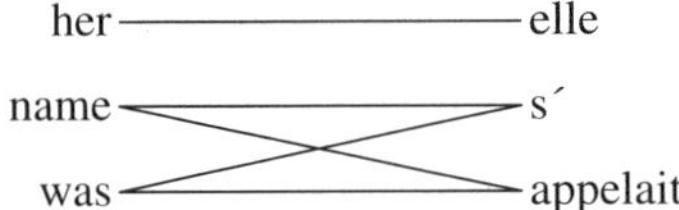

Figure A.8
Example 11.

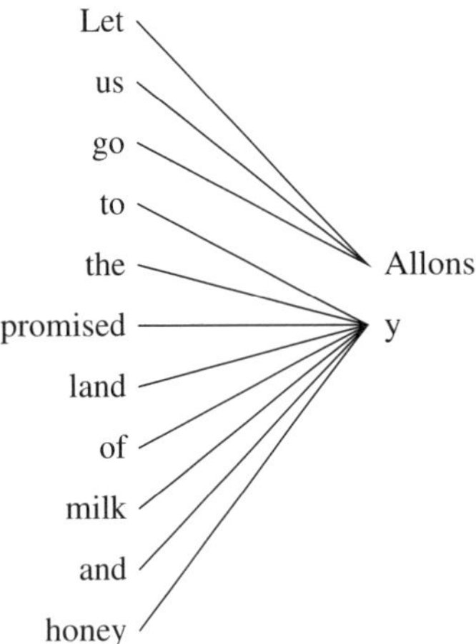

Figure A.9
Example 12.

A.2.2   Referring Expressions

Pronouns and Definite Descriptions   Divergent descriptions of the same thing should be linked as wholes, as in figure A.4. This rule holds even when one description is a pronoun. See figure A.9.

Resumptive Pronouns   *Resumptive pronouns* refer to something previously described in the same sentence, called the *antecedent*. When a resumptive pronoun occurs in a verse, but not in its translation, both the resumptive pronoun and its antecedent should be linked to the translation of the antecedent. Relative markers should be treated the same way. See figures A.10–A.12.

Conjunctive Non-Parallelism   When a piece of text is repeated in a verse but not in its translation, all instances of that piece of text in the first verse should be linked to the one translation. See figures A.13 and A.14.

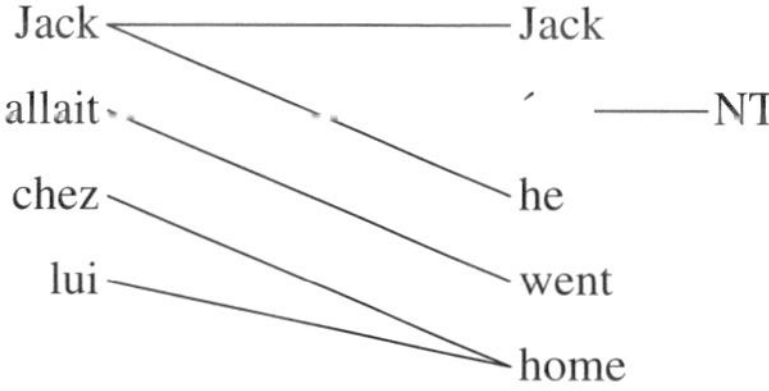

Figure A.10
Example 13.

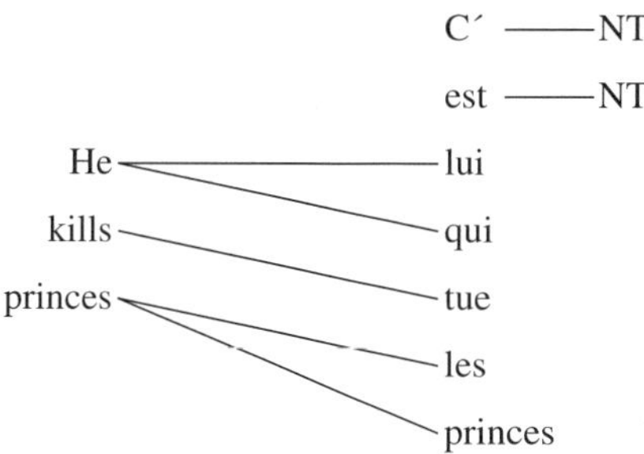

Figure A.11
Example 14.

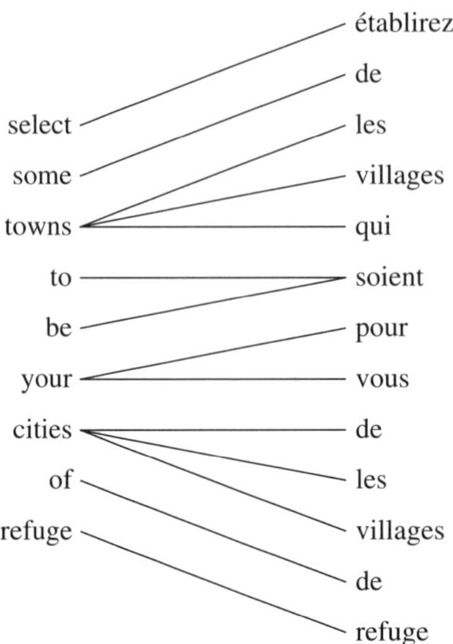

Figure A.12
Example 15.

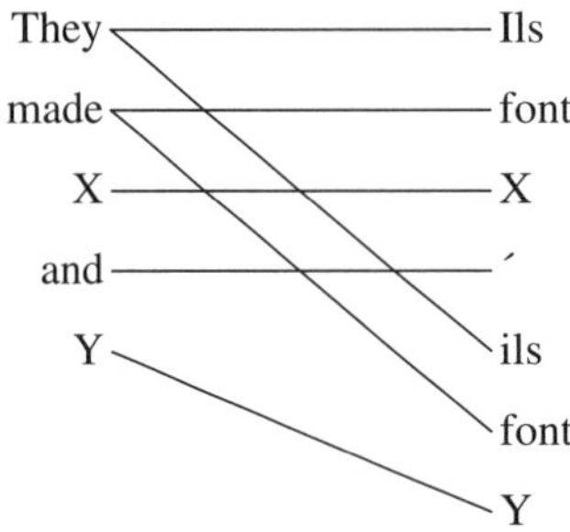

Figure A.13
Example 16.

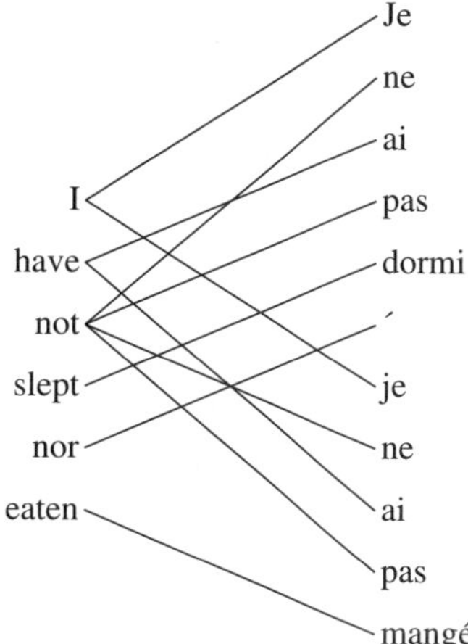

Figure A.14
Example 17.

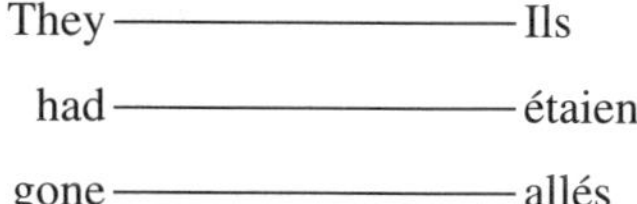

Figure A.15
Example 18.

A.2.3   Verbs

Negation   French negation often involves two words where English uses only one. In all such cases, *both* pieces of the French negation should be linked to the English negation. Examples include *ne . . . pas, ne . . . point, ne . . . rien, ne . . . jamais, ne . . . que.*

Auxiliary Verbs   Auxiliary verbs should *not* be linked to the main verb in the translation whenever that main verb also has auxiliaries attached. However, auxiliaries often do not match, especially when the verb tenses are slightly altered in translation. When there are auxiliaries in a verse but not in its translation, both the auxiliaries and the main verb should be linked to the main verb in the translation. See figures A.15 and A.16.

But consider *May . . . be / soit* in figure A.17.

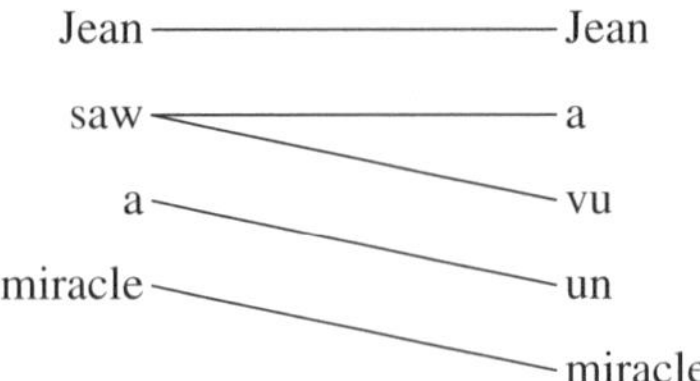

Figure A.16
Example 19.

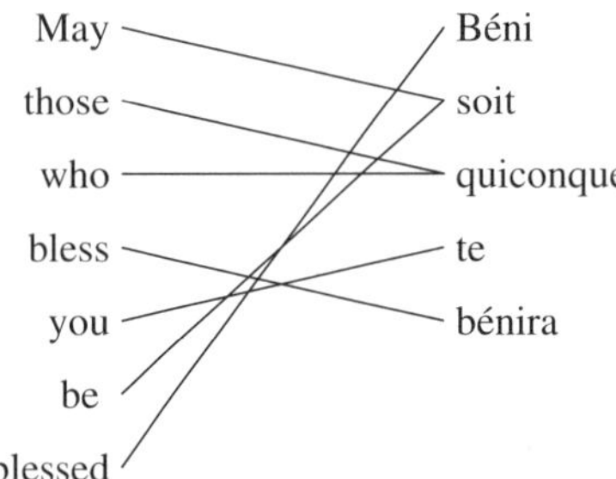

Figure A.17
Example 20.

Passivization   The order of corresponding words in a pair of verses may be very different when one verse is in the *passive voice* and the other is in the *active voice*. You should make an effort to tease apart the correspondences, instead of linking whole phrases. See figures A.18 and A 19.

A.2.4   Prepositions

Extra Prepositions   When a verse contains a preposition that does not appear in the translation, the preposition should be linked to the translation of the preposition's object, not the translation of its subject. See figures A.20 and A.21.

Divergent Prepositions   When a piece of text is slightly paraphrased, two prepositions that never mean the same thing literally may need to be linked anyway. See figure A.22.

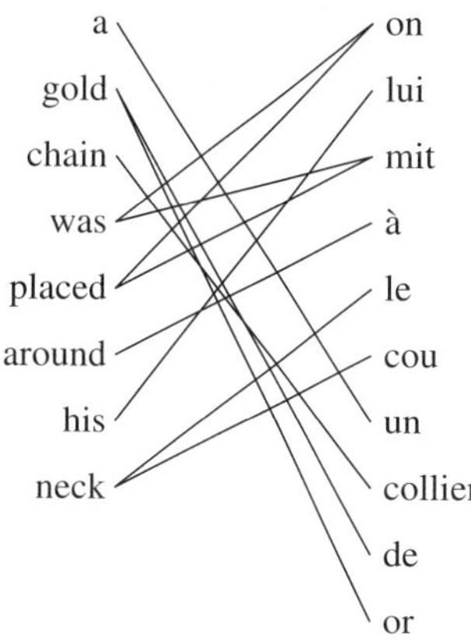

Figure A.18
Example 21.

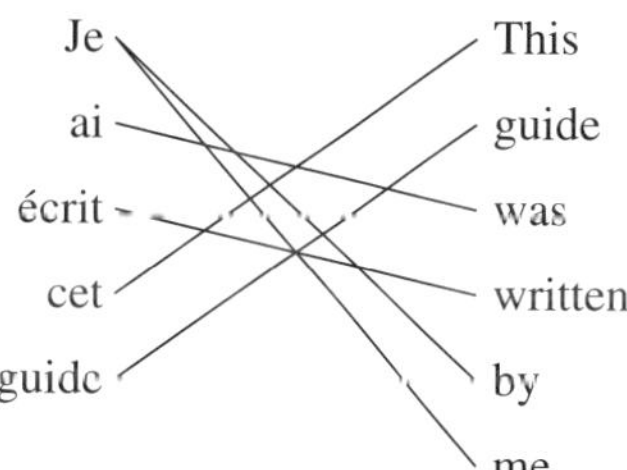

Figure A.19
Example 22.

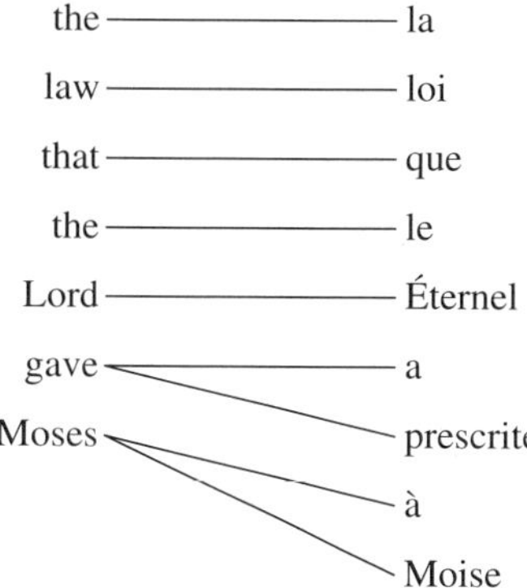

Figure A.20
Example 23.

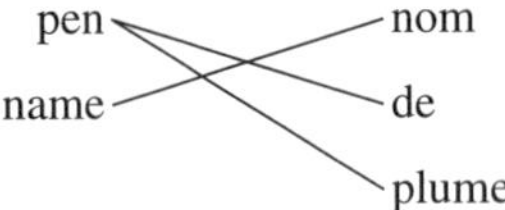

Figure A.21
Example 24.

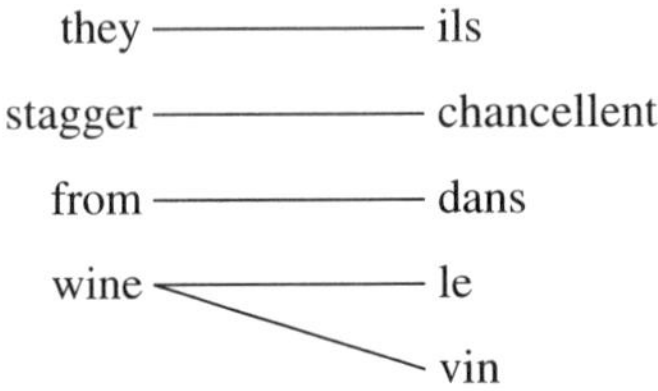

Figure A.22
Example 25.

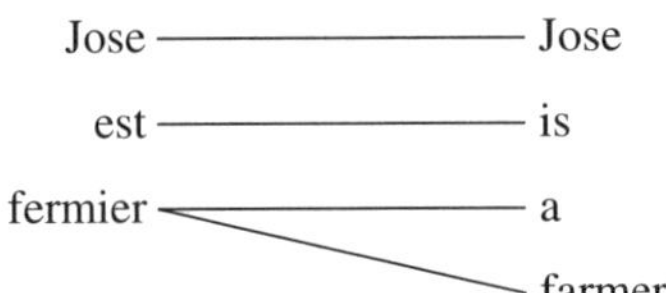

Figure A.23
Example 26.

A.2.5   Determiners

Extra Determiners   Extra determiners in a verse should be linked together
with their noun to the noun's translation. See figures A.23 and A.24.

Possessives   English and French possessive markers are different but easy to
identify. They should be linked separately from their nouns. See figure A.25.
The English plural possessive marker is just an apostrophe. See figure A.26.

A.2.6   Punctuation

Punctuation Series   Sometimes a verse pair contains several identical (or
similar) punctuation marks on each side, but in different quantities. In such
cases, the best linking strategy is to link all the words other than the punctu-

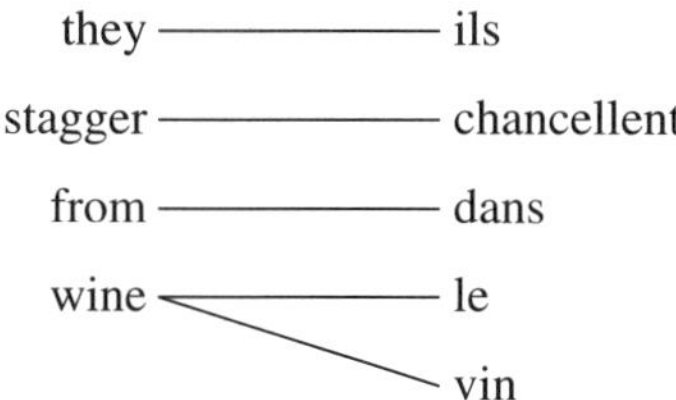

Figure A.24
Example 27.

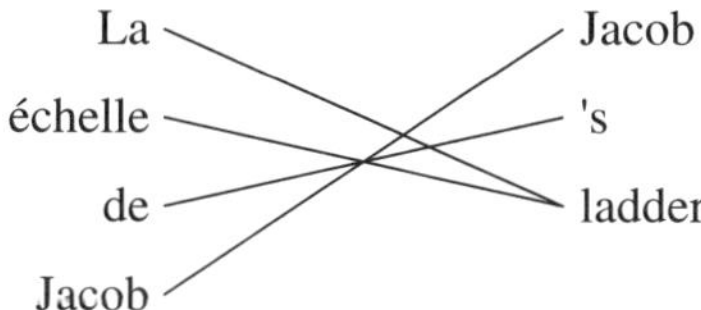

Figure A.25
Example 28.

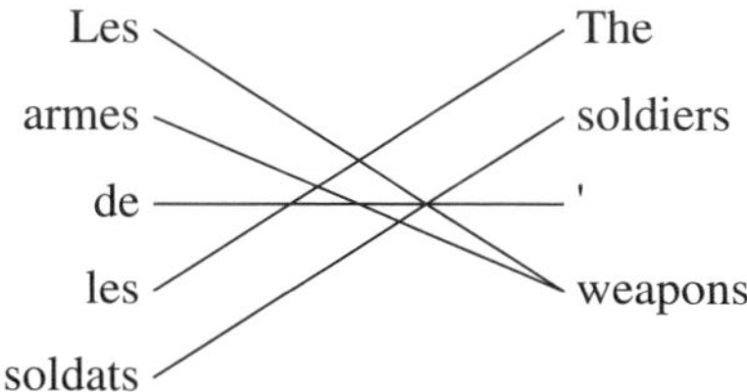

Figure A.26
Example 29.

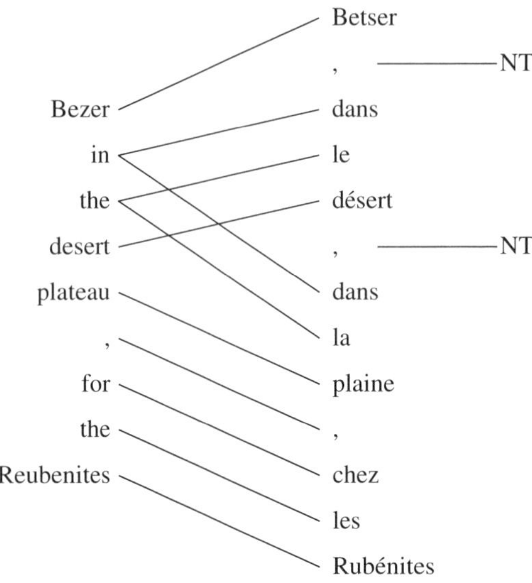

Figure A.27
Example 30.

ation marks first. Then link the punctuation marks to minimize the number of "crossing" links. See figure A.27.

Punctuation and Conjunction   When a series of conjunctions in one verse corresponds to a series of punctuation marks in the other verse, don't hesitate to link words to punctuation marks; e.g., English "and" will often correspond to a French comma.

Notes

Chapter 1

1. Note that the term *translation model*, which is standard in the literature, refers to a static mathematical relationship between two data sets. In this usage, the term says nothing about the *process* of translation, automated or otherwise.

Chapter 2

1. Larger chunks of text can be coordinated the same way, if we assign them the positions of their median character. If multiple TPCs arise at the same x- or y-position as a result, then we can maintain the bijectivity of the TBM by giving precedence to TPCs that coordinate the smallest text units.

2. See chapter 4 for more evidence.

3. Most published methods for automatically constructing translation lexicons require a pre-existing bitext map, which seems to render them useless for the purposes of bitext mapping algorithms. Fortunately, only one seed translation lexicon is required for each language pair, or at worst for each sublanguage. If we expect to map many bitexts in the same language pair, then it becomes feasible to spend a few hours creating one bitext map by hand. Melamed (1996b) explains how to do so quickly and efficiently. Better yet, Fung (1995b) shows how it may be possible to extract a small translation lexicon and a rough bitext map simultaneously.

4. Displacement can be negative.

5. Error measurements at the character level are less susceptible to random variation than measurements at the word level. Character-level measurements also have the advantage of being universally applicable to all languages, including those in which words are difficult to identify automatically.

6. Multi-word expressions in the translation lexicon can be treated just like any other character string.

Chapter 4

1. The misalignments listed in section 4.3 had been corrected.

2. SIMR can map English/French bitexts using cognates and/or a translation lexicon. Use of both kinds of information results in more accurate bitext maps, which make omission detection easier. However, wide-coverage translation lexicons are rarely available. To make the evaluation more representative, SIMR was run using cognates only.

Chapter 5

1. The translation models in chapter 7 are based on this assumption.

2. A *maximum matching* is a subgraph that solves the cardinality matching problem (Ahuja et al., 1993, pp. 469-470).

3. The algorithm is folklore, but Phillips & Warnow (1996) describe relevant methods.

Chapter 6

1. Resnik et al. (1997) discuss exceptions.

2. Both are on-line at `http://bible.gospelcom.net`. Use of the NIV requires a research license (International Bible Society, Attn: NIV Permission Director, 1820 Jet Stream Drive, Colorado Springs, CO 80921-3969). LSG is freely downloadable for research purposes; see `http://cedric.cnam.fr/ABU/`.

Chapter 7

1. "Sentence-to-sentence" might be a more transparent term, but all the models that I'm aware of apply equally well to sequences of words that are not sentences.

2. Assignments are different from Brown et al. (1993b)'s alignments in that assignments can range over pairs of arbitrary labels, not necessarily sequence position indexes. Also, unlike alignments, assignments must be one-to-one.

3. The exact nature of the bag size distribution is immaterial for the present purposes.

4. Since they are put into bags, $\vec{u}_i$ and $\vec{v}_i$ could just as well be bags instead of sequences. I make them sequences only to be consistent with more sophisticated models that take into account non-compositional compounds, such as those described in chapter 8.

5. The number of permutations is smaller when either bag contains two or more identical elements, but this detail does not affect the estimation algorithms presented here.

6. Rapp (1995) discovered the same thing at about the same time.

7. This expression is obtained by substituting Brown et al. (1993b)'s equation (17) into their equation (14).

8. Or, equivalently, if the notion of segments were dispensed with altogether, as under the distance-based model of co-occurrence (see chapter 5).

9. For example, the expectation in step 2 would need to be computed exactly, rather than merely approximated.

10. At least for my current very inefficient implementation.

11. The competitive linking algorithm can be generalized to stop searching before the number of possible assignments is reduced to one, at which point the link counts can be computed as probabilistically weighted averages over the remaining assignments. I use this method to resolve ties.

12. Except for the case when multiple tokens of the same word type occur near each other, which I hereby sweep under the carpet.

13. I.e., γ is the same as Dagan et al. (1993b)'s window width.

14. A more difficult question is whether it would be useful to include NULL links in this evaluation. I decided to exclude them for the sake of simplicity.

15. I.e., Method C and more recent versions of Method B should perform better.

Chapter 8

1. In the context of symmetric translation models, the words "source" and "target" are merely labels.

2. $s \in \mathcal{S}$ means that $\Pr_{\mathcal{S}}(s) > 0$.

3. See Cover & Thomas (1991) for a good introduction to information theory.

4. The threshold ϕ reduces errors due to noise in the data and in the translation model. It also ameliorates the overtraining tendencies of the objective functions described in this chapter. I use $\phi = 2$.

5. Although these alignments were less accurate than what might have been produced by the method in chapter 3, they were already available. Given more accurate alignments, the results can only improve.

6. These experiments were done before my translation model estimation methods were improved into the ones described in chapter 7. Given more accurate translation models, the results can only improve.

7. These results differ from those reported earlier (Melamed, 1997d), because source words that were not in the training data were no longer copied to the output.

Chapter 9

1. Li & Abe (1998) independently started working on agglomerative clustering at about the same time as I did.

2. The tags for different senses need not reflect any pre-existing sense inventory; they need only be distinct.

3. The average polysemy of this random sample is much higher than one might expect from table 9.2, but such was the luck of the draw.

References

A. Abeillé, Y. Schabes, & A. K. Joshi. (1990) "Using Lexicalized Tree Adjoining Grammars for Machine Translation," *13th International Conference on Computational Linguistics*. Helsinki, Finland.

L. Ahrenberg, M. Andersson, & M. Merkel. (1998) "A Simple Hybrid Aligner for Generating Lexical Correspondences in Parallel Texts," *36th Annual Meeting of the Association for Computational Linguistics*. Montreal, Canada.

R. K. Ahuja, T. L. Magnati, & J. B. Orlin. (1993) *Network Flows: Theory, Algorithms, and Applications*. Prentice Hall, Englewood Cliffs, NJ.

Y. Al-Onaizan, J. Curin, M. Jahr, K. Knight, J. Lafferty, I. D. Melamed, F. J. Och, D. Purdy, N. A. Smith, & D. Yarowsky. (1999) "Statistical Machine Translation," CLSP Technical Report, Baltimore, MD. Available from *www.clsp.jhu.edu/ws99/projects/mt/final_report/mt-final-report.ps*

S. Aster. (1997) Personal communication.

R. H. Baayen & R. Lieber. (1997) "Word Frequency Distributions and Lexical Semantics," *Computers and the Humanities 30*, pp. 281–291.

Y. Bar-Hillel. (1964) *Language and Information*. Addison-Wesley, Reading, MA.

A. Blum & T. Mitchell. (1998) "Combining Labeled and Unlabeled Data with Co-Training," *11th Annual Conference on Computational Learning Theory*, Madison, WI, pp. 92-100.

R. Bellman. (1957) *Dynamic Programming*. Princeton University Press, Princeton, NJ.

J. Brousseau, C. Drouin, G. Foster, P. Isabelle, R. Kuhn, Y. Normandin, & P. Plamondon. (1995) "French Speech Recognition in an Automatic Dictation System for Translators: The TransTalk Project," *EuroSpeech'95*. Madrid, Spain.

P. F. Brown, J. Cocke, S. A. Della Pietra, V. J. Della Pietra, F. Jelinek, R. L. Mercer, & P. Roossin. (1988) "A Statistical Approach to Language Translation," *12th International Conference on Computational Linguistics*. Budapest, Hungary.

P. F. Brown, J. C. Lai, & R. L. Mercer. (1991a) "Aligning Sentences in Parallel Corpora," *29th Annual Meeting of the Association for Computational Linguistics*. Berkeley, CA.

P. F. Brown, S. A. Della Pietra, V. J. Della Pietra, & R. L. Mercer. (1991b) "Word Sense Disambiguation Using Statistical Methods," *29th Annual Meeting of the Association for Computational Linguistics*. Berkeley, CA.

P. F. Brown, V. J. Della Pietra, P. V. deSouza, J. C. Lai, & R. L. Mercer. (1992) "Class-Based *n*-gram Models of Natural Language," *Computational Linguistics 18*(4). 467–479.

P. F. Brown, S. A. Della Pietra, V. J. Della Pietra, M. J. Goldsmith, J. Hajic, R. L. Mercer & S. Mohanty. (1993a) "But Dictionaries Are Data Too," *ARPA Workshop on Human Language Technology*. Princeton, NJ.

P. F. Brown, S. A. Della Pietra, V. J. Della Pietra, & R. L. Mercer. (1993b) "The Mathematics of Statistical Machine Translation: Parameter Estimation," *Computational Linguistics 19*(2). 263–311.

C. Buckley. (1993) "The Importance of Proper Weighting Methods," *DARPA Workshop on Human Language Technology*. Princeton, NJ.

M.-H. Candito. (1998) "Building Parallel LTAG for French and Italian," *17th International Conference on Computational Linguistics*. Montreal, Canada.

R. Catizone, G. Russell, & S. Warwick. (1989) "Deriving Translation Data from Bilingual Texts," *First International Lexical Acquisition Workshop*. Detroit, MI.

H.-H. Chen, S.-J. Huang, Y.-W. Ding, & S.-C. Tsai. (1998) "Proper Name Translation in Cross-Language Information Retrieval," *36th Annual Meeting of the Association for Computational Linguistics*. Montreal, Canada.

S. Chen. (1993) "Aligning Sentence in Bilingual Corpora Using Lexical Information," *31st Annual Meeting of the Association for Computational Linguistics*. Columbus, OH.

K. W. Church, I. Dagan, W. Gale, P. Fung, J. Helfman, & B. Satish. (1993). "Aligning Parallel Texts: Do Methods Developed for English-French Generalize to Asian Languages?" *PacfoCol'93*. Taipei, Taiwan.

K. W. Church & E. H. Hovy. (1993) "Good Applications for Crummy Machine Translation," *Machine Translation 8*, 239–258.

K. W. Church. (1993) "Char_align: A Program for Aligning Parallel Texts at the Character Level," *31st Annual Meeting of the Association for Computational Linguistics*. Columbus, OH.

P. H. Cousin, L. Sinclair, J. F. Allain, & C. E. Love. (1990) *The Harper Collins French Dictionary*. Harper Collins Publishers, New York, NY.

P. H. Cousin, L. Sinclair, J. F. Allain, & C. E. Love. (1991) *The Collins Paperback French Dictionary*. Harper Collins Publishers, Glasgow.

T. M. Cover & J. A. Thomas. (1991) *Elements of Information Theory*. John Wiley & Sons, New York, NY.

I. Dagan, A. Itai, & U. Schwall. (1991) "Two Languages Are More Informative than One," *29th Annual Meeting of the Association for Computational Linguistics*. Berkeley, CA.

I. Dagan, S. Marcus & S. Markovitch. (1993a) "Contextual Word Similarity and Estimation from Sparse Data," *31st Annual Meeting of the Association for Computational Linguistics*. Columbus, OH.

I. Dagan, K. Church, & W. Gale. (1993b) "Robust Word Alignment for Machine Aided Translation," *Workshop on Very Large Corpora: Academic and Industrial Perspectives*. Columbus, OH.

I. Dagan & K. Church. (1994) "TERMIGHT: Identifying and Translating Technical Terminology," *Fourth ACL Conference on Applied Natural Language Processing*. Stuttgart, Germany.

I. Dagan. (1997) Personal communication.

B. Daille, É. Gaussier, & J.-M. Langé. (1994) "Towards Automatic Extraction of Monolingual and Bilingual Terminology," *15th International Conference on Computational Linguistics*. Kyoto, Japan.

F. Debili & E. Sammouda. (1992) "Appariement des Phrases de Textes Bilingues," *14th International Conference on Computational Linguistics*. Nantes, France.

W. E. Deming & F. F. Stephan. (1940) "On a Least Squares Adjustment of a Sampled Frequency Table When the Expected Marginal Totals Are Known," *Annals of Mathematical Statistics 11*, pp. 427-444.

A. P. Dempster, N. M. Laird, & D. B. Rubin. (1977) "Maximum Likelihood from Incomplete Data via the EM Algorithm," *Journal of the Royal Statistical Society 39(B)*, 1–38.

L. R. Dice. (1945) "Measures of the Amount of Ecologic Association Between Species," *Journal of Ecology 26*, pp. 297-302.

B. J. Dorr. (1992) "The Use of Lexical Semantics in Interlingual Machine Translation," *Machine Translation 7(3)*, pp. 135–193.

T. Dunning. (1993) "Accurate Methods for the Statistics of Surprise and Coincidence," *Computational Linguistics 19(1)*, 61–74.

D. Elworthy. (1998) "Language Identification with Confidence Limits," *Sixth Workshop on Very Large Corpora*. Montreal, Canada.

D. A. Evans & C. Zhai. (1996) "Noun-Phrase Analysis in Unrestricted Text for Information Retrieval," *34th Annual Meeting of the Association for Computational Linguistics*. Santa Cruz, CA.

G. Foster, P. Isabelle, & P. Plamondon. (1996) "Word Completion: A First Step Toward Target-Text Mediated IMT," *16th International Conference on Computational Linguistics*. Copenhagen, Denmark.

P. Fung. (1995a) "Compiling Bilingual Lexicon Entries from a Non-Parallel English-Chinese Corpus," *Third Workshop on Very Large Corpora*. Boston, MA.

P. Fung. (1995b) "A Pattern Matching Method for Finding Noun and Proper Noun Translations from Noisy Parallel Corpora," *33rd Annual Meeting of the Association for Computational Linguistics*. Boston, MA.

P. Fung and K. W. Church. (1994). "K-vec: A New Approach for Aligning Parallel Texts," *15th International Conference on Computational Linguistics*. Kyoto, Japan. 1096-1102.

P. Fung and K. McKeown. (1994). "Aligning Noisy Parallel Corpora across Language Groups: Word Pair Feature Matching by Dynamic Time Warping," *1st Conference of the Association for Machine Translation in the Americas*. Columbia, MD. 81-88.

W. Gale & K. W. Church. (1991a) "A Program for Aligning Sentences in Bilingual Corpora," *29th Annual Meeting of the Association for Computational Linguistics*. Berkeley, CA.

W. Gale & K. W. Church. (1991b) "Identifying Word Correspondences in Parallel Texts," *DARPA Speech and Natural Language Workshop*. Asilomar, CA.

W. A. Gale & G. Sampson. (1995) "Good-Turing Frequency Estimation Without Tears" *Journal of Quantitative Linguistics 2*, pp. 217-237. Swets & Zeitlinger Publishers, Sassenheim, The Netherlands.

D. Graff, I. D. Melamed, & P. Morgovsky. (1997) "Hansard Corpus: Parallel Text in English and French" on CD-ROM, Linguistic Data Consortium.

B. Harris. (1988) "Bi-Text, a New Concept in Translation Theory," *Language Monthly #54*.

D. Hiemstra. (1996) *Using Statistical Methods to Create a Bilingual Dictionary*, Master's Thesis, University of Twente, The Netherlands.

D. Hiemstra. (1998) "Multilingual Domain Modeling in Twenty-One: Automatic Creation of a Bidirectional Translation Lexicon from a Parallel Corpus," *8th Meeting of Computational Linguistics in the Netherlands (CLIN)*.

J. W. Hunt & T. G. Szymanski. (1977) "A Fast Algorithm for Computing Longest Common Subsequences," *Communications of the ACM 20(5)*, pp. 350-353.

P. Isabelle. (1992). "Bi-Textual Aids for Translators," *8th Annual Conference of the UW Centre for the New OED and Text Research*. Waterloo, Canada. 1-15.

P. Isabell. (1995). Personal communication.

M. Kay & M. Röscheisen. (1993) "Text-Translation Alignment," *Computational Linguistics 19*(1).

G. Kikui. (1998). "Term-list Translation Using Mono-lingual Word Co-occurrence Vectors," *36th Annual Meeting of the Association for Computational Linguistics*. Montreal, Canada.

A. Kilgarriff. (1997a) "I Don't Believe in Word Senses," *Computers and the Humanities 31*(2), 91–113.

A. Kilgarriff. (1997b) "What is Word Sense Disambiguation Good For?" *NLP Pacific Rim Symposium '97*. Phuket, Thailand.

K. Kita, T. Omoto, Y. Yano, & Y. Kato. (1993) "Application of Corpora to Second Language Learning: The Problem of Collocational Knowledge Acquisition," *2nd Workshop on Very Large Corpora*. Columbus, OH.

K. Knight & J. Graehl. (1997) "Machine Transliteration," *35th Annual Meeting of the Association for Computational Linguistics*. Madrid, Spain.

A. Kumano & H. Hirakawa. (1994) "Building an MT Dictionary from Parallel Texts Based on Linguistic and Statistical Information," *15th International Conference on Computational Linguistics*. Kyoto, Japan.

J. Kupiec. (1993) "An Algorithm for Finding Noun Phrase Correspondences in Bilingual Corpora," *31st Annual Meeting of the Association for Computational Linguistics*. Columbus, OH.

P. Langlais, M. Simard, & J. Véronis. (1998) "Methods and Practical Issues in Evaluating Alignment Techniques," *36th Annual Meeting of the Association for Computational Linguistics*. Montreal, Canada.

L. Langlois. (1996) "Bilingual Concordances: A New Tool for Bilingual Lexicographers," *2nd Conference of the Association for Machine Translation in the Americas*. Montreal, Canada.

H. Li & N. Abe. (1996) "Clustering Words with the MDL Principle," *16th International Conference on Computational Linguistics*. Copenhagen, Denmark.

H. Li & N. Abe. (1996) "Word Clustering and Disambiguation Based on Co-occurrence Data," *Proceedings of the 17th International Conference on Computational Linguistics*. Montreal, Canada.

J. M. Lucassen & R. L. Mercer. (1984) "An Information-Theoretic Approach to the Automatic Determination of Phonemic Baseforms," *IEEE International Conference on Acoustics, Speech and Signal Processing*. San Diego, CA.

E. Macklovitch. (1994) "Using Bi-textual Alignment for Translation Validation: The TransCheck System," *1st Conference of the Association for Machine Translation in the Americas*. Columbia, MD.

E. Macklovitch. (1995) "Peut-on verifier automatiquement la coherence terminologique?" *I V^{es} Journées scientifiques, Lexicommatique et Dictionnairiques*, organized by AUPELF-UREF. Lyon, France.

M. P. Marcus, B. Santorini, & M. A. Marcinkiewicz. (1993) "Building a Large Annotated Corpus of English: The Penn Treebank," *Computational Linguistics 19*(2).

J. S. McCarley. (1999) "Should We Translate the Documents or the Queries in Cross-Language Information Retrieval?" *37th Annual Meeting of the Association for Computational Linguistics*. College Park, MD.

T. McEnery & M. Oakes. (1995) "Cognate Extraction in the CRATER Project: Methods and Assessment," *From Texts to Tags: Issues in Multilingual Language Analysis, SIGDAT Workshop*. Dublin, Ireland.

I. D. Melamed. (1995) "Automatic Evaluation and Uniform Filter Cascades for Inducing N-best Translation Lexicons," *Third Workshop on Very Large Corpora*. Cambridge, MA.

I. D. Melamed. (1996a) "Automatic Construction of Clean Broad-Coverage Translation Lexicons," *2nd Conference of the Association for Machine Translation in the Americas*. Montreal, Canada.

I. D. Melamed. (1996b) "Porting SIMR to New Language Pairs," IRCS Technical Report 96-26. University of Pennsylvania, Philadelphia, PA.

I. D. Melamed. (1997a) "Measuring Semantic Entropy," *SIGLEX Workshop on Tagging Text with Lexical Semantics*. Washington, DC.

I. D. Melamed. (1997b) "A Portable Algorithm for Mapping Bitext Correspondence," *35th Conference of the Association for Computational Linguistics*. Madrid, Spain.

I. D. Melamed. (1997c) "A Word-to-Word Model of Translational Equivalence," *35th Conference of the Association for Computational Linguistics*. Madrid, Spain.

I. D. Melamed. (1997d) "Automatic Discovery of Non-Compositional Compounds," *Second Conference on Empirical Methods in Natural Language Processing*. Providence, RI.

G. A. Miller (ed.). (1990) *WordNet: An On-Line Lexical Database*. Special issue of *International Journal of Lexicography 4*(3).

J. Nerbonne, L. Karttunen, E. Paskaleva, G. Proszeky, & T. Roosmaa. (1997) "Reading More into Foreign Languages," *5th ACL Conference on Applied Natural Language Processing*. Washington, DC.

D. W. Oard (1997) "Adaptive Filtering of Multilingual Document Streams," *5th RIAO Conference*. Montreal, Canada.

F. J. Och. (1999) "An Efficient Method for Determining Bilingual Word Classes," *15th Annual Meeting of the European Association for Computational Linguistics*. Bergen, Norway.

H. Papageorgiou, L. Cranias, & S. Piperidis. (1994) "Automatic Alignment in Parallel Corpora," *32nd Annual Meeting of the Association for Computational Linguistics (Student Session)*. Las Cruces, NM.

F. Pereira, N. Tishby, & L. Lee. (1993) "Distributional Clustering of English Words," *31st Annual Meeting of the Association for Computational Linguistics*. Columbus, OH.

C. Phillips & T. J. Warnow. (1996) "The Asymmetric Median Tree—A New Model for Building Consensus Trees," *Discrete Applied Mathematics 71(1-3)*, pp. 331-335.

R. Rapp. (1995) "Identifying Word Translations in Non-Parallel Texts," Student Session, *33rd Annual Meeting of the Association for Computational Linguistics*. Boston, MA.

P. Resnik. (1997) "Evaluating Multilingual Gisting of Web Pages," *AAAI Symposium on Cross-Language Text and Speech Retrieval*. Stanford University, Stanford, CA.

P. Resnik & I. D. Melamed. (1997) "Semi-Automatic Acquisition of Domain-Specific Translation Lexicons," *5th ACL Conference on Applied Natural Language Processing*. Washington, DC.

P. Resnik, M. B. Olsen, & M. Diab. (1997) "Creating a Parallel Corpus from the Book of 2000 Tongues," *10th TEI User Conference*. Providence, RI.

P. Resnik & D. Yarowsky. (1997) "A Perspective on Word Sense Disambiguation Methods and Their Evaluation," *SIGLEX Workshop on Tagging Text with Lexical Semantics*. Washington, DC.

P. Resnik. (1999) "Mining the Web for Bilingual Text," *37th Annual Meeting of the Association for Computational Linguistics*. College Park, MD.

P. Resnik & T. Kanungo. (1999). Personal communication.

K. Ries, F. D. Buo, & A. Waibel. (1996) "Class Phrase Models for Language Modeling," *Fourth International Conference on Spoken Language Processing*. Philadelphia, PA.

L. Rüschendorf. (1995) "Convergence of the Iterative Proportional Fitting Procedure," *Annals of Statistics 23(4)*, 1160-1174.

V. Sadler & R. Vendelmans. (1990) "Pilot Implementation of a Bilingual Knowledge Bank," *13th International Conference on Computational Linguistics*. Helsinki, Finland.

H. Schuetze & J. O. Pedersen. (1995) "Information Retrieval Based on Word Senses," *Fourth Annual Symposium on Document Analysis and Information Retrieval*, pp. 161-175. Las Vegas, NV.

H. Schuetze. (1998) "Automatic Word Sense Discrimination," *Computational Linguistics 24(1)*, pp. 97-124.

S. Shieber. (1994) "Restricting the Weak-Generative Capacity of Synchronous Tree-Adjoining Grammars," *Computational Intelligence 10:4*, pp. 371-385.

J. H. Shin, Y. S. Han, & K.-S. Choi. (1996) "Bilingual Knowledge Acquisition from Korean-English Parallel Corpus Using Alignment Method (Korean-English Alignment at Word and Phrase Level)," *16th International Conference on Computational Linguistics*. Copenhagen, Denmark.

M. Simard, G. F. Foster, & P. Isabelle. (1992) "Using Cognates to Align Sentences in Bilingual Corpora," *Fourth International Conference on Theoretical and Methodological Issues in Machine Translation*. Montreal, Canada.

M. Simard, G. F. Foster, & F. Perrault. (1993) "TransSearch: A Bilingual Concordance Tool." Centre d'Innovation en Technologies de l'Information, Laval, Canada.

M. Simard. (1995) Personal communication.

M. Simard & P. Plamondon. (1996) "Bilingual Sentence Alignment: Balancing Robustness and Accuracy," *2nd Conference of the Association for Machine Translation in the Americas*. Montreal, Canada.

F. Smadja. (1992) "How to Compile a Bilingual Collocational Lexicon Automatically," *AAAI Workshop on Statistically-Based NLP Techniques*. San Jose, CA.

N. A. Smith & M. E. Jahr. (2000) "Cairo: An Alignment Visualization Tool," *Second Conference on Language Resources and Evaluation*. Athens, Greece.

R. Sproat, C. Shih, W. Gale, & N. Chang. (1996) "A Stochastic Finite-State Word-Segmentation Algorithm for Chinese," *Computational Linguistics* 22(3):377-404.

J. Svartvik. (1992) *Directions in Corpus Linguistics*. Mouton de Gruyter, Berlin.

D. Turcato. (1998) "Automatically Creating Bilingual Lexicons for Machine Translation from Bilingual Text," *36th Annual Meeting of the Association for Computational Linguistics*. Montreal, Canada.

R. V. V. Vidal. (1993) *Applied Simulated Annealing*. Springer-Verlag, Heidelberg, Germany.

S. Vogel, H. Ney, & C. Tillmann. (1996) "HMM-Based Word Alignment in Statistical Translation," *16th International Conference on Computational Linguistics*. Copenhagen, Denmark.

E. M. Voorhees. (1993) "Using Wordnet to Disambiguate Word Senses for Text Retrieval," *SIGIR '93*, pp. 171–180.

P. Vossen (ed.). (1998) *Eurowordnet: A Multilingual Database with Lexical Semantic Networks*. Kluwer Academic Publishers, Dordrecht, the Netherlands.

S. Wan & M. Verspoor. (1998) "Automatic English-Chinese Name Transliteration for Development of Multilingual Resources," *36th Annual Meeting of the Association for Computational Linguistics*. Montreal, Canada.

Y. Wang, J. Lafferty, & A. Waibel. (1996) "Word Clustering with Parallel Spoken Language Corpora," *Fourth International Conference on Spoken Language Processing*. Philadelphia, PA.

W. Weaver. (1955) "Translation." In William N. Locke and Donald A. Booth, eds., *Machine Translation of Languages*. MIT Press, Cambridge.

J. S. White & T. A. O'Connell. (1993) "Evaluation of Machine Translation," *ARPA Workshop on Human Language Technology*. Princeton, NJ.

D. Wu. (1994) "Aligning a Parallel English-Chinese Corpus Statistically with Lexical Criteria," *32nd Annual Meeting of the Association for Computational Linguistics*. Las Cruces, NM.

D. Wu & P. Fung. (1994) "Improving Chinese Tokenization with Linguistic Filters on Statistical Lexical Acquisition," *4th Conference on Applied Natural Language Processing*. Stuttgart, Germany.

D. Wu & X. Xia. (1994) "Learning an English-Chinese Lexicon from a Parallel Corpus," *First Conference of the Association for Machine Translation in the Americas*. Columbia, MD.

D. Wu. (1995) "Grammarless Extraction of Phrasal Translation Examples from Parallel Texts," *Sixth International Conference on Theoretical and Methodological Issues in Machine Translation*. Leuven, Belgium.

D. Yarowsky. (1993) "One Sense Per Collocation," *DARPA Workshop on Human Language Technology*. Princeton, NJ.

D. Yarowsky. (1996) *Three Machine Learning Algorithms for Lexical Ambiguity Resolution*. Ph.D. Dissertation, University of Pennsylvania, Philadelphia, PA.

G. K. Zipf. (1936) *The Psycho-biology of Language: an Introduction to Dynamic Philology*. Routledge, London, UK.

Index